Entertaining

Entertaining

Robert Carrier

Sidgwick and Jackson   London

First published in Great Britain 1977 by Sidgwick and Jackson Limited
Copyright © 1977 Robert Carrier
ISBN 0 283 98348 5

Design by Mike Ricketts, assisted by Martin Atcherley
Line drawings by Vana Haggerty
Extra photography by Rod Shone

Printed in Great Britain by Hazell, Watson & Viney Limited,
Aylesbury, Bucks., for
Sidgwick and Jackson Limited, 1 Tavistock Chambers,
Bloomsbury Way, London WC1A 2SG

Contents

Tips on Entertaining

Many of us approach entertaining with mixed emotions. While there is the pleasant prospect of gaiety and conviviality in the offing, there is also, for the host or hostess who wants to give a memorable luncheon or dinner party, a lot of real hard work. And yet party giving can be great fun if we learn to be realistic about our budget – and our capabilities – and remember that the true purpose of getting friends and family together is enjoyment.

I receive many letters every day from readers of my monthly columns in *Homes and Gardens* and *High Life* – letters from cities as far apart as Saigon and Sydney, Portland and Rome – and most of these letters deal in one way or another with the problems of party giving:

'What menus can I serve to a house party of six for a week-end in the country?'
'What wines should I choose for a cold buffet meal?'
'What is an inexpensive way of entertaining if I have no dining room?'
'What are easy dishes based on rice to feed a crowd?'

Finding the right answer to these queries began to fascinate me. And my letters, recipe suggestions, menus and party ideas became the central core of this book, *Entertaining*. Its aim is to broaden the scope of everyday entertaining beyond the traditional luncheons or dinners we are so used to. There are so many other opportunities for welcoming friends and relations to our homes – breakfast parties, brunches, teas, wine tastings, barbecues, after theatre or cinema suppers, picnics, punch parties, cocktail parties, children's parties and all kinds of buffet meals.

Hostmanship

Good food and good conversation are the two inseparable ingredients of a good party. I think it was the famous host Alfred Hitchcock who said 'For truly great conversation, there should never be more than six to dinner . . . if more, the conversation tends to dissipate, ideas begin to founder.'

Impromptu parties can be fun. Deciding what kind of party to give is a simple matter of finding out what you've got and what you can do with it, and not trying to do a classic dinner party in a situation that doesn't fit a classic dinner party.

To entertain apparently effortlessly, do as much 'do-it-ahead' preparation as possible, either in the morning or preferably the day before.

Plan your meals to leave yourself as free as you can so that you can enjoy your guests – and perhaps, even more important – so your guests can enjoy you.

Don't go in for numbers of courses. It is too difficult to manage.

If you have no help: serve the first course with the drinks.

If you specialize in small dinner parties, build your table wardrobe around one or two beautiful centre pieces or serving dishes. If buffets are your forte, start with cook-and-serve pieces you'll be proud to show off on the table.

Develop a trio of dishes that you do especially well and feel completely at ease in preparing. Then add a few new specialities each year.

Keep a record of the parties you give and the guests who attend them and what you gave them to eat. A hostess friend of mine – noted for the charm and gaiety of her parties – even keeps a list of the table decorations and china used for each party.

If you are trying out a new dish that sounds fabulous: (1) try it out on the family or close friends so that you can have a taste and time rehearsal. Nothing worse than being flustered at the last minute if the flavour is not exactly as you had wanted it; (2) check that it doesn't take twice as long to cook in your oven as you had counted on.

7

There's No Such Thing as a Born Cook

If you have ever wondered whether you had a talent for real cooking—the ability to prepare and serve a perfect dinner—here is your opportunity to find out. *Entertaining* is designed to sweep you along dish by dish, menu by menu, to heights of culinary skill which you never before imagined possible. After a few short chapters, you too will be able to prepare delicious meals based on savoury French casseroles and *quiches*, Italian pasta dishes, perfect omelettes, fragile soufflés and a host of really super sweets.

You will learn professional tips and special dishes to stretch your budget . . . international cooking secrets . . . and what utensils to use. You will discover what wines to serve with meals, what drinks and what snacks to serve at cocktail parties. From now on, you will know how to plan a buffet party, a barbecue, a picnic; how to cook delicious Continental summer meals and how to combine hundreds of exciting dishes in everyday and party menus, that you, your family and your friends will long remember.

Cooking is fun – and it is easy. I've always said: if you can read, you can cook! All you need is a little know-how and a little practice. But, a word of warning: there is no such thing as a born cook. You must learn step by step, one dish at a time. Of course, we all have some friends who cook better than others; *the truth is they have enough patience, time, curiosity and imagination to cook really well.*

Bored?

How often have you asked yourself: 'What shall I cook tonight?' If you are bored with serving the same kind of basic meal week after week, take advantage of this opportunity to get out of your everyday cooking rut. Next time you are serving gammon, for instance, try it in a creamy casserole combined with noodles liberally laced with a little dry sherry. Or surprise your guests with quickly made Beef Stroganoff, thin strips of lean beef simmered in butter and sour cream with mushrooms and onions. Follow with a salad with a special hard-boiled egg dressing and the day is made. It's that easy.

You will need no exotic equipment to follow this book; no hard-to-find ingredients. Of course, you will require a certain number of utensils – good solid kitchen tools – to help you on your way to being top cook in your neighbourhood. So buy the best quality heavy-duty cookware you can find. Make sure it is handsome enough to go straight from oven to table. Buy just one or two pieces at a time, for good cookware is expensive. And only buy just what you need. You will be amazed at how many complete luncheons and dinners you will be able to turn out with one or two frying pans, a medium-sized saucepan and a good-sized casserole. My old friend, the late Nancy Spain, descendant of the great Mrs Beeton, used to boast that given a sharp knife, a wooden spoon and a saucepan with a thick bottom that she could trust, she could happily cook up a storm.

'The whole secret', according to a really famous cook – Alexandre Dumaine, often called the greatest chef in France – 'is enhancing the intrinsic flavour of the ingredient to be cooked. If one *just* cooks, it is not worth the trouble.' Take a tip from this great chef: you don't have to be a genius to cook really well. Take it slowly as you would any other branch of learning and you can astound your friends and delight yourself. For there is something vastly satisfying about cooking.

Learn to experiment with flavours, with textures, with heat. For heat is the most important friend – or foe – that any cook can have. Just how a fish or a piece of meat is 'seized' in butter or oil at its first contact with the heat is as important to its final flavour and texture as its freshness and quality. You'll find that meat tends to dry out and toughen if cooked at too high a temperature; so watch your oven heats and make sure your cooker really does simmer at the lowest possible temperature. Many a dish has been ruined, many an otherwise delicious meal spoiled because the meat was boiled when it should only have simmered.

Don't make the mistake of trying to economize on the basic necessities of good cooking. You will need good butter and cooking oils to cook with; fat green bacon to add flavour and substance to stews and casseroles; a few packets of dried herbs – bay leaves, rubbed thyme, rosemary and sage – as well as coarse salt and freshly ground black pepper to add a little zest and excitement to your cooking. And your larder should always contain a few Spanish onions, some carrots and garlic. You'll find it makes all the difference and means that you don't have to run out to the shops every time a recipe reads 'take an onion' or 'add a pinch of thyme'.

For best results all butter, cooking fats and cooking oils (the most practical and most pleasant to use are olive, corn and peanut) should be of the best quality. For slow frying, I like to mix olive oil and butter in equal quantities, putting the oil in the pan first to keep the butter from browning; or I use a combination of olive oil and corn or peanut oil for lighter casseroles of chicken, rabbit or vegetables. For the earthier casseroles, I combine olive oil and butter and add diced green bacon to create a rich emulsion with plenty of flavour. But whatever cooking you intend to do, a supply of good olive oil is essential for salads and as a sauce for spaghetti and bean dishes in the Italian manner.

The onion family – onions, shallots, leeks and garlic – are a must for all casserole dishes and stews. Try the French cook's trick of browning a little finely chopped onion and garlic in olive oil and butter before adding meat and vegetables for a meat casserole. These lusty aromatics will greatly enhance your dish. (But, a word of warning: do not let onions or garlic turn colour before adding your meat, or they will become bitter.) For a simple sauce that will add much to the savour of grilled steak, lamb chops or fish, try a little finely chopped onion – just a tablespoon or two, no more – simmered in butter with a little finely chopped parsley and a hint of garlic.

Working Girl

I often get letters from young working girls about to get married who have never before cooked anything more ambitious than a TV dinner: 'Give me some simple dishes I can cook for my husband and friends that do not take too much time; that are not too expensive and that I can do without being a master chef in the kitchen.' Two dishes that answer these specifications perfectly are Beef Stroganoff and Spaghetti Parmesan—dishes I often rely on at weekends when a hungry look comes into my guests' eyes and it is time to rustle up something quick and easy.

Overleaf: Beef Pot Roast (page 126)

I'm a social cook, working at my best when I'm being jostled by a kitchenful of people. Beef Stroganoff is easy to serve to a lot of people at once or as a quick knock-up dinner for two or four. Spaghetti Parmesan is one of my favourite pasta dishes. The recipe here I learned when I lived in Rome. It's never failed me on weekends in the country when I've found myself in charge of the kitchen. All three recipes serve four people.

Easy Beef Stroganoff

with these recipes I suggest the following Inexpensive Red Wines
Macon Rouge
Gigondas
Chianti Red Ruffino

Trim fat from 1½ lb (675g) rump steak or sirloin and cut into steaks a little over 1 inch (2.5cm) thick. Then cut each steak across the grain into slices ¼ inch (0.5cm) thick. Season meat generously with salt and freshly ground black pepper and then flatten each strip with a wooden steak mallet. This will tenderize the steak and make each slice bigger. If no wooden mallet is available, use a wooden potato masher or the side of a kitchen cleaver.

Devilled Whitebait
(page 34)

Simmer 4 level tablespoons finely chopped onions in 4 level tablespoons butter in a

thick-bottomed frying pan, stirring constantly, until it just begins to turn golden in colour. Add sliced, seasoned beef and continue to cook for about 3 minutes longer, turning slices with the prongs of a kitchen fork until they are brown on all sides. Remove meat from frying pan and keep warm.

Add 2 tablespoons olive oil to the pan; pour in any juices from the meat; add $\frac{1}{4}$ lb (100g) thinly sliced mushrooms and simmer, stirring constantly, until they begin to turn brown. Season to taste with salt, freshly ground black pepper and a dash of cayenne.

Return meat strips to the pan and add $\frac{1}{4}$ pint (1.5dl) sour cream. Stir well over low heat to blend juices and make sure each strip is coated with the creamy sauce. Heat through.

Transfer to a heated serving dish; sprinkle with 2 level tablespoons and serve with **boiled rice** (see page 70) or **mashed potatoes** (see page 42).

Spaghetti Parmesan

Bring 3 to 4 quarts (3 to 4 litres) well-salted water to the boil in a large saucepan. Add 1 lb (450g) spaghetti and cook for about 12 to 15 minutes or until it is tender but still firm—*al dente*, as the Italians say, which means just firm enough to bite comfortably but not so soft that it is mushy.

Melt 2oz (50g) butter in a large saucepan. Drain spaghetti and while it is still very hot toss it in the butter.

Pour beaten yolks of 4 eggs and $\frac{1}{4}$ pint (1.5dl) cream over spaghetti; add salt, freshly ground black pepper and a dash of nutmeg. Stir for a minute; remove from heat and add more butter. The sauce and the eggs should not begin to solidify. Serve immediately in a large heated bowl or serving dish with freshly grated Parmesan and additional butter.

Follow either of the above two dishes with a salad of tender lettuce leaves dressed with a special dressing. The dressing has lots of character without garlic, but include it if you like a touch of the South of France in your cooking.

Salad Carrier

Wash the leaves of 1 or 2 heads of lettuce well in a large quantity of water. They should be left whole, never cut. Drain well and dry thoroughly in a cloth or salad basket.

To make a dressing: combine 1 chopped hard-boiled egg with 6–8 tablespoons olive oil and 2 tablespoons wine vinegar, seasoned to taste with a little dry mustard, salt, freshly ground black pepper and a squeeze of lemon juice. Add a little finely chopped parsley and spring onion or chives, plus 1 small clove of garlic finely chopped, if desired.

Pour dressing over lettuce just before serving and toss until each leaf is glistening.

Utensils

Most young cooks begin their culinary experiments with the minimum of equipment: a roasting tin and a grill pan – they come with the cooker – a small saucepan, a heatproof casserole and that old standby, a frying pan. Add to this a few knives, a wooden spoon or two, a strainer and a colander, and you are in business. But for those cooks who intend to do a little more in the kitchen, I suggest the following basic cook's tools:

Basic Cook's Tools

FRYING PANS
1 small frying pan
1 large frying pan
1 omelette pan

SAUCEPANS AND CASSEROLES
3 enamelled saucepans
1 oval casserole
1 large oval casserole
1 round casserole
1 rectangular baking dish
1 double saucepan

CUTTING TOOLS
1 paring knife
1 cook's knife, 7 inches(18cm)
1 cook's knife, 9 inches(23cm)
1 ham knife
1 bread knife
1 carving knife and fork
1 pair kitchen scissors, or poultry shears

OTHER BASICS
1 pair kitchen scales
1 graduated measuring jug
1 set measuring spoons
1 chopping board
1 mortar and pestle
1 chopping bowl and round-bladed chopper
1 hanging kitchen set (fish slice, ladle, slotted spoon, fork, etc.)
1 sieve
1 colander
1 salad shaker
1 grater
1 peppermill
1 salt mill
1 can opener
skewers

MIXING BOWLS AND MIXERS
1 set graduated kitchen bowls
4–6 wooden spoons
1 wire whisk
1 large wire whisk
1 rotary whisk

Specialized Equipment

The more advanced cook will need more specialized equipment for making pastry, cakes, *pâtés* and soufflés.

TARTS, CAKES AND BREADS

1 pastry board
1 rolling pin
1 pastry blender
1 flour sifter
1 pastry wheel
2 bread pans
2 large tart tins, with removable bottoms
6 individual tart tins, with removable bottoms
1 baking sheet

2 layer-cake tins
1 round ring mould
1 kugelhupf mould
1 piping bag
candy thermometer

PÂTÉS AND SOUFFLÉS

2 rectangular or oval pâté dishes
2 large soufflé dishes
6 individual ramekins

Electrical Equipment

1 blender/mixer

And, if you are feeling rich, an electric cook's tool you will never regret: 1 Magi-mix blender, for blending pastry and cake doughs, and for grinding vegetables, cheeses, breadcrumbs and minced meats for *pâtés, terrines, mousses* and *quenelles* quicker than you can talk about it.

Tips for the Cook

How to Follow a Recipe Successfully

1 Read recipe carefully through to the end, working out the total preparation time, including hold-ups while marinating, chilling, etc.

2 Make sure you have all the necessary ingredients and utensils, and that the latter are of the correct size.

3 Remove eggs, butter, meat, etc., from refrigerator one hour before using so that they will be at room temperature by the time you start to cook.

4 Light oven if a preheated oven is required. Set refrigerator to required setting if this is called for.

5 Do any advance preparation indicated in list of ingredients. The preparation of cake tins, etc., should also be attended to before you start.

6 Measure or weigh ingredients carefully.

7 Do not be tempted to alter a recipe in midstream until you have prepared it faithfully at least once, and do not telescope or ignore directions and procedures for combining ingredients unless you are a very experienced cook.

8 Follow cooking and/or baking times and temperatures given, but test for doneness about two-thirds of the way through; be prepared to increase cooking time if it appears insufficient.

How to Measure Correctly

Accurate measurement is essential to any kind of cooking. A standard set of individual measuring spoons in plastic or metal – 1 tablespoon, 1 teaspoon, $\frac{1}{2}$ teaspoon and $\frac{1}{4}$ teaspoon – is ideal for small quantities, and can be bought in many kitchen departments throughout the country. When a recipe calls for a fraction not catered for in the standard set, a dry ingredient can be measured by taking a whole spoonful, then carefully halving or quartering the amount with the tip of a knife and discarding the excess.

WHITE SUGAR
Make sure there are no lumps. Lift out a heaped spoonful and level off with a spatula or a straight knife.

BROWN SUGAR
Pack firmly into spoon so that when turned out the sugar will hold the shape of the spoon. (**Note:** If brown sugar has hardened into a brick, leave it in the bread bin for a few hours to soften again.)

WHITE FLOUR
Sift once. Dip spoon into flour, taking a heaped spoonful, and level off top with a spatula or a straight knife.

OTHER FLOURS/FINE MEALS AND FINE CRUMBS
Stir instead of sifting. Measure like flour.

BAKING POWDER/CREAM OF TARTAR/ CORNFLOUR/GROUND HERBS AND SPICES
Stir to loosen if necessary. Measure like flour.

SOLID FATS
Soften before measuring. Then dip spoon into fat, scoop out, and level off top.

SYRUP/TREACLE/LIQUID HONEY
Dip spoon in hot water for 30 seconds before measuring to prevent syrup sticking to sides.

LARGER QUANTITIES
For measuring larger quantities of ingredients you will also need:

A measuring jug, marked off in fluid ounces, and heatproof to withstand boiling liquids. You will also find this useful with American recipes, but remember that the American pint measures only 16 fl oz(450ml) and the American cup or ½ pint measures 8 fl oz(225ml).

KITCHEN SCALES
Select a pair with a large enough pan to hold the quantities you are likely to be measuring.

Oven Temperatures
All the recipes in this book were tested in both gas and electric ovens which conformed to the temperatures and gas settings given below. If in doubt about your own oven, invest in an oven thermometer, which will also allow you to make spot checks in the future. Remember, though, to light the oven at least 15 to 20 minutes before taking a reading, and be prepared for a slight variance in temperature between top and bottom of oven.

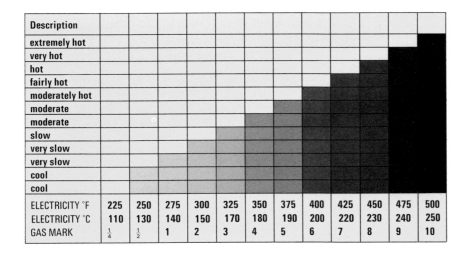

Description												
extremely hot												
very hot												
hot												
fairly hot												
moderately hot												
moderate												
moderate												
slow												
very slow												
very slow												
cool												
cool												
ELECTRICITY °F	225	250	275	300	325	350	375	400	425	450	475	500
ELECTRICITY °C	110	130	140	150	170	180	190	200	220	230	240	250
GAS MARK	¼	½	1	2	3	4	5	6	7	8	9	10

Vegetables without Water

Water is the enemy of the well-cooked vegetable. Remember this and you're well on the way to giving vegetables the importance they deserve in our daily diet. They're full of nutritive value and their vitamin content is high. But all too often they end up as a soggy, colourless, tasteless mess.

The secret of cooking vegetables is simply this – use no water! Any cooking water you throw away is waste water. So it follows that if you use less water, your food will have that much more flavour. This is the secret of Chinese cookery, with its delicious, crisp and colourful vegetables. Little liquid is used. No liquid is thrown away. Therefore, no flavour is lost. Simple, isn't it?

In this way, you *add* flavour rather than subtract it. Even the firmest vegetables – like carrots and turnips – if cut in chunks and blanched before being simmered in a very little chicken stock and butter, are twice as flavourful as those boiled to death in the usual manner.

So whatever you do, don't drown your vegetables. My favourite method of cooking them is to use a little butter or olive oil, with just enough chicken stock (or water, white wine, or even steam) to bring out their delicate flavours and textures. And always serve vegetables slightly crisp.

I know what you are thinking. You're going to ask 'Won't the vegetables burn or dry up?'

No. And I'll tell you why.

By combining equal amounts of butter and chicken stock – 4 tablespoons of each for an average serving for four – you will find that the chicken stock will reduce while the vegetables are cooking, leaving the cooked vegetables in a few tablespoons of beautifully flavoured butter.

And, remember, it is better to undercook than to overcook. A fact which 999 people out of 1,000 forget.

Method

Melt 2 to 4 level tablespoons butter in a saucepan; place washed fresh vegetables or frozen vegetables (prepared as below) in the pan; sprinkle with a little sugar to bring out their natural sweetness and add 2 to 4 tablespoons chicken stock (made with a cube) for extra flavour. Stir vegetables over fairly high heat for a minute or two; then *cover tightly* and simmer on the lowest possible heat for about 15 minutes, or until vegetables are fork tender. Taste vegetables, then add salt and freshly ground black pepper, as necessary, just before serving.

Green beans: whole, or cut into 2-inch(5-cm) segments.
Baby marrows or **courgettes:** sliced, not peeled.
Spinach: whole leaves, with stems removed.
New carrots: peeled or scraped, whole, sliced, or cut into 1-inch(2·5-cm) segments. Old carrots must be blanched first.
New turnips: peeled, quartered, sliced or diced. Old turnips must be blanched first.
Small white onions: whole, but must be skinned and blanched first.
Peas: whole.
Asparagus: cut into $\frac{1}{2}$-inch(1-cm) or 1-inch(2·5-cm) segments. Use tender part only.
Celery: sliced or cut into $\frac{1}{2}$-inch(1-cm) or 1-inch(2·5-cm) segments but must be blanched first.

To Blanch Vegetables Before Cooking

Place prepared vegetables in a saucepan large enough to hold them comfortably; add cold water to cover vegetables; place saucepan over high heat and bring rapidly to the boil. Drain and use as directed.

Great Cabbage

1 small head cabbage
Butter
4 tablespoons chicken stock
1 level teaspoon sugar
Grated nutmeg
Freshly ground black pepper
2 level tablespoons finely chopped
    parsley
Salt
Lemon juice

1 Wash 1 small head of cabbage well and cut into wedges about 1 inch(2·5cm) thick, removing all the core.

2 Combine 4 level tablespoons butter and chicken stock in a large shallow saucepan (you will want all the cabbage wedges to spread out in the pan so that they can cook evenly and quickly); then add cabbage and sprinkle with sugar, a dash of grated nutmeg and freshly ground black pepper, to taste. Cover saucepan tightly and place over high heat until it starts to steam. Then reduce heat and simmer cabbage gently for about 15 minutes, or until cooked through.

3 Transfer to a heated serving bowl; sprinkle with finely chopped parsley and serve with melted butter seasoned with salt, freshly ground black pepper and lemon juice, to taste.

Glazed White Onions

1 lb(450g) small white onions
4 level tablespoons butter
4 tablespoons chicken stock
1 level tablespoon sugar
Salt

1 Peel onions and place them in a small saucepan; cover with cold water and cook over high heat until water boils. Remove from heat and drain.

2 Replace blanched onions in the saucepan; add butter and chicken stock; season with sugar and salt, to taste, and simmer over low heat until onions have absorbed the liquid without burning and have taken on a little colour.

Buttered Carrots

1 lb(450g) small carrots
4 level tablespoons butter
4 tablespoons chicken stock
1 level tablespoon sugar
Salt

1 Scrape carrots; slice thickly and place in a small saucepan; cover with cold water and blanch. Drain.

2 Simmer blanched carrots with butter, chicken stock, sugar and salt, to taste, until they have absorbed the liquid without burning and have taken on a little colour.

Green Beans–Chinese Style

1 lb(450g) green beans
2 tablespoons peanut oil or lard
½ level teaspoon salt
Soy sauce or dry sherry

1 Wash and trim green beans; break or cut them into sections about 1 inch(2·5cm) long.

2 Heat peanut oil or lard in a thick-bottomed frying pan; add beans and cook over medium heat for 1 minute, stirring continually. Add salt and ¼ pint(1·5dl) water; cover pan and cook beans for 3 minutes; remove cover and simmer, stirring from time to time, until all the water has evaporated (about 5 minutes). Add soy sauce or dry sherry to taste.

Courgettes

4–6 courgettes
2 tablespoons peanut oil or lard
½ level teaspoon salt
Soy sauce or dry sherry

1 Wash courgettes; cut off ends and slice thinly.

2 Heat peanut oil or lard in a thick-bottomed frying pan; add sliced courgettes and salt and cook over medium heat for 3 minutes, stirring continually. Add ¼ pint(1·5dl) water, and continue to simmer, stirring until the water has evaporated, about 5 minutes. Add soy sauce or dry sherry to taste.

French Style Peas

1 lb(450g) frozen peas
4 level tablespoons butter
4 tablespoons chicken stock
1 level tablespoon sugar
Salt

1 Place frozen peas in a small saucepan; cover with cold water and blanch. Drain.

2 Simmer blanched peas with butter, chicken stock, sugar and salt, to taste, until peas have absorbed the liquid and are tender.

Spinach

2 lb(900g) fresh spinach leaves
3 tablespoons peanut oil or lard
½ level teaspoon salt
Soy sauce or dry sherry

1 Wash spinach leaves in several changes of water; drain thoroughly.

2 Heat peanut oil or lard in a thick-bottomed frying pan; add spinach and salt and cook over medium heat for 3 minutes, stirring continually. Add soy sauce or dry sherry to taste.

STOCKS

Real Chicken Stock *(Quick Method)*

Place 1 chicken (about 4 lb/1·8kg) and 1 lb/450g veal knuckle in a large stock-pot with 3 quarts/3·4 litres water and bring to the boil, skimming until the scum no longer rises to the surface. Simmer for 1 hour. Add 2 leeks (white parts only), 1 Spanish onion stuck with cloves, 2 coarsely chopped carrots, 2 stalks celery, tops included, 1 large clove garlic and 4 sprigs parsley; add salt and pepper to taste and continue to simmer for 1 hour. Correct seasoning and strain the stock through a fine sieve. Cool, remove fat and reheat, or store in the refrigerator.

Real Beef Stock *(Quick Method)*

Have 1 lb/450g veal knuckle and 1 lb/450g beef knuckle coarsely chopped by your butcher; brush with 4 tablespoons meat dripping (beef, veal or pork) and brown them in the oven. Place in a large stock-pot with 2 lb/900g lean stewing beef, 2 chicken feet, if you have any, 2 leeks (white parts only), 1 large onion stuck with 2 cloves, 2 stalks celery, tops included, 2 coarsely chopped carrots, 4 sprigs parsley and 1 large clove garlic. Cover with 3 quarts/3·4 litres cold water and bring slowly to the boil, removing the scum as it accumulates on the surface. Simmer gently for 1 hour; add salt and pepper and continue to simmer for another hour, or until the meat is tender. Correct seasoning and strain the stock through a fine sieve. Cool, remove fat and reheat, or store in the refrigerator for later use.

Fish Stock *(Quick Method)*

Ask your fishmonger for some fish heads, fish bones and trimmings. Wash them well, discarding any black looking skin, and break the bones in pieces. Put them in an enamelled saucepan with 1 lb (450g) haddock, cod, halibut or flounder, 3 to 4 parsley stalks, 1 sliced Spanish onion, 2 sliced carrots, 1 bay leaf, a few white peppercorns and a little salt. Cover with equal parts water and dry white wine and simmer for 30 minutes. Strain before using.

Other optionals for a more flavoursome stock: $\frac{1}{2}$ chicken stock cube, a little canned clam juice, a lobster shell, or the heads and shells of prawns and shrimps.

Chicken Consommé

Strain 2 to 2$\frac{1}{2}$ quarts (1·5–2 litres) well-flavoured chicken stock into a large saucepan. Add whites and crushed shells of 2 eggs and bring to the boil. Simmer for 1 hour; strain through a fine cloth and cool. Skim.

Beef Consommé

Strain 2 to 2$\frac{1}{2}$ quarts (1·5–2 litres) beef stock into a large saucepan; add $\frac{1}{2}$ lb (225g) minced beef, 2 chopped leeks, $\frac{1}{2}$ chopped onion, the whites and crushed shells of 2 eggs and bring to the boil. Simmer for 1 hour; correct seasoning and strain through muslin lined sieve. Cool and skim.

Fish Consommé

Strain 2 to 2$\frac{1}{2}$ quarts (1·5–2 litres) fish stock into a large saucepan; add $\frac{1}{2}$ lb (225g) chopped fish, 2 chopped leeks, $\frac{1}{2}$ chopped onion, $\frac{1}{2}$ chicken stock cube and a little saffron. Simmer for $\frac{1}{2}$ hour. Add lemon juice and salt and freshly ground black pepper, to taste. Strain, cool and skim.

One-Dish Meals for Easy Entertaining

If you are a beginner cook – the kind who whimpers 'I can't even boil water without burning it' – or if you are one of those who stick to steaks and chops because you can't be bothered with all those 'fussy little bits' – I say *cook it in a casserole*. For with a casserole your very first recipe will turn out as if you had been cooking – flawlessly and effortlessly – for years. Casseroles can open the door for you to a whole school of cooking that has produced some of the greatest dishes of the world. Each country has its native one-dish meals, usually brought to the table in the classic earthenware or iron pots in which they have been cooked. These basic, slow-cooked dishes are simple to prepare, improve with keeping and reheating and are much more time-saving, economical and delicious than the so-called short-cut foods that so many cooks rely on today.

The great thing about casserole cooking is that there is no last minute fuss; no worry about plates getting cold while you cope with the carving. If you are giving a dinner party, guests can be late; if it's just you and the family, you can linger over that last drink while your casserole simmers gently in the lowest of ovens.

Most cooks, I think, tend to make things too difficult. They get nervous and tend to over-decorate and be too ambitious with what they want to do. Casserole cookery can be relied on to make even the least desirable cuts of meat taste delicious. Just seize the meat in a little butter or olive oil; flavour it with aromatic herbs – marjoram, rosemary, thyme or tarragon – add a touch of onion or garlic, and then let it simmer in the oven for an hour or two in a sauce made rich with stock, a little wine or a little cream. And even these additives need not be too expensive. A good light stock for a casserole can be made with a cube, perfectly good wines for cooking are still reasonably cheap (especially when you consider that most casserole recipes use no more than a few fluid ounces/millilitres) and cream is well within the budget for most of us. You'll find that most casseroles seem to go further, too.

I make no bones about it. I far prefer to serve economical cuts of meat for earthy stews and casseroles where long slow cooking brings out the utmost in flavour and tenderness. French lamb stew, my favourite combination of low-budget meats and vegetables, simmered in a little light stock flavoured with tomatoes, makes for delicious eating. A plump chicken, cooked in a little light stock with aromatic vegetables – onions, turnips, and mushrooms – and then bathed in a sauce made rich with egg yolks and cream, makes a Sunday spectacular your friends will rave about.

So be adventurous in trying out new cuts of beef or lamb, and make the most of our battery-bred chickens by adding flavour and moisture to them. You will find the long, slow cooking cuts are good bargains. They are moist and well flavoured; they cut well; and they will not turn stringy if simmered in a very slow oven (275°F to 300°F/140°C to 150°C/Mark 1 to Mark 2) for beef and veal or a slow oven (325°F/170°C/Mark 3) for lamb and pork. Or, if you prefer, you can cook them slowly in a casserole on top of the stove. But either way, make sure that the liquid in which they are cooked barely bubbles.

On lecture tours through Australia and the United States I always tell the cooks in my audience that the liquid in a casserole must never boil or even bubble merrily. It should just go 'plop, plop … plop' at one side of the casserole if the meat is to be tender and moist. Too quick cooking in liquid tends to make meat stringy and tough. So use this gentle bubbling of the steam escaping from the bottom of the casserole as your guide. You will be able to see at a glance: if the liquid is bubbling all over the casserole your heat is too high.

It is always difficult for me to give exact measurements for a casserole, but as a general rule 2 lb (900g) meat makes an adequate stew for four persons. But then, if you trim the pieces of meat of skin, bones and surplus fat (leaving some fat with the meat, of course, for succulence and flavour) you should allow an extra $\frac{1}{2}$ lb(225g) meat; and if, like me, you are apt to favour ample helpings, it is best to add another $\frac{1}{2}$ lb(225g). So let us say $2\frac{1}{2}$ to 3 lb(1·1 to 1·4kg) meat when boned for a comfortable meal for four persons, allowing just that little bit extra for larger helpings, or for an unexpected guest. You'll find you can't really have too much of a good thing.

Most casserole dishes are better if allowed to cool, so that the fats may be skimmed off the top, and then brought slowly to the correct temperature before serving. In this way the main dish for your dinner can be prepared in the morning or even the night before, and thus free you for the other pains and pleasures of entertaining.

If you desire, other seasonings may be added while your casserole is reheating. It is really a dash of this or that seasoning that turns an ordinary dish into something special. Here are three super casserole dishes, all of which need little more than a salad to turn them into a meal to be proud of. Each one of them could be the basis for a fine little dinner to invite friends to, or a weekend 'special' for you and the family to enjoy. All three recipes serve four people.

Osso Bucco
(illustrated overleaf)

The joy of this traditional Italian dish is that the bone with its marrow filling gives substance and flavour. Don't forget to supply a small teaspoon for each guest to extract the deliciously flavoured marrow.

4 pieces shin of veal
Flour
Salt and freshly ground black pepper
Olive oil
3 cloves garlic, finely chopped
$\frac{1}{2}$ Spanish onion, finely chopped
$\frac{1}{4}$ pint(1·5dl) chicken stock (made with a cube)
$\frac{1}{4}$ pint(1·5dl) dry white wine
4–6 level tablespoons tomato concentrate
4 anchovy fillets, finely chopped
4 tablespoons finely chopped parsley
Grated rind of 1 lemon

1 Choose a shin of veal with plenty of meat and have your butcher saw it through the bone into 4 pieces about 2 inches(5cm) thick and 4 to 6 inches(10–15cm) in diameter. Dust pieces with flour and season generously; simmer in olive oil in a thick-bottomed casserole on top of the stove until lightly browned on each side.

2 Add 1 clove of finely chopped garlic and finely chopped onion; pour over chicken stock, white wine and tomato concentrate. Cover the casserole and continue to simmer over low heat for $1\frac{1}{2}$ hours, adding a little water if sauce gets too dry.

3 Then add finely chopped anchovy fillets and remaining finely chopped garlic cloves. Blend thoroughly, heat through and serve sprinkled with finely chopped parsley and the grated lemon rind. In Italy this richly coloured, highly flavoured dish is always served with **saffron rice** (see overleaf).

with this recipe I suggest the following Inexpensive Red Wines
Valpolicella
Chianti Red Ruffino

Easy Saffron Rice

½ level teaspoon powdered saffron
6 tablespoons dry white wine
1½ pints(8·5dl) chicken stock
¾ lb(350g) rice
Salt and freshly ground black pepper

1 Dissolve powdered saffron in dry white wine; add it to hot chicken stock and combine in a large saucepan with rice and salt and freshly ground black pepper to taste.

2 Cover pan and simmer until all the liquid is absorbed and the rice is tender, about 30 minutes.

Beef in Beer

with this recipe I suggest the following Inexpensive Red Wines
Beaujolais
Châteauneuf-du-Pape
or Lager

Osso Bucco with Easy Saffron Rice

2½ lb(1·1 kg) raw beef
2 tablespoons olive oil
Salt and freshly ground black pepper
2 level tablespoons butter
2 large Spanish onions (or 4 medium-sized), thinly sliced
2 level tablespoons flour

1 bottle Guinness
Light beef stock (made with a cube)

1 Heat olive oil in a thick-bottomed frying pan. Cut the beef – I sometimes use rump steak, at other times less expensive shin of beef – into cubes about 1½ inches(4cm) square. Season cubes generously with salt and freshly ground black pepper and then brown on all sides in the heated oil. Transfer meat to an ovenproof casserole.

2 Add butter to the frying pan and gently simmer thinly sliced onions until they are soft and just beginning to turn colour. Sprinkle onions with flour; stir well and then add mixture to meat in casserole.

3 Add bottle of Guinness and just enough light beef stock (or water, if no stock available) to cover the meat. Cover the casserole and simmer over a very low heat – or in a very slow oven (275°F to 300°F/140°C to 150°C/Mark 1 to Mark 2) for about 2 hours, or until beef is tender. Check occasionally to make sure that the liquid in the casserole is just simmering, not

bubbling. In this way you will ensure that your beef is meltingly tender.

4 Correct seasoning and serve with **mashed potatoes** (see page 42) or boiled noodles or **boiled rice** (see page 70).

Sunday Chicken Tarragon

1 roasting chicken, 3½–4 lb(1·6–1·8kg)
Olive oil
Salt and freshly ground black pepper
1 level tablespoon dried tarragon
4 carrots, scrubbed and halved
4 medium-sized onions
4 mushrooms
4 3-inch(8-cm) pieces celery
4 sprigs fresh parsley
Light chicken stock (made with a cube)

SAUCE:
3 level tablespoons butter
2 level tablespoons flour
½ pint(3dl) chicken broth
¼ pint(1·5dl) dry white wine
1 level tablespoon dried tarragon
¼ pint(1·5dl) cream
2 egg yolks

1 Wash a plump, tender roasting chicken, and pat dry. Rub a little olive oil inside and out, then dust chicken with salt, freshly ground black pepper and dried tarragon.

2 Place the chicken in a large heatproof casserole with halved carrots, onions, mushrooms, celery and sprigs of fresh parsley. Add light chicken stock to almost cover bird; then cover casserole and cook gently on top of the stove or in a slow oven (325°F/170°C/Mark 3) until chicken is tender, removing cover of casserole and skimming froth from time to time. A bird of this size – if simmered at a very low heat to keep it moist and tender – will take from 1 to 1½ hours to cook. Test for tenderness at end of first hour by sticking thigh of bird with the prongs of a cooking fork. When chicken is

tender, remove the casserole from the heat and allow chicken to steep in its own liquids while you make the accompanying sauce.

3 To make sauce: melt butter in a thick-bottomed saucepan or in the top of a double saucepan. Add flour and stir over medium heat until flour and butter are bubbling and well blended. Then remove pan from heat. Strain hot chicken broth into a measuring jug and pour it, stirring continuously, into the butter and flour mixture. Return the saucepan to low heat – or, if using a double saucepan, place top part over boiling water – and cook, stirring, until sauce begins to thicken. Add white wine and dried tarragon and allow sauce to simmer gently until you are ready to use it.

4 Remove chicken and vegetables from the casserole and cut the bird into serving pieces, removing skin from each part, if desired, to make a more presentable dish.

5 Strain remaining broth into a bowl and put in the refrigerator to use on another day.

6 Wash casserole and return chicken pieces to it. Return carrots, onions and mushrooms to casserole with chicken. Put casserole in the lowest of ovens to keep warm.

7 Combine cream and egg yolks in a bowl and you are ready to complete the dish.

8 To complete dish: pour a little of the hot sauce into the egg yolk and cream mixture and mix well. Remove remaining sauce from heat and slowly add the egg yolk and cream mixture to it, stirring continuously. Then return pan to the lowest of heats (or over hot but not boiling water) and let sauce simmer gently until it thickens. Check seasoning. Do not let the sauce boil or it will curdle.

9 Spoon hot creamy sauce over chicken and vegetables and serve immediately from the casserole.

with this recipe I suggest the following Inexpensive White Wines
Muscadet
Sancerre
or
the following Medium-priced White Wines
Chablis
Pouilly Blanc Fumé

25

WINE MAGIC

You will find cooking with wine is as easy as opening the bottle and taking a sip. If like some of my friends, you are a little inhibited in your use of this magic cook's aid, don't be: think of it as just another good ingredient, like butter, olive oil, fresh herbs, or cream. Firstly, remember: the alcohol evaporates in cooking. Secondly, you don't have to use great quantities. Even a tablespoon or two, a quarter bottle, or at the most a half bottle, will work wonders for a delicious dish to feed four to six people.

Easy-to-prepare casserole recipes with wine are literally as old as time. The manner of cooking fish and shellfish, and meat, poultry and game in a combination of wine and stock or wine and cream probably originated centuries ago on the sun-washed hillsides of southern France when the early Romans were first teaching the natives of the region how to cultivate the local grapes to make wine. In those days, the casserole was undoubtedly cooked in the ashes. Today, we use modern electricity and gas to make our task even easier. But two magic 'constants' remain:

Slow Even Cooking

All wine-simmered casseroles – vegetables as well as meats, poultry, fish and game – respond wonderfully well to 'low heat' cookery. Over the many years I have been experimenting with heat, I have gradually lowered the temperature at which I like to cook stews, *daubes, ragoûts* and casseroles to cool, (225°F/110°C/Mark $\frac{1}{4}$, or 250°F/130°C/Mark $\frac{1}{2}$). And when cooking this type of dish on top of the stove, I always use an asbestos or wire mat to help keep the cooking down to a faint, barely perceptible simmer. It is a good idea, the first few times you follow this method of cooking, to check up on your casserole frequently. Thermostats vary, and you may find you have to adjust the setting slightly to keep the casserole at its low, 'barely simmering' point. And always make sure that you bring the ingredients up to a bubble on top of the stove before you put the casserole into the oven.

The Reduction of Wine to Give Added 'Fillip'

Wine 'reduced' to a quarter of its original quantity by fast boiling over a high heat is one of the best ways of adding savour to a casserole. Professional cooks often use this method of seasoning to 'correct' and intensify the depth of flavour of their wine cooked dishes. I like to reduce stock, too, in the same manner, adding a combination of the two separate reductions – stock and wine – to the dish at the last minute to give hidden depth and interest to a *ragoût* of meat, poultry or game. Try adding separate reductions of fish stock and dry white wine in this way to add excitement to a fish soup, casserole, or fish-based cream or *velouté* sauce.

Small Quantities of Wine Can Make a Great Difference to Your Cooking

1 Add 2 tablespoons dry white wine to your usual salad dressing; add a little finely chopped spring onion, onion or garlic and mix with sliced, boiled new potatoes for a delicious potato salad. Always remember to toss the potato slices with the dressing when potatoes are still a little warm.

2 Combine 6 tablespoons each olive oil and dry white wine with 2 crumbled bay leaves, a little finely chopped onion and parsley and salt and freshly ground black pepper, to taste. Use to marinate *brochettes* of lamb, chicken or fish before grilling. Good, too, for marinated lamb chops. This is one of the best and easiest marinades I know.

3 Combine 1 glass red wine with 1 clove crushed garlic, $\frac{1}{4}$ level teaspoon dried marjoram or thyme (or a combination of the two), $\frac{1}{4}$ chicken stock cube and freshly ground black pepper, to taste. Reduce these ingredients over a high heat to half the original quantity and use this aromatic sauce with a little butter swirled in to baste lamb, veal or chicken.

4 Always add 2 or more table-spoons of red wine just before serving a casserole of meat or game which you have marinated or simmered in red wine. You will find it helps the flavour of the finished dish.

5 Toss fresh strawberries in a few tablespoons of red wine. Chill before serving.

6 Spike a fresh fruit salad with half a quarter bottle of champagne. Leave just enough champagne for a glass for the cook! A double delight.

Super Meals Built around Four Family Favourites

Ring the changes with exciting appetizers and puddings to these four family favourites: Roast Leg of Lamb, Roast Chicken, Steak and Kidney Pudding and the 'No-roast' Roast Beef, to give yourself sixteen different menus.

Marinated Mushrooms

2 lb (900g) small button mushrooms
Juice of $\frac{1}{2}$ lemon
Salt
$\frac{1}{4}$ pint (1·5dl) wine vinegar
$\frac{1}{4}$ pint (1·5dl) olive oil
4 cloves garlic, crushed
1 sprig thyme
2 sprigs parsley
1 bay leaf
4–6 peppercorns
12 coriander seeds

1 Trim stems and wash mushrooms thoroughly. Drain and place in a saucepan with cold water, lemon juice and salt to taste. Bring gently to the boil; lower heat and simmer for 10 minutes. Place blanched mushrooms in a shallow earthenware dish.

2 Combine the remaining ingredients in an enamelled saucepan; bring to the boil, lower heat and simmer for 20 minutes. Pour mixture over mushrooms and allow to marinate in the refrigerator for 24 hours.

Or

*Opposite: Marinated Mushrooms
Below: Roast Leg of Lamb with Garlic, Lemon and Parsley Dressing (page 30)*

Menu

Marinated
Mushrooms
or
Avocado Soup

Roast Leg of
Lamb with Garlic,
Lemon and
Parsley Dressing

Old English Trifle
or
Elizabeth
Moxon's Lemon
Posset

Serves 4

*with this menu I suggest
the following Inexpensive
Red Wines*
**Pomerol
Beaujolais
Bourgueil**

Avocado Soup

2 ripe avocado pears
1 teaspoon curry powder
Salt and freshly ground black pepper
$\frac{1}{4}$ pint(1·5dl) double cream
1 pint(6dl) stock
2 teaspoons lemon juice
Cayenne pepper
Finely chopped parsley

1 Peel avocados thinly and halve each one lengthwise; remove stones and dice flesh, retaining a little of the darker green flesh for garnish. Blend diced avocado in an electric blender together with the curry powder, salt and freshly ground pepper, and double cream.

2 Combine stock and lemon juice. Bring gently to the boil; add a little to the avocado and cream mixture, and then blend all together with the remaining stock and reheat gently.

3 Correct seasoning, adding a little cayenne pepper, and more lemon juice if desired. Serve in individual dishes, garnished with chunks of dark green avocado and a little finely chopped parsley.

Roast Leg of Lamb with Garlic, Lemon and Parsley Dressing

(illustrated on the previous page)

1 leg of lamb $3\frac{1}{2}$–4 lbs (1·5–1·8kg)
1 tablespoon butter
1$\frac{1}{2}$ lb(675g) potatoes, peeled and sliced
Salt and freshly ground black pepper
$\frac{1}{2}$ pint(3dl) rich chicken stock
GARLIC, LEMON AND PARSLEY
DRESSING:
6 cloves garlic, finely chopped
6 tablespoons finely chopped parsley
6 tablespoons fresh breadcrumbs
6 tablespoons softened butter
Juice of 1 lemon
Salt and freshly ground black pepper

1 Have your butcher trim and tie a leg of lamb. Butter a shallow fireproof casserole or gratin dish just large enough to hold leg of lamb comfortably.

2 Peel and cut potatoes in thick slices and arrange in the bottom of the dish in overlapping rows. Salt and pepper the potatoes generously.

3 Place lamb on the potatoes and moisten with chicken stock. Season generously with salt and freshly ground black pepper.

4 Roast lamb in a preheated, moderately hot oven (400°F/200°C/Mark 6) for 25 minutes per lb/450g or until lamb is pink and tender. If you prefer lamb well done, increase to 30 minutes per lb/450g.

5 **To make dressing:** make a smooth paste of finely chopped garlic, parsley, fresh breadcrumbs, butter and lemon juice and season to taste with salt and freshly ground black pepper.

6 One hour before lamb is due to come out of the oven, remove it; allow it to cool for 15 minutes, spread it with dressing and return it to the oven for an hour.

Old English Trifle

1 can peeled whole apricots
1 jam roll
$\frac{1}{4}$ pint(1·5dl) sweet Marsala
2 tablespoons cornflour
2 tablespoons sugar
$\frac{1}{2}$ pint(3dl) hot milk
3 egg yolks
1 cup crumbled macaroons

TOPPING:
1 pint(6dl) double cream
$\frac{1}{2}$ teaspoon vanilla essence
Sugar
Fresh strawberries or crystallized
    fruits, to garnish

1 Drain syrup from a tin of peeled whole apricots. Remove pits and purée apricots in an electric blender. Cut jam roll into slices. Arrange slices in the bottom of a large glass serving bowl, reserving 4 to 6 for decoration. Pour Marsala over slices and spread apricot purée over them.

2 **To prepare custard:** mix cornflour and sugar to a smooth paste with a little milk; combine with remaining hot milk in the top of a double saucepan and bring to the boil. Cook over water, stirring continuously, until the mixture thickens. Remove from heat and beat in egg yolks one by one. When well blended, simmer gently over water, stirring constantly, for 10 minutes. Stir in crumbled macaroons and leave to soak until soft; then beat well to dissolve them. Cool custard. Arrange reserved jam roll slices around dish and fill dish with custard. Chill for 2 hours.

3 Just before serving, whisk double cream with vanilla essence and sugar until thick. Then, either cover custard with whipped cream and decorate with fresh strawberries or crystallized fruits, or pipe whipped cream over custard, serving remainder separately, and decorate with strawberries or fruits.

Elizabeth Moxon's Lemon Posset

1 pint(6dl) double cream
Grated rind and juice of 2 lemons
¼ pint(1·5dl) dry white wine
Icing sugar
3 egg whites
Freshly grated orange peel

Add the grated lemon rind to double cream and whisk until stiff. Stir in lemon juice and dry white wine. Add sugar to taste. Whisk egg whites until they form peaks and fold into whipped cream mixture. Serve garnished with a little freshly grated orange peel.

Avocado Stuffed Tomatoes

8–12 large ripe tomatoes

GUACAMOLE FILLING:
2 ripe avocado pears
Juice of 1 lemon
1 tablespoon onion juice
1 clove garlic, mashed
Salt and freshly ground black pepper
Mexican chili powder to taste
4 tablespoons finely chopped celery
** or green pepper**
1 tablespoon finely chopped fresh
** coriander or parsley**

1 Plunge tomatoes into boiling water, one by one, and holding each tomato in a clean towel, peel off the skin with a sharp knife. Slice off cap and carefully scoop out all pulp and seeds. Cover tomatoes loosely with aluminium foil and chill until ready to use.

2 **To make Guacamole filling:** peel and mash avocados lightly with a wooden spoon. Add lemon juice and seasonings. Fold in celery or pepper and chill.

3 Just before serving, fill each tomato case with *Guacamole* mixture; sprinkle with finely chopped coriander or parsley.

Mussel Soup
(illustrated overleaf)

1 Spanish onion, finely chopped
1 clove garlic, finely chopped
½ pint(3dl) dry white wine
1 quart(1·1 litres) mussels, cooked in
** 1 pint(6dl) water**
Salt and freshly ground black pepper
Dry mustard
2 oz(50g) butter
2 oz(50g) flour
Coarsely chopped parsley
Heart-shaped croûtons
Turmeric (optional)

Menu

**Avocado
Stuffed Tomatoes
or
Mussel Soup**

**Roast Chicken
with Watercress
Stuffing**

**Orange Dessert
or
Iced Coffee
Soufflés**

Serves 4

*with this menu I suggest
the following Inexpensive
White Wines*
**Muscadet
Chablis
Vinho Verde**

1 Cook the onion and garlic in white wine, 1 pint(6dl) water and strained mussel liquor until vegetables are soft. Season to taste with salt, freshly ground black pepper and mustard.

2 Make a *roux* with the butter and flour, and thicken soup. Add the mussels in their shells and reheat soup.

3 Serve sprinkled with coarsely chopped parsley and accompanied by heart-shaped *croûtons*. Tint the soup with a little turmeric if desired.

Roast Chicken with Watercress Stuffing

1 roasting chicken, $3\frac{1}{2}$–4 lb(1·6–1·8kg)
1–2 rashers fat bacon
Butter, for basting
Flour
Watercress, to garnish

STUFFING:
6 tablespoons finely chopped onion
6 tablespoons finely chopped celery
6 tablespoons butter
1 bunch watercress, finely chopped
Salt and freshly ground black pepper
$\frac{1}{4}$ lb(100g) dry breadcrumbs

1 **To make stuffing:** simmer onion and celery in half the butter until soft. Add watercress and season to taste with salt and freshly ground black pepper. Cook until all liquids evaporate.

2 Melt remaining butter; stir in breadcrumbs and add to watercress mixture.

3 Stuff chicken with this mixture; tie 1 or 2 rashers of fat bacon over the breast, making 1 or 2 slits in the bacon to prevent it from curling. Cover the bird with waxed paper and roast in a slow oven (325°F/170°C/Mark 3), removing paper from time to time to baste chicken with butter. Cook bird for 1 to $1\frac{1}{2}$ hours, according to size and age. Test it by piercing the flesh of the leg with a skewer or sharp pointed knife. When juices seem clear, it is cooked. But don't be worried if the meat near the bone of the thigh is still a little pink, your chicken will only be more moist if this is so.

4 A few minutes before the end of cooking time, remove the paper and bacon; sprinkle the breast lightly with flour; baste well and brown quickly.

5 **To serve:** put bird on a hot serving dish, and garnish with watercress.

Orange Dessert

3 tablespoons sugar
I level tablespoon cornflour
$\frac{1}{4}$ pint (1·5dl) orange juice
$\frac{1}{2}$ teaspoon finely sliced orange rind
2 tablespoons Cointreau
2 tablespoons cognac
Pinch of salt
Knob of butter
6 navel oranges
Sprigs of mint

I Combine sugar, cornflour, 6 tablespoons water and orange juice in the top of a double saucepan. Cook over low heat, stirring constantly, until thickened. Remove from heat and stir in orange rind, Cointreau, cognac, salt and butter. Cool.

2 To prepare oranges: cut through the rind of each orange vertically from the stem almost to the bud end, forming 8 segments, and curl each segment of peel inwards under the fruit at the base of each orange.

3 Loosen orange segments just enough so that they can be eaten easily with a knife and fork. Trim away any excess membrane and glaze oranges lightly with sauce. Chill. Just before serving, spoon a little more sauce over orange sections and decorate with sprigs of mint.

Iced Coffee Soufflés

4 eggs
$\frac{1}{4}$ lb (100g) sugar
2 tablespoons powdered coffee
2 oz (50g) chocolate
2 tablespoons rum
$\frac{1}{2}$ pint (3dl) double cream
Grated chocolate

I Separate eggs and beat yolks with sugar and powdered coffee until mixture is thick and creamy. Melt chocolate with 2 tablespoons water in a small saucepan; add rum and stir into egg and coffee mixture.

2 Whip cream and fold into soufflé mixture. Whisk egg whites and fold into mixture. Fold in 2 tablespoons grated chocolate; pour into individual soufflé dishes or custard cups and freeze for 4 hours. Decorate with a little grated chocolate.

Opposite: Mussel Soup
Below: Orange Dessert

**Devilled
Whitebait
or
Crab Salad**

**Steak and Kidney
Pudding**

**Apple Snow
or
Burnt Pudding**

Serves 4

*with this menu I suggest
the following Inexpensive
White Wines*
**Muscadet
Sancerre**
*or the following Medium-
priced white Wines*
**Felstar
Adgerstone
Hambledon**
*or the following Inexpensive
Red Wines*
**Cabernet (Yugoslavian)
Beaujolais Fleurie
Châteauneuf-du-
Pape**

Devilled Whitebait

(illustrated on page 12)

1½ lb(675g) whitebait
Ice cubes
Salt and freshly ground black pepper
Flour
Lard, for frying
Cayenne pepper
Lemon wedges

1 Put whitebait to firm in a shallow bowl with ice cubes and a little water. Just before frying, spread fish on a clean tea cloth to dry. Place on paper liberally dusted with well-seasoned flour and dredge with more flour; place in a wire basket, a portion at a time, and shake off surplus flour. Then plunge the basket into very hot lard and fry quickly for 3 to 5 minutes, shaking basket continually to keep fish apart while cooking.

2 Lift basket from fat and shake it well before transferring fish to paper towels to drain. Place whitebait on a serving dish in a warm oven while remainder are fried. Season with freshly ground black pepper and cayenne and serve with lemon wedges.

Crab Salad

½ pint(3dl) well-flavoured
    mayonnaise (see page 152)
2 tablespoons tomato ketchup
Tabasco or Worcestershire sauce
3 tablespoons olive oil
1 tablespoon wine vinegar
2 level tablespoons finely grated onion
2 tablespoons finely chopped parsley
6 tablespoons double cream, whipped
Salt, freshly ground black pepper and
    cayenne pepper
1–2 tablespoons chopped olives
1 lb(450g) cooked crabmeat, flaked
4–6 large tomatoes
Lettuce and sliced hard-boiled eggs, to
    garnish

1 Blend together mayonnaise, tomato ketchup, Tabasco or Worcestershire sauce, olive oil, wine vinegar, finely grated onion, finely chopped parsley and whipped cream. Season to taste with salt, freshly ground black pepper and a dash of cayenne. Stir in chopped olives and chill for 1 or 2 hours before serving. This sauce is delicious for all seafood cocktails.

2 Add flaked crabmeat.

3 Slice tomatoes in half; place on salad plates; pile crab salad on tomatoes and garnish with lettuce and sliced hard-boiled eggs.

Steak and Kidney Pudding

(illustrated on page 36)

1½–2 lb(675–900g) steak
½ lb(225g)calf's kidney
2 tablespoons flour
Salt and freshly ground black pepper
6 oz(175g) freshly grated or packaged
    suet
¾ lb(350g) self-raising flour
Dripping
4 tablespoons finely chopped shallot
    or onion
¼ pint(1·5dl) rich beef stock
2–4 tablespoons port wine (optional)

1 Cut steak and kidney into rather small pieces, and shake well in a bowl containing flour and ½ level teaspoon each salt and freshly ground black pepper, until all the pieces are well coated.

2 Combine freshly grated suet with self-raising flour, adding pepper and salt to taste, to make a light suet crust.

3 Grease a pudding basin with dripping, line it with pastry and put in the seasoned meat and finely chopped shallot or onion. Combine stock and port wine (if desired) and fill the basin nearly to the top with this

mixture, adding a little water if necessary. Put on the pastry lid, making sure that the edges are well sealed to keep in the steam. Cover the whole pudding with a floured cloth and simmer or steam for 3 to 4 hours. The crust should be rather damp.

Apple Snow

1½ lb(675g) cooking apples
6 oz(175g) castor sugar
Juice of ½ lemon
2 egg whites
Whipped cream
Toasted slivered almonds

1 Core apples, cut in thick slices and put with very little water in a covered saucepan. Cook until soft; sieve and measure off ½ pint(3dl) purée. Add sugar and lemon juice. Cool.

2 Whisk egg whites until stiff, fold in apple mixture and continue whisking until stiff and fluffy.

3 Pile into tall glasses and decorate with a swirl of whipped cream and toasted almond slivers.

Burnt Pudding

Castor sugar
½ pint(3dl) single cream
4 egg yolks, well beaten
Grated lemon rind
½–1 teaspoon vanilla essence

1 Add 2 tablespoons castor sugar to cream in the top of a double saucepan and bring mixture to the boil, stirring constantly. Then gradually pour the cream over well-beaten egg yolks, stirring until well blended. Return egg and cream mixture to the top of the double saucepan; add grated lemon rind to taste and cook over simmering water,

stirring, until mixture thickens to a custard-like consistency. When thick enough, flavour with vanilla essence and pour into a heatproof soufflé dish or individual soufflé dishes to set. Chill.

2 When thoroughly set cover with a thick layer of sugar and place under a preheated grill until the sugar caramelizes. Cool.

Artichoke Soup

1½ lb (675g) Jerusalem artichokes
1½ pints well-flavoured chicken stock
3 large potatoes, peeled and quartered
1 Spanish onion, quartered
Salt and freshly ground black pepper
Freshly grated nutmeg
1 egg yolk
½ pint (3dl) single cream

GARNISH:
Lemon rings
Cream
Cayenne pepper

1 Put artichokes in a saucepan of cold water and bring gradually to the boil. Drain; cool in running water and then peel.

2 Simmer artichokes in well-flavoured chicken stock with potatoes and onion until all vegetables are soft, 15 to 20 minutes.

3 Purée with stock in an electric blender, or press through a fine sieve; season to taste with salt, pepper and a little nutmeg.

4 Beat egg yolk into cream; add to soup and heat, stirring constantly, until soup is heated through. Do not allow it to come to the boil, or the egg will curdle.

5 Decorate with rings of lemon, topped with a swirl of cream sprinkled with cayenne.

Menu

Artichoke Soup
or
Watercress Salad
with Mushrooms

The 'No-roast'
Roast Beef

English Spring
Pudding
or
Pineapple
Romanoff

Serves 4

with this menu I suggest the following Inexpensive Red Wines
**Bordeaux Supérieur
Côtes-du-Rhône
Châteauneuf-du-
Pape**
or the following Medium-priced Red Wines
**Beaune
Pommard
Nuits-St-Georges**

Steak and Kidney
Pudding (page 34)

Watercress Salad with Mushrooms

1 bunch watercress
1 head lettuce
8-12 walnuts
4-6 oz (100-175g) mushrooms
Vinaigrette sauce (see below)
2 tablespoons finely chopped parsley
2 tablespoons finely chopped chives

1 Wash and trim the watercress. Wash and dry the lettuce leaves. Shell and halve the walnuts. Wash mushrooms, trim stem ends and slice mushrooms thinly.

2 Make a vinaigrette sauce with 2 tablespoons wine vinegar, 6 to 8 tablespoons olive oil, coarse salt and pepper.

3 Toss walnut halves and sliced mushrooms in the vinaigrette sauce.

4 Line a salad bowl with lettuce leaves. Arrange the prepared watercress in the centre. Scatter nuts and sliced mushrooms over, together with vinaigrette sauce. Garnish with finely chopped fresh herbs. Toss at the table in front of guests.

The 'No-roast' Roast Beef

Lovers of perfectly rare beef, pink and juicy from end to end, with just the outer surface richly crusted, should try the following method when next cooking a joint weighing 5 lb (2·25 kg) or more. I have attempted to adapt it to smaller pieces of beef, too, but have had to admit defeat, which is sad, as the method is otherwise foolproof.

Rib roast of beef, 3 or 4 ribs, 6-9lb
 (2·7-4 kg)
Salt and freshly ground black pepper
4 level tablespoons dripping or butter
6-8 tablespoons red wine, stock or water

1 Ask your butcher to trim off rib bones close to the meat.

2 Turn the thermostat up to 500°F/ 250°C/Mark 10 and give the oven at least 20 minutes to heat up before proceeding.

3 Rub joint all over with salt and freshly ground black pepper, and spread it with 4 level tablespoons dripping or butter. Lay it on a rack over a roasting tin.

4 Place meat in the oven. Roast for 5 minutes per lb/450g; then, without opening the oven door, switch off the heat and leave for a further 2 hours. *Do not, under any circumstances, open the oven door during this time.*

5 When the 2 hours are up, open the door and, without removing the tin from the oven, touch the beef with your finger. If it

Watercress Salad with Mushrooms

feels hot, go ahead and serve it. However, as some ovens do not retain their heat as well as others (electricity is often rather better than gas in this instance), you may find the beef on the lukewarm side. If so, close the door, relight the oven, still at 500°F/250°C/Mark 10, and give it a further 10 minutes or so. This will raise the temperature of the beef without affecting its rareness.

6 To serve roast beef: when the joint is done to your liking, season it with additional salt and freshly ground black pepper. Transfer it to a well-heated platter, large enough to allow the carver to operate comfortably, and leave it to stand for 15 to 20 minutes at the front of the turned off oven with the door open. This will allow the cooking to stop and the juices to subside, making it easier to carve neatly.

7 In the meantime, pour off most of the fat in the roasting pan and use the juices and sediment that remain, reinforced with a little red wine, stock or water, and the juices that poured from the roast as it 'set', to make your gravy. Make sure your sauceboat and plates are very hot, too. Congealed gravy is unpleasant.

English Spring Pudding

2 lb (900g) rhubarb
1 lb (450g) sugar
3 tablespoons lemon juice
Butter
Thin slices of white bread
Custard sauce or whipped cream

1 Wash and trim young rhubarb stalks; cut them into 1-inch (2·5-cm) lengths. Combine rhubarb, sugar, lemon juice and 3 tablespoons butter in a thick-bottomed saucepan; bring gently to the boil, stirring continuously; lower heat and simmer, stirring all the while, for about 5 minutes, or until rhubarb becomes soft but still keeps its identity. Don't let stalks disintegrate

entirely; they must remain a trifle firm to be at their best. (Rhubarb varies enormously in flavour when cooked; so add a little more sugar if too tart, a little more lemon juice if too sweet.)

2 Lightly butter a soufflé dish; trim crusts from bread; cut each slice in half lengthwise and line sides of soufflé dish. Then cut enough slender triangles of bread to cover bottom of dish, and trim off standing bread slices at rim of dish.

3 Fill dish with rhubarb mixture, reserving a little of the juice. Cut additional bread triangles to cover pudding. Chill in refrigerator overnight to firm.

4 Just before serving, turn pudding out on a serving dish. Pour over reserved rhubarb juice. Serve with custard or whipped cream.

Pineapple Romanoff

1 large pineapple
6 tablespoons icing sugar
3 tablespoons Cointreau
3 tablespoons rum
½ pint(3dl) double cream
3 tablespoons Kirsch
Grated rind of 1 orange

1 Slice top off pineapple. Scoop out flesh to within 1 inch(2·5cm) of the bottom, being careful not to damage shell. Dice flesh and toss segments in a bowl with 2 tablespoons icing sugar. Pour over them a mixture of Cointreau and rum; chill in the refrigerator.

2 One hour before serving: whip cream; add remaining icing sugar and flavour with Kirsch. Spoon whipped cream into marinated pineapple pieces, tossing until every piece is coated with creamy liqueur mixture. Spoon into pineapple shell – or into individual dishes – and dust with grated orange rind. Keep cold until time to serve.

Cost-Wise Entertaining Three Simple Menus Based on Minced Beef

Good cooks the world over favour minced meat because it is as easy to cook as it is to eat; because it is economical to buy and a little can be made to go a long way; and because it gives free rein to their inventiveness, for it can be stretched, shaped, seasoned and sauced in a variety of ways. For the best results, of course, it pays to mince the meat yourself, or ask your butcher to do it especially for you. In this way you know exactly what you are getting. Minced meat must not be too fat, for instance; 2 oz(50g) fat to 1 lb(450g) beef is about right.

I have enjoyed super hamburgers and meat loaves in America, *pâtés* and mousses in France and meatballs in almost every country of the world. Whether the origin of the dish is Moroccan or Egyptian, French or Scandinavian, Greek or Italian, it all comes down to the same basic recipe: *take a pound of mince*.

Fettuccine al Burro e Formaggio

1 lb(450g) Italian noodles
Salt
Freshly grated Parmesan cheese
    (garnish)

SAUCE:
$\frac{1}{4}$ lb(100g) butter
4–6 tablespoons double cream
$\frac{1}{4}$ lb(100g) freshly grated Parmesan
    cheese

1   Cook the noodles in boiling salted water for 5 to 8 minutes until just tender, or a little longer if you like your pasta more thoroughly cooked, stirring it with a fork from time to time to separate the strands.

2   **Meanwhile, prepare the sauce:** beat the butter until light, then gradually beat in the cream, followed by the grated cheese.

3   Drain the *fettuccine* when cooked and turn immediately into the Parmesan mixture. Toss with a serving fork and spoon to coat the strands thoroughly with the sauce.

Sprinkle with additional Parmesan and serve immediately.

Italian Stuffed Peppers

(illustrated overleaf)

4–6 green peppers
Olive oil
Butter
Salt and freshly ground black pepper
1 Spanish onion, finely chopped
1 lb(450g) minced beef
Freshly grated nutmeg
2 level tablespoons grated Parmesan
    cheese
12 black olives, pitted and chopped
3 level tablespoons seedless raisins
2 level tablespoons chopped chives
2 level tablespoons chopped parsley
$\frac{1}{2}$ pint(3dl) chicken stock (made with a
    cube)
Strips of canned pimento

1   Remove the tops of the peppers and scoop out pith and seeds. Place peppers in boiling water, to cover; add 2 tablespoons olive oil and leave for 5 minutes. Drain well and dry.

Menu

Fettuccine al
Burro e
Formaggio

Italian Stuffed
Peppers

Green Salad
with
Italian Dressing

Cassata alla
Siciliana

Serves 4–6

with this menu I suggest the following Inexpensive White Wines
**Soave
Verdicchio
Lachryma Christi**

39

2 Place a small piece of butter in the bottom of each pepper and season well. Sauté finely chopped onion in 4 tablespoons olive oil until onion is soft. Add minced beef and continue to cook, stirring constantly, until meat just begins to brown. Add salt and freshly ground black pepper, freshly grated nutmeg, grated Parmesan cheese, chopped black olives, seedless raisins, chopped chives and parsley and mix well.

3 Stuff peppers with this mixture and place in a flat ovenproof dish. Pour chicken stock over peppers and bake in a preheated moderate oven (375°F/190°C/Mark 5) for 30 to 40 minutes or until done, basting them frequently. Just before serving garnish each pepper with thin strips of canned pimento. Serve hot as a main course; cold as an appetizer.

Green Salad with Italian Dressing

1–2 heads lettuce

ITALIAN DRESSING:
1 tablespoon lemon juice
1–2 tablespoons wine vinegar
$\frac{1}{4}$ teaspoon dry mustard
1 pinch dried oregano
Coarse salt and freshly ground black pepper
6–8 tablespoons olive oil

1 Wash lettuce leaves well in a large quantity of water. They should be left whole, never cut. Drain well and dry thoroughly in a cloth or a salad basket so that there is no water on them to dilute the dressing.

2 To make dressing: mix together lemon juice, wine vinegar, dry mustard and oregano, and season to taste with coarse salt and freshly ground black pepper. Add olive oil and beat with a fork until the mixture emulsifies.

Cassata alla Siciliana

1 pint (6dl) vanilla ice cream
$\frac{1}{2}$ pint (3dl) strawberry or raspberry ice cream
Chopped crystallized fruits
Chopped nuts
$\frac{1}{2}$ pint (3dl) pistachio ice cream
Crystallized fruits for decoration

1 Mould vanilla ice cream around the inside of a 2-pint (1-litre) *bombe* mould or pudding basin, and place a smaller mould or basin in the centre to hold the ice cream in position. Freeze.

2 Carefully remove the inner mould. Mould the strawberry or raspberry ice cream inside the vanilla layer and, as before, place a still smaller mould or basin in the centre. Freeze.

3 Carefully remove the centre mould. Stir the chopped crystallized fruits and chopped nuts into the pistachio ice cream. Remove the centre mould and fill with the pistachio ice cream. Freeze once more.

4 To serve: unmould and decorate with crystallized fruits.

Cassata alla Siciliana

41

Moroccan Meatballs

1 lb(450g) minced beef or lamb
2 oz(50g) beef or lamb fat
½ Spanish onion, finely chopped
6 mint leaves, finely chopped
6 sprigs parsley, finely chopped
¼ level teaspoon dried marjoram
¼ level teaspoon powdered cumin
¼ level teaspoon cayenne pepper
¼ level teaspoon paprika
¼ level teaspoon cinnamon
Salt and freshly ground black pepper
Butter

SAUCE:
1 lb(450g) tomatoes, peeled, seeded
   and coarsely chopped
½ Spanish onion, finely chopped
2 tablespoons finely chopped parsley
1 clove garlic, finely chopped
4 tablespoons olive oil
Paprika
Cayenne pepper
Salt

1 Combine meat and fat with onion, mint leaves and parsley. Mix well and add dried marjoram, powdered cumin, cayenne pepper, paprika and cinnamon, with salt and freshly ground black pepper to taste.

2 Form into little balls the size of a marble and poach gently in water for 10 minutes. Then sauté gently in butter until lightly browned.

3 **To make sauce:** combine tomatoes with finely chopped onion, parsley and garlic, olive oil, ½ pint (3dl) water and paprika, cayenne pepper and salt, to taste (the sauce too should be very highly flavoured) in a saucepan and simmer for 1 hour, uncovered.

4 Finally, simmer meatballs in sauce for at least 10 minutes before serving. Serve in sauce or on a bed of **boiled rice** (see page 70), steamed couscous, or **mashed potatoes** (see next column) with sauce separate.

Mashed Potatoes

2 lb(900g) floury potatoes
Salt
¼ pint (1·5dl) hot milk
2 oz(50g) butter, melted
3 level tablespoons double cream
Freshly ground black pepper
Freshly grated nutmeg

1 Peel potatoes and, if they are very large, cut them up into roughly even-sized pieces.

2 Boil potatoes in salted water until they feel soft when pierced with a fork but are not disintegrating. (Overcooked potatoes will produce a water-sodden purée, not a fluffy one as you might expect.)

3 As soon as potatoes are cooked, drain them thoroughly and toss in the dry pan over moderate heat until remaining moisture has completely evaporated.

4 Mash potatoes to a smooth purée or rub them through a fine wire sieve; return them to the pan.

5 Gradually beat in hot milk with a wooden spoon. (If potatoes are particularly dry, you may need to use more milk.) Then add melted butter and cream and continue to beat vigorously until purée is light and fluffy.

6 Season purée to taste with salt, freshly ground black pepper and a grating of fresh nutmeg, and beat over a moderate heat until purée is thoroughly hot again. Take great care not to let purée boil, or it may discolour. Serve immediately.

Note: Although ideally a potato purée should be served as soon as it is prepared, you can keep it hot for up to half an hour by putting it in a buttered mixing bowl over hot water, covered with well-buttered greaseproof paper. Just before serving, beat purée up again to restore its texture.

Sautéed Courgettes and Tomatoes

(illustrated on page 105)

12 courgettes
Salt
6 tablespoons flour
6 tablespoons freshly grated Parmesan
   cheese
Freshly ground black pepper
4 tablespoons olive oil
4 tablespoons butter
1 Spanish onion, coarsely chopped
8 tomatoes, peeled, seeded and
   chopped
4 coriander seeds, crushed

1 Slice courgettes thickly and poach in boiling salted water until just tender, about 5 minutes. Drain thoroughly, then dry slices on absorbent kitchen paper.

2 Combine flour with freshly grated Parmesan, salt and freshly ground black pepper to taste. Toss courgette slices in this mixture until lightly coated.

3 Heat oil in a heavy sauté pan and sauté courgettes over a moderate heat until golden brown on all sides. Remove from pan with a slotted spoon; drain thoroughly on absorbent paper. Pile in centre of a suitable serving dish and keep hot.

4 Melt butter in pan and sauté coarsely chopped onion until soft and transparent. Add chopped tomatoes and crushed coriander seeds and simmer for 2 to 3 minutes longer.

5 Surround courgettes with sautéed onion and tomato mixture. Serve hot.

Moroccan Orange Salad

4–6 ripe oranges
6–8 dates, chopped
6–8 blanched almonds, slivered
Orange flower water (or lemon juice
   and powdered sugar)
Powdered cinnamon

1 Peel oranges, removing all pith, and slice crosswise. Place in a salad bowl with chopped dates and slivered almonds and flavour to taste with orange flower water or lemon juice and powdered sugar.

2 Chill. Just before serving, sprinkle lightly with powdered cinnamon.

Meat Loaf

2 lb(900g) lean beef, minced – or 1½ lb
   (675g) minced beef and ½ lb(225g)
   minced pork or sausage meat
1 Spanish onion, finely chopped
2 level teaspoons salt
Freshly ground black pepper
½ level teaspoon dried rosemary,
   marjoram or sage
2 eggs, well beaten
4 slices white bread
¼ pint(1·5dl) milk or light beef or
   chicken stock
Butter
2 rashers bacon

1 Combine minced beef in a large mixing bowl with onion, salt, freshly ground black pepper, rosemary, marjoram or sage and well-beaten eggs.

2 Trim crusts from bread and shred into milk or stock. Add bread and liquid to the meat mixture and mix well.

3 Pack mixture into a lightly buttered loaf pan 9 × 5 × 2½ inches (23 × 13 × 6·5cm) mounding it slightly on top (or, if you prefer, shape it into a long, thin loaf on a baking sheet); top with two bacon rashers and bake in a moderate oven (350°F/180°C/ Mark 4) for 1¼ hours. Serve hot – or cold as a picnic loaf.

Menu

Meat Loaf
with
Baked Stuffed
Potatoes
and
Tomatoes
Provençale

Italian Fruits in
Marsala
or
Strawberries with
Marsala
and
Pernod

Serves 4

with this menu I suggest the following Inexpensive Red Wines
Macon Rouge
Beaujolais
Valpolicella

Baked Stuffed Potatoes

6 medium-sized cold baked potatoes
4 tablespoons single cream
2 oz(50g) softened butter
4-6 level tablespoons freshly grated
   Parmesan cheese
Salt and freshly ground black pepper

1 Preheat oven to moderate (375°F/190°C/ Mark 5).

2 Cut a thin slice from each potato and with a spoon scoop out the pulp into a bowl, leaving a firm shell.

3 Mash potato pulp smoothly with cream, butter and Parmesan and season with salt and freshly ground black pepper.

4 Pile potato purée back into shells and place potatoes on a wire rack.

5 Bake for 25 to 30 minutes or until potatoes are thoroughly heated.

Tomatoes Provençale

4-6 firm tomatoes
Butter
$\frac{1}{4}$-$\frac{1}{2}$ level teaspoon French mustard
Salt and freshly ground black pepper
1-1$\frac{1}{2}$ oz(25-40g) soft white
   breadcrumbs
1-1$\frac{1}{2}$ level tablespoons finely chopped
   parsley
2-3 teaspoons olive oil

1 Grease a wide, shallow baking dish lightly with butter.

2 Cut tomatoes in half horizontally and arrange them side by side in the dish, cut sides up. Spread lightly with mustard and season with salt and freshly ground black pepper.

3 Toss breadcrumbs with parsley and sprinkle over tomatoes. Trickle a little olive oil over each tomato.

4 Bake on shelf below meat for 20 minutes, or until breadcrumbs are golden.

Italian Fruits in Marsala

$\frac{1}{2}$ lb(225g) sugar
Juice of 1 lemon
$\frac{1}{4}$ pint(1·5dl) Marsala
4-6 small peaches
1 small pineapple
1 small punnet strawberries

1 Dissolve the sugar in $\frac{1}{4}$ pint (1·5dl) water and lemon juice, and boil to form a heavy syrup. Allow to cool. Stir in Marsala and leave to become quite cold.

2 Blanch the peaches by plunging quickly into boiling water, then remove the skins. Immerse in the syrup.

3 Peel the pineapple and cut into thick slices. Add to the peaches. Wash the strawberries, but do not remove the stems and leaves. Stir into the syrup.

4 Chill thoroughly before serving.

Strawberries with Marsala and Pernod

3 small punnets of ripe strawberries
Juice of 1 lemon
6 tablespoons Marsala
3 tablespoons Pernod
Sugar

Wash and hull strawberries, discarding any berries that are not perfect. Slice strawberries in half and sprinkle with lemon juice, Marsala and Pernod. Toss well and add sugar, to taste. Chill until ready to serve.

Kidneys that are the Cat's Whiskers

My cat Somi – a pale Siamese with lilac grey points – is a super talker. From a low, contented growl of greeting at breakfast time to a high frequency shriek as he shoots up the curtains in an occasional spurt of jungle abandon, he's a never-failing source of wonder to me.

His chatty, catty conversation rises to new heights whenever he can smell kidneys. For Somi is crazy about kidneys and hangs around for a taste.

However, it's not entirely to please Somi that we have kidneys, cooked in one way or another, quite often at our house. I particularly like halved lambs' kidneys grilled on a skewer – each half-kidney topped just before serving with a savoury knob of 'snail' butter, which is butter mashed with lemon juice, finely chopped parsley and a hint of garlic.

First take your kidneys . . . . Remove skin and excess fat and then cut out the hard core with a pair of pointed kitchen scissors. Soak kidneys (especially ox kidneys) for at least 15 minutes in cold salted water before cooking – changing water at least once during this time. Since they are rather perishable, kidneys should be purchased fresh when needed and carefully refrigerated, loosely covered to permit circulation of air, until ready to cook. French cooks serve kidneys, except pork, juicily pink within. So if you want to get the best from these kidney recipes, don't overcook. Kidneys tend to toughen if they are cooked too long.

Menu

Mussels cooked like Snails

Creamed Kidney Stew with Buttered Carrots

Bananas with Orange

Serves 4

with this menu I suggest the following Inexpensive Rosés
Tavel
Rosé de Provence

Mussels cooked like Snails

(illustrated on page 48)

48 mussels
2 tablespoons chopped shallots
2 sprigs thyme
2 sprigs parsley
1 bay leaf
Salt
¼ pint(1·5dl) dry white wine

BEURRE D'ESCARGOTS:
½ lb(225g) butter
3 cloves garlic, finely chopped
¾ cup finely chopped parsley
¼ cup finely chopped chives

1 Choose fine fat mussels and scrape, beard and wash them. Place in a saucepan together with finely chopped shallots, thyme, parsley and a bay leaf.

2 Season lightly with salt and moisten with dry white wine. Steam for 4–5 minutes, or until the shells are well opened. Remove 1 half-shell from each.

3 **To make beurre d'escargots:** knead together butter, finely chopped garlic, parsley and chives. If chives are not available, add more parsley. Chill butter again before using.

4 Butter mussels copiously with *beurre d'escargots*; place them in their half-shells in 4 individual ovenproof dishes and bake in a hot oven for 2–3 minutes.

Creamed Kidney Stew

2 veal kidneys
4 lambs' kidneys
Butter
2 tablespoons olive oil
Salt and freshly ground black pepper
1 can (approx. 10 fl oz [275ml]) creamed chicken soup

12 cooked button onions
4 small cooked carrots, sliced
$\frac{1}{4}$ lb(100g) button mushrooms, sliced

1 Trim fat and skin from kidneys, remove cores and cut kidneys into lengthwise slices.

2 Melt 2 tablespoons each butter and olive oil in a pan; add kidneys and brown for 3 minutes on each side. Season with salt and freshly ground black pepper. Pour off fat and drain kidneys.

3 Return kidneys to pan; add chicken soup, onions, sliced carrots and sliced button mushrooms which you have simmered in a little butter until tender.

4 Season with salt and pepper and simmer for 4–6 minutes. Serve with **buttered carrots** (see page 19).

Bananas with Orange

4 large or 8 small bananas
Juice of $\frac{1}{2}$–1 lemon
1 oz(25g) butter
Juice and finely grated rind of
** 1 orange**
1 oz(25g) castor sugar

1 Peel bananas. Brush each one with lemon juice as soon as you peel it to avoid discolouration; then leave to absorb lemon flavour for a few minutes.

2 Melt butter in a large, heavy frying pan

into which bananas will fit side by side; add orange juice, grated orange rind and sugar. Stir over low heat until sugar has dissolved.

3 Arrange bananas side by side in the pan and brown them gently all over, taking care not to burn sauce or overcook bananas. Serve immediately.

Greek Egg and Lemon Soup

1 chicken joint (leg or breast)
2$\frac{1}{2}$ pints(1·4 litres) chicken stock
** (see page 21)**
3 eggs
2 tablespoons lemon juice
6–8 level tablespoons cooked long-
** grain rice**
Salt and freshly ground black pepper
2–3 level tablespoons finely chopped
** parsley**

1 Bring chicken stock to the boil in a pan and poach chicken joint for 15–20 minutes.

2 Remove joint from stock and leave until cool enough to handle. Strain stock through a fine sieve into a clean pan and return to heat to keep hot but not boiling.

3 Skin and bone chicken joint, cutting flesh into very thin slivers.

4 In a bowl, beat eggs lightly with lemon juice. Add a ladleful of hot stock to the egg mixture, beating vigorously with a whisk.

5 Now bring remaining stock to the boil. Remove from heat; add cooked rice and slivered chicken and stir in egg mixture. Season to taste with salt and freshly ground black pepper and return to very low heat for 3–4 minutes, stirring constantly, until soup is hot and creamy. Do not allow it to boil again, or eggs will curdle.

6 Stir in finely chopped parsley and serve immediately.

Greek Egg and
Lemon Soup

Lambs' Kidneys
Italian Style
with
Pommes
Parisiennes

Gooseberry Fool

Serves 4–6

*with this menu I suggest
the following Inexpensive
Red Wines*
Bourgueuil
Beaujolais Villages
Chianti Ruffino Red

Lambs' Kidneys Italian Style

1 lb(450g) frozen peas
$\frac{1}{4}$ lb(100g) button mushrooms, sliced
$\frac{1}{2}$ pint(3dl) Italian tomato sauce
Salt and freshly ground black pepper
8 lambs' kidneys
2 tablespoons olive oil
2 level tablespoons butter
$\frac{1}{2}$ Spanish onion, finely chopped
3 slices cooked ham, finely chopped
Lemon juice

1 Simmer peas and sliced button mushrooms in tomato sauce. Season with salt and freshly ground black pepper.

2 Strip kidneys of fat; remove skin; cut out hard cores and then cut kidneys into $\frac{1}{4}$-inch (0·5-cm) slices. Sauté sliced kidneys in olive oil and butter with finely chopped onion and finely chopped ham.

Mussels cooked like Snails (page 46)

3 When kidneys are tender (3–5 minutes), add a little lemon juice and combine in a serving dish with peas and mushrooms in tomato sauce.

Pommes Parisiennes

2 lb(900g) large potatoes
3 level tablespoons butter
1 tablespoon olive oil
Salt and freshly ground black pepper
Finely chopped parsley, to garnish

1 Peel, wash and dry potatoes.

2 Holding a potato firmly in one hand, press the bowl of a 1-inch (2·5-cm) Parisienne cutter (the same gadget you use to make melon balls) into the flesh, open side down. Twist gently from side to side until you can scoop out a neat ball of potato. Scoop as many balls as you can out of each potato – the trimmings can be used in a *vichyssoise* (leek and potato soup), see page 168, or boiled and mashed.

3 Dry potato balls thoroughly.

4 Select a large, heavy frying pan which will hold all the potato balls in one layer. Melt butter and oil in it and, when foaming subsides, add potato balls. Sauté over moderate heat, shaking pan frequently so that potato balls brown evenly, for 15 minutes, or until they are crisp and golden on the outside and feel soft when pierced with the point of a knife. Season to taste.

5 Drain potato balls thoroughly and serve sprinkled with finely chopped parsley.

Gooseberry Fool

(illustrated on page 52)

$1\frac{1}{2}$ lb(675g) gooseberries
$\frac{1}{4}$–$\frac{1}{2}$ lb(100–225g) sugar
$\frac{1}{4}$ pint(1·5dl) double cream, whipped

CUSTARD:
$\frac{1}{4}$ pint(1·5dl) milk
$\frac{1}{2}$ teaspoon cornflour
Sugar
2 egg yolks, well beaten
Vanilla extract

1 Clean and wash gooseberries and remove stems; put them in an enamelled saucepan with $\frac{1}{4}$ pint(1·5dl) water and sugar. Cook until they are quite soft and then rub them through a fine sieve.

2 To make custard: combine milk with cornflour and sugar to taste in the top of a double saucepan. Bring to the boil. Pour a little of the hot liquid into well-beaten egg yolks, mix well, then return the egg yolk mixture to the milk and cornflour and cook over hot, but *not* boiling water, stirring constantly with a wooden spoon, until custard is thick and smooth. Do not let the mixture boil. Flavour to taste with vanilla extract, strain and cool.

3 Mix custard and whipped cream (reserving a little cream for garnish) with the gooseberry purée and serve in a glass bowl or in individual glasses. Garnish with whipped cream.

Cold Ratatouille (page 51)

What's French for Rissoles?

Everyday British cooking is laced with splendiferous French terms – fricassé, marinade, daube – which have entered easily into our language. A case in point is croquettes – the most glamourous way of serving leftovers ever invented!

Croquettes – from the French word *croquer*, meaning 'to crunch' or 'to crackle under the teeth' – are delicate little morsels (generally shaped into diminutive sausages, rounds or squares) deep-fried in hot fat or oil until they are wonderfully crisp on the outside and meltingly creamy on the inside.

Croquettes are absolutely delicious when properly made. You'll find this great speciality of French cooking makes even the most ordinary leftovers interesting. Make your croquettes of minced, cooked or canned fish, chopped hard-boiled eggs, minced cooked meats or finely chopped cooked vegetables, held together by a thick white sauce, coated with egg and breadcrumbs and then deep-fried to a crisp gold.

Basic rule for easy croquette making:
Use $\frac{1}{3}$ pint(2dl) thick white sauce to bind 1 lb(450g) ground or minced solid food. Always drain moisture from solid food before combining with sauce.

THICK WHITE SAUCE:
2 level tablespoons butter
4 level tablespoons flour
$\frac{1}{3}$ pint(2dl) milk
1 level teaspoon finely chopped onion
1 level teaspoon finely chopped parsley
Salt and pepper
1 level teaspoon lemon juice

1 Melt butter in a saucepan. (I like to use the top of a double saucepan for making sauces so that I can stir them over gently bubbling water without danger of scorching.) Add flour and mix well. Then add milk, onion, parsley, salt and pepper and cook until sauce is thick, stirring continuously. Stir in lemon juice.

2 To shape croquettes: spread croquette mixture – the white sauce combined with the minced solid food of your choice – about 1 inch(2·5cm) thick in a greased baking tray. Chill until ready to use. Then cut mixture into squares, dust with a little flour and form into the shape desired – squares, oblongs, sausages, balls, or even perfectly shaped apples and pears.

3 To coat croquettes with egg and breadcrumbs: dip each croquette, formed as above, into 1 egg beaten with 2–3 tablespoons of water and then roll in fine dry breadcrumbs to make a crisp crust when croquettes are deep-fried. You'll find that it is often wise to dip each croquette into the egg and breadcrumb mixture one more time to make sure that the filling cannot ooze out of its crisp case during the cooking.

4 To fry croquettes: croquettes are usually fried in deep cooking fat or oil (375°F/190°C on frying thermometer) for 1–5 minutes, or until they are evenly browned all over. Drain croquettes on kitchen paper, keeping them warm in a slow oven (325°F/170°C/Mark 3) until serving.

Cold Ratatouille
(illustrated on page 49)

8 tablespoons olive oil
2 Spanish onions, sliced
2 green peppers, diced
2 aubergines, diced
2 baby marrows, cut in slices
4–6 ripe tomatoes, peeled, seeded
     and chopped
Salt and freshly ground black pepper
1 tablespoon chopped parsley
Pinch of marjoram or oregano
Pinch of basil
1 large clove garlic, crushed

1 Heat olive oil in a heatproof casserole; add onion slices and sauté until they are transparent. Add green peppers and aubergines and, 5 minutes later, baby marrows and tomatoes. The vegetables should not be fried but stewed in the oil, so simmer gently in a covered pan for 30 minutes.

2 Add salt and pepper to taste, chopped parsley, marjoram or oregano, basil and crushed garlic; then cook uncovered for about 10 to 15 minutes, or until *ratatouille* is well mixed and has the appearance of a *ragoût* of vegetables – which it is.

3 Serve cold as a delicious beginning to a summer meal.

Salmon Croquettes

Thick white sauce (see previous page)
Two 7-oz(200-g) cans of salmon,
    flaked
4 level tablespoons freshly grated
    Parmesan cheese
Salt and freshly ground black pepper
Finely chopped onion
Lemon juice
Fine dry breadcrumbs
1 egg, lightly beaten
Fat, for frying

1 Add flaked salmon to sauce together with Parmesan cheese. Taste mixture, adding salt and freshly ground black pepper, finely chopped onion and lemon juice to taste.

2 Spread mixture about 1 inch (2·5cm) thick in a greased baking tray. Chill.

3 Shape into 8 croquettes; roll in fine dry breadcrumbs, dip into egg, lightly beaten with 2 to 3 tablespoons water, roll again in breadcrumbs and chill until ready to fry.

4 Fry in deep fat (375°F/190°C on frying thermometer) until golden.

Rice Pilaff

¾ lb(350g) long-grain rice
½ Spanish onion, finely chopped
Butter
¾ pint(4dl) well-flavoured stock
Thyme
Salt and freshly ground black pepper

1 Wash rice; drain and dry with a cloth.

2 Sauté finely chopped onion in butter until a light golden colour.

3 Add rice and continue to cook, stirring constantly, until it begins to take on colour.

4 Pour in hot stock and season with thyme, salt and freshly ground black pepper.

5 Cover saucepan and place in a moderate oven (350°F/180°C/Mark 4) for 15 to 20 minutes, or until the liquid has been absorbed and the rice is tender but not mushy. Serve with additional butter.

Or

Rice Pilaff with Pine Nuts
Toss 2 oz(50g) pine nuts in butter until crisp and golden. Just before serving, scatter over **rice pilaff** (see recipe above).

Menu

Cold Ratatouille

Salmon
Croquettes
with
Rice Pilaff
or
Rice Pilaff
with
Pine Nuts

Normandy Baked
Apples

Serves 4

*with this menu I suggest
the following Inexpensive
White Wines or
Rosés*
**Muscadet
Sancerre
Rosé de Provence**

Normandy Baked Apples

1 lb(450g) frozen puff pastry
6 large eating apples
1½ oz(40g) castor sugar
Ground cloves
3–4 level tablespoons butter
1 egg, beaten, to glaze

1 Defrost puff pastry. Preheat oven to hot (450°F/230°C/Mark 8).

2 Peel apples; core them carefully from the stem end without going quite to the bottom. Roll pastry out into a sheet about ⅛ inch (0·3cm) thick and cut out 6 6-inch(15cm) squares.

3 Moisten apples slightly and place each one in the centre of a pastry square. Sprinkle each apple with a little castor sugar and a generous pinch of ground cloves. Push a knob of butter into each cavity.

4 Bring pastry squares up around apples to enclose them completely; seal them tightly, moistening seams with a drop of water if necessary and trimming off any excess pastry. Roll out pastry trimmings and cut out 'leaves' to decorate tops of apples. Alternatively, you can make a slightly more elaborate and very pretty decoration as follows: roll out remaining pastry thinly and cut out circles to fit tops of apples like little caps; press down lightly but firmly, then make 'leaves' from remaining scraps of pastry and arrange on top so that the tips of the leaves overlap the edges of the caps.

5 Brush apples with beaten egg. Place them on a baking sheet and bake for 10 minutes at 450°F/230°C/Mark 8; then lower oven temperature to 425°F/220°C/Mark 7 and continue to bake for a further 20 minutes, or until pastry is puffed and a rich golden colour.

6 Delicious hot, sprinkled with a little more castor sugar. Serve with cream.

Gooseberry Fool
(page 48)

Onions à la Grecque
(page 56)

Chicken Croquettes

Thick white sauce (see page 50)
1 lb(450g) cooked chicken, minced
Dash of Tabasco or Worcestershire sauce
Salt and freshly ground black pepper
1 level tablespoon finely chopped onion
Lemon juice
Fine dry breadcrumbs
1 egg, lightly beaten
Fat, for frying

1 Combine sauce with cooked chicken and Tabasco or Worcestershire sauce. Taste mixture, adding salt, pepper, onion and lemon juice as desired.

2 Spread mixture about 1 inch(2·5cm) thick in a greased baking tray. Chill; then cut mixture into 8 portions.

3 Shape each portion into a round or oblong-shaped patty and roll in fine dry breadcrumbs. Dip croquettes into a lightly beaten egg mixed with 2 to 3 tablespoons water; roll again in breadcrumbs and chill until ready to fry.

4 Fry croquettes in deep fat (375°F/190°C on frying thermometer) for about 5 minutes, or until golden brown. Serve immediately with **glazed courgettes** (see below) and **boiled rice** (see page 70).

Glazed Courgettes

2 lb(900g) or 12 small courgettes
Butter
Salt and freshly ground black pepper
Sugar
Light stock

1 Cut unpeeled courgettes into quarters lengthwise; slice each quarter into 2-inch (5-cm) segments and blanch in boiling water for about 3 minutes. Drain.

2 Combine courgettes in a shallow saucepan with a little butter, salt, freshly ground black pepper and sugar to taste. Add a little light stock and simmer gently, covered, until liquid has almost disappeared and courgettes are glazed and tender.

Port-'n'-Pippins

1½ lb(675g) small Cox's Orange Pippins, peeled and cored
½ lb(225g) sugar
1 inch(2·5cm) cinnamon stick
1 inch(2·5cm) whole ginger
Rind of 1 lemon
1 glass port
Red food colouring (optional)
Whipped cream (optional)

1 Combine sugar, 1 pint(6dl) water, cinnamon and ginger in a saucepan with the thinly peeled rind of 1 lemon, and boil for 10 minutes. Strain and cool. Pour this syrup over the apples in a bowl; cover with a plate and marinate overnight.

2 The following day, transfer apples and syrup to an enamelled saucepan and simmer until tender.

3 Remove apples with a slotted spoon and arrange in a shallow serving bowl. Add port to syrup and strain it over apples. A few drops of red food colouring may be added to syrup if desired, and apples may be decorated with a little whipped cream.

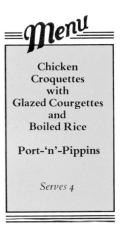

Menu

Chicken Croquettes with Glazed Courgettes and Boiled Rice

Port-'n'-Pippins

Serves 4

with this menu I suggest the following Inexpensive White Wines or Rosés
Sancerre
Chablis
Tavel

It's all a Skewer

Turkish Lamb Kebabs
(page 56)

Skewered meats are famous the world over. Whether they are called *kebabs* (as they are in Turkey and the Middle East), *brochettes* (in France and North Africa) or *satés* (the Far East and Polynesia) these tender morsels of meat, fish, or poultry – first marinated, then threaded on metal skewers and grilled – add up to the same thing: a delicious *meal-on-a-stick*.

If you have never tried making *kebabs* or *brochettes* in your own kitchen now is the time to start. You will find they are wonderfully easy to make, for most of the preparation is done in advance, and the actual cooking time is a matter of minutes only. And cutting up the meat, fish or poultry into small squares makes a little go a long way.

The secret of all skewer cookery lies in the marinade. One of the simplest I know – and equally good for beef, lamb, pork, chicken, fish or shellfish – is the following: combine 4 tablespoons each olive oil and lemon juice with 2 level tablespoons finely chopped parsley, 2 crumbled bay leaves, a little finely chopped onion or garlic, salt and freshly ground black pepper to taste.

MOROCCAN SPICE MARINADE

White part of 1 leek, chopped
½ Spanish onion, chopped
1 level teaspoon sea salt
½ level teaspoon each of powdered cumin and ginger, and crushed black pepper
4 tablespoons olive oil
Cayenne pepper and paprika

Pound leek, onion and salt in a mortar; add to meat and sprinkle with powdered cumin, ginger and crushed black pepper. Add olive oil and cayenne pepper and paprika, to taste. Mix well.

TURKISH MARINADE

White part of 1 leek, chopped
½ Spanish onion, chopped
6 level tablespoons parsley, chopped
6 tablespoons olive oil
Salt and freshly ground black pepper

Combine chopped leek, onion and parsley and olive oil. Add generous amounts of salt and freshly ground black pepper. Mix well.

Let it remain in this mixture for at least 2 hours, or overnight. Then thread the cubed meat on long metal skewers (the flat-edged variety are the best) alternately with the vegetables of your choice.

Do not push the pieces of meat and vegetables too closely together or the meat will not cook all the way through. To grill, place skewers about 3 or 4 inches (7.5 or 10cm) from the heat and cook – turning skewers occasionally – until the meat is medium brown, basting with the marinade juices from time to time. I like lamb and beef cooked until they are well browned on the outside, but still moist and pink on the inside. Try grilling a test skewer – with just a vegetable or two on it – to see how many minutes you should cook *kebabs* so that they are done to your liking.

The choice of *kebab* variations is practically limitless: arrange meats, poultry or fish on skewers alternately with your choice of small white onions, either raw or poached, strips of green pepper, cubes of poached potato, mushroom caps, sliced baby marrow or aubergine, thin wedges of apple or tomato (wrapped in bacon to keep them from falling off the skewer), whole small tomatoes or cubes of fat salt pork.

Menu

Onions à la
Grecque

Turkish Lamb
Kebabs
with
Saffron Rice Salad

Raspberry
Bavarois

Serves 4

*with this menu I suggest
the following Inexpensive
Red Wines*
**Médoc
Beaujolais
Macon**

Onions à la Grecque

(illustrated on page 52)

2 lb(900g) small onions
$\frac{1}{4} - \frac{1}{2}$ pint (1·5–3dl) dry white wine
5 oz(150g) sugar
5 oz(150g) raisins
4 tablespoons tomato concentrate
4 tablespoons olive oil
2–4 tablespoons wine vinegar
Salt and freshly ground black
  pepper
Cayenne pepper
Coarsely chopped parsley

1 Peel onions. Combine in a saucepan with 1 pint(6dl) water, dry white wine, sugar, raisins, tomato concentrate and olive oil. Add wine vinegar, salt, freshly ground black pepper and cayenne pepper, to taste, and simmer for about $\frac{1}{4}$ hour, or until onions are tender but still quite firm.

2 Serve cold, garnished with coarsely chopped parsley.

Turkish Lamb Kebabs

(illustrated on previous page)

2 lb(900g) lamb, cut from the leg
4 tiny green peppers, caps and
  seeds removed (or 4 squares cut
  from 1 green pepper)
4 small tomatoes
2 baby marrows, thickly sliced
4 mushroom caps

MARINADE SAUCE:
6 tablespoons olive oil
4 tablespoons sherry
1–2 cloves garlic, finely chopped
$\frac{1}{4}$ Spanish onion, finely chopped
2 tablespoons finely chopped parsley
1 level teaspoon oregano
Salt and freshly ground black pepper

1 Combine marinade ingredients in a mixing bowl. Cut meat into 1-inch(2·5-cm) squares and place in marinade mixture, making sure each piece of meat is properly covered. Cover bowl with a plate and refrigerate for 12 to 24 hours. Turn meat several times during marinating period.

2 When ready to cook, place meat on 4 large skewers alternately with green peppers, tomato, sliced baby marrows and mushroom caps.

3 Brush meat and vegetables with marinade sauce and cook over charcoal or under grill until done, turning skewers frequently and basting several times during cooking. Serve with **saffron rice salad** (see below).

Saffron Rice Salad

$\frac{1}{2}$ level teaspoon powdered saffron
$\frac{1}{4}$ level teaspoon powdered cumin
6 tablespoons dry white wine
1 pint(6dl) hot chicken stock
$\frac{3}{4}$ lb(350g) Italian rice for risotto
$\frac{1}{2}$ green pepper, seeded and cut into
  squares
$\frac{1}{2}$ red pepper, seeded and cut into
  squares
$\frac{1}{2}$ Spanish onion, coarsely chopped
Salt and freshly ground black pepper

DRESSING:
6–8 tablespoons olive oil
2–3 tablespoons wine vinegar
2 tablespoons finely chopped parsley
Salt and freshly ground black pepper

1 Dissolve saffron and cumin in white wine and chicken stock, and combine in a large saucepan with rice, pepper squares, chopped onion, salt and freshly ground black pepper, to taste. Cover pan and simmer until all the liquid is absorbed and the rice is tender. Add some more liquid if necessary.

2 Drain well and toss with dressing. Allow to cool. Add more oil or vinegar if necessary.

Raspberry Bavarois

1 lb(450g) frozen raspberries
3 oz(75g) castor sugar
3 egg yolks
½ pint(3dl) milk
½ oz(14g) powdered gelatine
Juice of 1 lemon
½ pint(3dl) double cream
Tasteless oil, for mould

1 Place raspberries in a sieve over a bowl and sprinkle with 1 oz(25g) castor sugar. Leave until completely defrosted.

2 Whisk remaining sugar with egg yolks until light and fluffy.

3 Scald milk. Pour over egg and sugar mixture gradually, beating constantly.

4 Transfer mixture to the top of a double saucepan and stir over simmering water until sauce thickens enough to coat the back of a wooden spoon. Take care not to let it boil, or egg yolks will curdle. Remove from heat and cool slightly.

5 Meanwhile, soften gelatine for 5 minutes in 4 tablespoons of the syrup from the raspberries; then stir over hot water until liquid is clear and gelatine completely dissolved.

6 Cool gelatine mixture slightly. Blend with cooling custard.

7 Crush two-thirds of the raspberries, reserving the best ones, and press them through a sieve to make a purée. Blend purée with custard; then fold in whole fruit, taking care not to crush them. Add lemon juice to taste.

8 Whip half the cream lightly. Fold into raspberry custard.

9 Brush a 2-pint(1-litre) decorative mould with about 1 tablespoon oil. Pour in the raspberry cream and chill until firm.

10 When ready to serve: whip remaining cream stiffly.

11 Dip mould for 1 or 2 seconds only into very hot water. Turn *bavarois* out on to a serving dish and pipe whipped cream in a decorative pattern over top and sides. Serve very cold.

Chinese Spiced Spareribs

(illustrated overleaf)

2 lb(900g) pork spareribs
4 tablespoons dry sherry
4 tablespoons soy sauce
1 level tablespoon sugar
2 cloves garlic, finely chopped
¼ level teaspoon each cinnamon,
grated nutmeg and powdered
cloves
Salt
Hot mustard

1 Combine the sherry, soy sauce, sugar, finely chopped garlic and spices. Add a little salt if desired. Marinate the spareribs in this mixture for at least 2 hours.

2 When ready to cook, place the spareribs on a rack in a roasting pan and cook in a preheated slow oven (325°F/170°C/Mark 3) for 1 hour, basting frequently with the marinade juices.

3 Cut into separate 'ribs' and serve with hot mustard.

menu

Chinese Spiced Spareribs

Chinese Skewered Beef or Chinese Skewered Pork with Steamed Rice

Watercress and Orange Salad

Candied Apple Fritters

Serves 4

with this menu I suggest China Tea or the following Inexpensive White Wines
Sancerre
Muscadet

Chinese Skewered Beef

1–1¼ lb(450–575g) tender rump
or sirloin steak
Freshly ground black pepper
1 tablespoon soy sauce
1 tablespoon oyster sauce
1–2 tablespoons fermented black
beans
1 level tablespoon sugar
1 tablespoon olive oil
2 tablespoons dry white wine

1 Cut beef into 1-inch(2·5-cm) cubes, re-moving fat and gristle. Put in a large bowl. Sprinkle with freshly ground black pepper.

2 Combine Chinese bottled or canned sauces: soy sauce, oyster sauce, fermented black beans (all available from Chinese supermarkets) and add sugar, olive oil and dry white wine. Pour marinade over meat and toss well. Leave to marinate for 2 hours.

3 Preheat grill at maximum for 20 minutes before cooking.

4 Divide marinated meat among 6 skewers. Assemble *brochettes*.

5 Grill 6 to 8 minutes for rare beef, turning skewers frequently to ensure even cooking; 8 to 10 minutes for medium rare; and 10 to 15 minutes for well done. Serve im-mediately.

Chinese Skewered Pork

2 lb(900g) lean pork
1 level teaspoon dry mustard
½ level teaspoon ground ginger
1 finely chopped Spanish onion
1 finely chopped garlic clove
4 tablespoons lemon juice
Salt and freshly ground black pepper
1–2 tablespoons liquid honey

1 Advance preparation: cut pork into 1-inch(2·5-cm) squares. Put these into a large mixing bowl and sprinkle with mus-tard, ginger, onion, garlic, lemon juice, salt and freshly ground black pepper, to taste.

2 Add liquid honey and toss well so that meat is impregnated with the aromatics. Allow to stand in this mixture for at least 2 hours, turning occasionally, so that meat is well flavoured.

3 When ready to grill: arrange pork on metal skewers and grill 3 to 4 inches(7·5 to 10cm) from heat until done. To test pork: cut a piece open with the point of a sharp knife. Pork is done only when there is no trace of pinkness in cut piece of meat.

4 Serve with **steamed rice** and a **water-cress and orange salad** (see page 60).

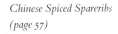

Chinese Spiced Spareribs
(page 57)

Steamed Rice

¾ lb(350g) long-grain rice
4 tablespoons lemon juice
Salt

1 Fill a large pan two-thirds full of water. Add lemon juice and a small handful of salt and bring to the boil.

2 When water is bubbling briskly, shower in rice. Stir well to dislodge any grains that have attached themselves to the bottom and boil, uncovered, for 10 to 12 minutes. Rice should be cooked, but still very firm.

3 Drain rice thoroughly in a colander.

4 Cut a large square of double-thickness muslin. Heap rice in the centre and wrap up in a loose bundle.

5 Place bundle in a steamer over boiling water. Cover tightly and steam for 20 to 25 minutes, or until rice grains are fluffy, tender, and quite separate.

Note: You can wrap the rice in a clean tea towel instead of muslin, but make sure that any washing soap has been thoroughly rinsed out of it to avoid tainting the rice.

Watercress and Orange Salad

4 bunches watercress
2 oranges

DRESSING:
6–8 tablespoons olive oil
2 tablespoons wine vinegar
1 teaspoon Dijon mustard
Salt and freshly ground black pepper
1–2 level tablespoons finely chopped spring onion or chives

1 Prepare watercress and chill in a damp towel. Peel oranges, cut into thin segments and chill.

2 Combine olive oil, wine vinegar and Dijon mustard. Season to taste with salt and freshly ground black pepper. Add finely chopped spring onion or chives and mix well.

3 Just before serving, place watercress in a salad bowl, arrange orange segments on top and pour over dressing.

Candied Apple Fritters
(illustrated on previous page)

3 oz(75g) plain flour
Pinch of salt
1 small egg, well beaten
Peanut oil, for deep-frying
4 dessert apples, peeled, cored and cut into eighths
6 tablespoons sugar
Sesame seeds
Butter

1 **To make batter:** sift the flour and salt into a mixing bowl. Gradually blend in the beaten egg and ⅓ pint(2dl) water. Beat together until smooth. Leave batter to stand in a cool place for at least ½ hour.

2 When ready to cook the fritters, heat the peanut oil to 375°F/190°C. Dip the apple wedges into the batter and deep-fry in hot oil until golden. Drain and keep hot.

3 **To make caramel:** very slowly melt the sugar in 3 tablespoons water in a thick-bottomed pan. Boil until a pale golden colour.

4 Remove from the heat. Quickly dip each apple fritter into hot caramel, sprinkle liberally with sesame seeds and serve on a hot buttered dish.

Making the Most of Lamb

Meat is expensive today. With the inevitable spiralling cost of living – both in this country and abroad – it is most important that we get the most out of the cheaper cuts of meat. A leg of lamb – lean, with a small amount of bone – fits the bill to perfection. It may be roasted as it is; boned by your butcher and then stuffed; poached in stock and served with caper sauce; or braised or casseroled in any number of ways. If a whole leg is too large for a small family, ask your butcher to cut it into two pieces; one to roast, the other to braise or stew. Or cook the whole roast and then use the leftovers for one or two delicious meals based on tender, succulent lamb.

Choosing Lamb

High-quality lamb is firm and fine-textured, varying in colour from dark pink to light red. It has a smooth covering of clear pinkish-white brittle fat over most of the exterior. Over this is a thin paperlike covering called the 'fell'. It is not necessary to remove this fell from the leg before roasting. In fact if you leave it on the leg it will hold its shape better, be juicier and cook faster.

Storing Lamb

Fresh lamb, like any other meat, should be wrapped loosely in waxed paper or foil and stored in the coldest part of the refrigerator. A whole raw roast can be kept on a refrigerator shelf for 5 to 6 days.

Cooking Lamb

Lamb should never be overcooked. It is at its succulent best – moist and richly flavoured – when it is just a little pink on the inside. So do not roast it until it is a dull greyish-brown in colour, with the meat falling off the bones, the flesh dry and stringy. Instead treat lamb gently, as the French do, roasting it until the juices run pink when it is cut. For maximum juiciness and minimum shrinkage, I like to sear it in a hot oven (450°F/230°C/Mark 8) for 15 minutes and then cook it at a relatively low temperature (325°F/170°C/Mark 3) for 15 to 20 minutes per lb/450g.

Taramasalata

I 6-oz(175-g) jar smoked cod's roe
6 slices white bread
$\frac{1}{4}$ Spanish onion, grated
1–2 cloves garlic, mashed
8 tablespoons olive oil
6 tablespoons double cream
Juice of 1 lemon
I level teaspoon gelatine dissolved
   in 3 teaspoons water
I tablespoon finely chopped parsley
Black olives
Hot toast

I Place roe in a mortar. Trim crusts from bread; soak bread in water; squeeze lightly and add to roe. Pound mixture to a smooth paste. Stir in grated onion and garlic. Then add olive oil, double cream and lemon juice alternately in small amounts, stirring well, until the mixture is smooth and uniform.

2 Strain through a fine sieve. (The mixing can be done in an electric blender, in which case there's no need to sieve.)

3 Beat in dissolved gelatine.

4 Pipe mixture into individual soufflé dishes or ramekins, sprinkle with chopped parsley and garnish with black olives.

5 Serve with hot toast. I also like to stuff 2-inch (5-cm) lengths of crisp celery with this mixture as a light appetizer.

Menu

Taramasalata

**Lamb Hash
Parmentier**

**Tossed Green
Salad**

Cheeses and Fruit

Serves 4–6

*with this menu I suggest
the following Inexpensive
White Wines*
**Retsina
Muscadet
Sancerre**

Above: French Cucumber Salad (page 64)
Below: Pommes au Beurre (page 64)

Right: the French are most imaginative in their ways of cooking lamb: garlic, parsley, watercress, rosemary and even orange are used to add savour to this delicious meat.

Lamb Hash Parmentier

1 lb(450g) cooked lamb, diced
6 medium potatoes
4 level tablespoons butter
1 egg, well beaten
Salt and freshly ground black pepper
Butter
Olive oil
1 Spanish onion, finely chopped
½ pint(3dl) well-flavoured tomato
   sauce (or thickened tomato-
   flavoured lamb gravy)
3–4 level tablespoons freshly grated
   Parmesan cheese

1 Peel and boil potatoes. Mash 4 of them with butter and well-beaten egg; season to taste with salt and freshly ground black pepper and force through a piping bag to make a border round a shallow ovenproof dish.

2 Dice remaining 2 potatoes and fry in equal quantities of butter and olive oil until golden. Drain and reserve.

3 Fry finely chopped onion in 2 table-spoons olive oil until transparent. Add diced lamb to onion in pan and continue to cook until both begin to turn golden. Season generously with salt and freshly ground black pepper. Stir in fried potatoes; pour over well-flavoured tomato sauce or tomato-flavoured lamb gravy and simmer gently for 10 to 15 minutes, stirring from time to time. Correct seasoning.

4 Spoon hash into centre of potato border; sprinkle with freshly grated Parmesan and cook in a hot oven (450°F/230°C/Mark 8) for 10 to 12 minutes, or until golden brown.

Tossed Green Salad

(for recipe, see **green salad and variations,** page 100)

Cheeses and Fruit

(for **cheeses,** see pages 240–1)

French Cucumber Salad

Lamb in the French Manner with Pommes au Beurre

Fresh Strawberries with Raspberry Purée

Serves 4–6

with this menu I suggest the following Inexpensive Red Wines
**Pomerol
Bourgueuil
Fleurie**

French Cucumber Salad
(illustrated on page 62)

1 **large cucumber**
1 **tablespoon salt**
French dressing (see below)
2 **tablespoons finely chopped fresh parsley**
1 **tablespoon finely chopped fresh tarragon**
Salted whipped cream

1 Peel and slice cucumber thinly; sprinkle with salt and place under a weighted plate in a glass bowl for at least 1 hour. Wash well; drain.

2 Make a French dressing with 3 tablespoons olive oil, 1 tablespoon wine vinegar, salt and freshly ground black pepper, to taste.

3 Place drained cucumber slices in a serving bowl; pour over dressing and toss. Chill in refrigerator for at least 30 minutes.

4 Just before serving, sprinkle with finely chopped parsley and tarragon, and garnish with whipped cream to which you have added salt to taste.

Lamb in the French Manner
(illustrated on previous page)

3½ – 4 lb(1·6 – 1·8kg) **leg of lamb**
1–2 **cloves garlic**
1 **level teaspoon crushed rosemary leaves**
Juice of ½ lemon
4 **level tablespoons softened butter**
Salt and freshly ground black pepper

1 Cut garlic cloves into slivers. Make small slits in lamb and insert slivers.

2 Combine crushed rosemary leaves with lemon juice, butter, salt and freshly ground black pepper, to taste.

3 Spread lamb with this mixture and place on a rack in an open roasting pan. Roast meat, uncovered, in a preheated hot oven (450°F/230°C/Mark 8) for 20 minutes; reduce oven heat to 325°F/170°C/Mark 3 and continue to cook for 20 minutes per lb/450g or until done as you like it.

4 When lamb is cooked, transfer it to a heated serving dish and let it stand for 15 minutes before carving.

Pommes au Beurre
(illustrated on page 62)

2 lb(900g) **potatoes**
Oil, for deep-frying
Salt and freshly ground black pepper
Butter
Finely chopped fresh parsley

1 Peel the potatoes and cut them into small balls with a melon scoop or a vegetable cutter. Soak the potato balls in iced water for 1 hour, then dry them well in absorbent towels.

2 Heat the oil to 370°F/185°C in a large frying pan or deep-fryer. Cook potato balls in fat until golden; then remove, drain and season generously with salt and freshly ground black pepper.

3 Just before serving, sauté potato balls in equal parts of butter and oil until brown and cooked through.

4 Drain; sprinkle with finely chopped fresh parsley and serve immediately.

Fresh Strawberries with Raspberry Purée

2 **punnets fresh strawberries**
2 **punnets fresh raspberries**
Lemon juice
Icing sugar

1 Wash and hull strawberries, and chill.

2 Put raspberries in electric blender with 2 tablespoons each lemon juice and icing sugar and blend until smooth, adding more sugar or lemon juice as desired. Strain into a bowl and chill.

3 **To serve:** pile strawberries into a glass serving bowl and spoon over raspberry purée, covering each berry with the purée. Serve immediately.

Italian Cauliflower Appetizer
(illustrated overleaf)

1 **cauliflower**
Salt
6 **anchovy fillets, finely chopped**
12 **black olives, pitted and finely chopped**
3 **tablespoons finely chopped parsley**
1 **clove garlic, finely chopped**
1 **tablespoon finely chopped capers**
6 **tablespoons olive oil**
2 **tablespoons wine vinegar**
Freshly ground black pepper

GARNISH (optional):
Anchovy fillets
Halved tomatoes

1 Remove green leaves from cauliflower, trim stem and cut off any bruised spots. Break or cut into flowerets and poach in lightly salted water for about 5 minutes. Drain and place in a bowl of cold, salted water for 1 hour. Drain well.

2 Mix anchovies, olives, parsley, garlic and capers with oil and vinegar in a large mixing bowl; add cauliflower and season with salt and pepper to taste. Allow cauliflower to marinate for at least 2 hours in this dressing.

3 **To serve:** arrange marinated cauliflower and dressing in a salad dish; garnish, if desired, with anchovy strips and tomatoes.

Italian Sauté of Lamb

1 **lb(450g) cooked lamb, cut into strips**
6 **large firm tomatoes**
4 **tablespoons olive oil**
Salt and freshly ground black pepper
2 **cloves garlic, finely chopped**
6 **spring onions, thinly sliced**
6 **tablespoons finely chopped parsley**
Grated peel of $\frac{1}{2}$ lemon

1 Drop tomatoes into boiling water for about 30 seconds. Peel them at once and cut them into quarters. Remove seeds from each quarter with a teaspoon, a small knife, or simply with your fingers; cut remaining outer shell and membranes of each tomato quarter into thin strips.

2 Heat olive oil in the bottom of a large thick-bottomed frying pan; add lamb strips and cook over a high heat until well browned on all sides. Season generously with salt and freshly ground black pepper and 1 clove of finely chopped garlic. Add tomato strips and continue to cook, stirring continuously, for about 3 minutes or until the tomato strips are barely cooked through.

3 Add the thinly sliced spring onions and finely chopped parsley. Toss well over heat; then sprinkle with grated lemon peel and remaining garlic; cover pan and allow aromatics to heat through for 3 minutes before serving. Serve with **boiled rice** (see page 70) and **courgettes à la Grecque** (see overleaf).

Menu

Italian Cauliflower
Appetizer

Italian Sauté of
Lamb
with
Courgettes à la
Grecque
and
Boiled Rice

Baked Vanilla
Custard

Serves 4

with this menu I suggest the following Inexpensive Red Wines
Valpolicella
Chianti Ruffino Red
Cabernet
(Yugoslavian)

salted water and 1 oz(25g) butter for 6 to 8 minutes, depending on size of courgettes. Keep warm in cooking liquid.

2 Sauté chopped onion and garlic in remaining butter until transparent. Add chopped tomatoes and cook until soft but not mushy. Season generously with salt and freshly ground black pepper.

3 Remove courgettes from cooking liquid, drain and arrange in a heated oblong *gratin* dish. Pour over tomato and onion mixture and serve immediately.

Baked Vanilla Custard

4 egg yolks
2 egg whites
Castor sugar
Pinch of salt
$\frac{1}{2}$ teaspoon vanilla extract
1 pint(6dl) milk
Butter

1 Beat the egg yolks and whites in a bowl with 2 tablespoons castor sugar, salt and vanilla extract.

2 Heat the milk without allowing it to boil and pour it slowly on to the beaten eggs, stirring constantly. Strain the mixture into a well-buttered soufflé dish.

3 Place the dish in a baking tin with a little cold water round it and cook in a moderate oven (375°F/190°C/Mark 5) for about 1 hour, or until the custard sets and the top is golden brown. The water in the tin will prevent the custard from becoming too hot and curdling.

4 Sprinkle with a little castor sugar before serving.

Courgettes à la Grecque

8 courgettes
Salt
2 oz(50g) butter
1 medium onion, chopped
1 clove garlic, finely chopped
4 ripe tomatoes, peeled, seeded and chopped
Freshly ground black pepper

1 Score courgettes lengthwise with a tin opener or the end of a pointed teaspoon. Poach courgettes lightly in $\frac{1}{4}$ pint(1·5dl)

66

Left: Italian Cauliflower Appetizer (page 65)

Right: Courgettes à la Grecque

White and Brown

SAUCES

Béchamel Sauce

Melt 2 tablespoons butter for the *roux* in the top of a double saucepan. Cook ½ onion and 1 stalk celery, finely chopped, in it over a low heat until onion is soft but not browned. (For a fuller flavour, I sometimes add 4 level tablespoons chopped cooked ham or chopped raw veal to the onion and celery mixture.) Remove pan from heat, stir in 2 tablespoons flour, return to heat and cook gently for 3 to 5 minutes, stirring constantly, until flour is cooked through. Add ¼ pint/1·5dl milk, heated to boiling point, and cook over hot water, stirring vigorously. As the sauce begins to thicken add a further ¾ pint/4dl hot milk, stirring constantly with a wooden spoon until sauce bubbles. Add 1 small sprig thyme, ½ bay leaf, white peppercorns and freshly grated nutmeg to taste, and simmer sauce gently for 15 minutes. Strain through a fine sieve and dot surface with butter. Makes about 1 pint/6dl.

Variations

Cream Sauce For fish, poultry, eggs and vegetables:
Add 4 tablespoons double cream to 1 pint/6dl hot Béchamel and bring to boiling point. Add a few drops lemon juice.

Mornay Sauce For fish, vegetables, poultry, poached eggs, noodle and macaroni mixtures:
Mix 2 slightly-beaten egg yolks with a little cream and combine with 1 pint/6dl hot Béchamel sauce.

Cook, stirring constantly, until it just reaches boiling point. Add 2 tablespoons butter and 2 to 4 tablespoons freshly grated cheese (Parmesan or Swiss cheese is best).

Aurore Sauce Excellent with eggs, chicken or shellfish:
Add 2 to 3 tablespoons tomato purée to 1 pint/6dl hot Béchamel sauce.

Velouté Sauce Melt 2 tablespoons butter in a saucepan; add 2 tablespoons flour and cook for a few minutes to form *roux blond*. Add 1 pint/6dl boiling white stock (chicken or veal), salt and white peppercorns and cook, stirring vigorously with a whisk. Add 4 chopped button mushrooms and cook slowly, stirring occasionally and skimming from time to time, until the sauce is reduced to two-thirds of its original quantity and is very thick but light and creamy. Strain through a fine sieve.

Espagnole Sauce

1 Melt 3 tablespoons beef dripping in a large, heavy saucepan; add 3 oz/75g diced fat salt pork (or green bacon), 3 carrots, 1 Spanish onion and 2 stalks celery, all coarsely chopped, and cook until golden. Sprinkle with 3 tablespoons flour and cook gently over very low heat, stirring frequently, until well browned. Divide 3 pints/1·7 litres of boiling home-made beef stock into three parts; add first third together with *bouquet garni* and 1 clove garlic to flour mixture and

cook, stirring frequently, until sauce thickens.

2 Add the second third of stock and cook very slowly over a very low heat, uncovered, stirring the sauce occasionally, for about 1½ to 2 hours. Skim off scum and fat rising to surface as it cooks. Add ¼ pint/1·5dl rich tomato sauce (or 3 to 4 tablespoons tomato concentrate) and cook for a few minutes longer. Then strain through a fine sieve into a bowl, pressing the vegetables against the sieve to extract all their juices.

3 Clean the saucepan; return the mixture to it; add remaining stock and continue cooking slowly until the sauce is reduced to about 2 pints/1·1 litres, skimming the surface from time to time.

4 Strain again. Cool, stirring occasionally. Store in a covered jar in the refrigerator until ready for use.

Variations

Madeira Sauce Reduce 1 pint/6dl *Espagnole* sauce until it is half the original quantity. Add 6 tablespoons Madeira. Heat the sauce well but do not let it boil, or the flavour of the wine will be lost.

Sauce Bordelaise Cook 2 finely chopped shallots in ¼ pint/1·5dl red wine until liquid is reduced to a third of its original quantity. Add ½ pint/3dl *Espagnole* sauce and simmer gently for 10 minutes.

Remove the marrow from a split beef bone; cut it into small dice and poach it in boiling salted water for 1 or 2 minutes. Drain, and just before serving sauce add 2 tablespoons diced beef marrow and a little finely chopped parsley.

Sauce Lyonnaise Sauté ½ Spanish onion, finely chopped, in 2 tablespoons butter until golden. Add 6 tablespoons dry white wine and simmer until reduced to half the original quantity. Add ½ pint/3dl *Espagnole* sauce; cook gently for 15 minutes; add 1 tablespoon chopped parsley and finish by swirling in 1 tablespoon butter.

French Onion Sauce Chop 1 Spanish onion finely; cover with water and parboil for 3 to 5 minutes. Drain and sauté onion in butter until soft. Add 1 pint/6dl hot Béchamel sauce and cook 15 minutes longer. Strain sauce through a fine sieve; return to heat; beat in 4 tablespoons double cream and flavour with nutmeg, lemon juice, salt and white pepper, to taste.

Sauce Fines Herbes Remove leaves from 3 sprigs each parsley, tarragon and chervil. Chop stems and sauté in butter with a few chopped shallots and mushrooms. Add 2 chopped tomatoes and 8 tablespoons dry white wine and cook until reduced to half original quantity. Add 1 pint/6dl *Espagnole* sauce and simmer for 20 minutes. Strain. Heat sauce with reserved leaves, juice of ½ lemon and 1 level tablespoon butter.

Four Meals Based on Rice

Rice is one of the easiest vegetables to cook really well. And yet it is rare to come across rice cooked to perfection – each grain separate and fluffy, just tender, not mushy.

If you would like to make perfect rice – every time – follow the simple rules for Basic Boiled Rice and Basic Risotto below before you go on to the special Summer Rice Dishes. And remember, the best rice for savoury dishes is long-grain rice. Keep the smaller grains for sweets and puddings only.

Basic Boiled Rice

There are countless ways of cooking plain boiled rice. Some cooks prefer to steam it; others insist that unless a knob of butter or a little oil is added to the cooking liquid, the grains won't be separate. I like to boil it in a large, heavy saucepan capable of holding a good quantity of water. The secret of getting separate grains of white, fluffy rice is very simple indeed; just salt the water, add a little lemon juice to keep the rice white, and, when the water is boiling well, dribble the grains into the liquid through your fingers, stirring all the while. Then simply allow rice to cook uncovered for 14 to 18 minutes. During the last 2 or 3 minutes of cooking time watch the rice carefully, for the only real test is the *taste test*. I always pick out a grain or two with a fork and test them. When the rice is just right, with the granular core tender, but not mushy, drain it in a large colander and keep warm over boiling water until ready to serve. Serve the rice as it is to accompany curries or Chinese dishes; or add butter and a little freshly grated Parmesan if the rice is served as an accompanying vegetable to grilled or roast meat or fish.

Basic Risotto

One of the most delicious ways to cook rice is the risotto. Wash $\frac{1}{2}$ lb(225g) long-grain or Italian rice in cold water. Drain thoroughly. Add 3 to 4 tablespoons butter, salt and freshly ground black pepper, to taste and $1\frac{3}{4}$ pints (1 litre) chicken stock or beef stock, flavoured with a little dry white white. Bring to the boil, stirring; reduce heat; cover tightly and simmer gently for 14 to 18 minutes; uncover, toss lightly with a fork, add a little extra butter and some grated Parmesan and serve. The rice should have absorbed all the liquid and the grains should be moist but separate.

Variations

If a good stock is used in cooking the rice, and you have sautéed it with a little finely chopped onion before adding the liquid, it will take on extra strength and flavour. Try adding to it $\frac{1}{2}$ lb(225g) diced, cooked chicken or lamb that has been heated in a little stock with half a Spanish onion, finely chopped, and cooked until golden in 2 tablespoons of butter or oil. Adding a teaspoon or two of curry powder, $\frac{1}{2}$ teaspoon of powdered saffron, chopped nuts, diced raw apple, or plumped-up raisins will also do much to change the taste and quality of your summer rice dish. This with a salad, followed by a sweet or cheese and fruit, will make a delicious and satisfying meal.

Three Rice Dishes:
Spanish Pork and Rice Casserole (page 77),
Kedgeree (page 75), and Harem Pilaff (page 74) 71

Menu

Salade de Moules

Lamb Fried Rice
with
Herbed Buttered
Carrots

Apple Pie with
Orange Juice

Serves 4

*with this menu I suggest
the following Inexpensive
White Wines*
**Muscadet
Sancerre
Chablis**

Salade de Moules

2 **quarts(2·3 litres) mussels**
2 **level tablespoons finely chopped
   shallots**
2 **sprigs parsley**
$\frac{1}{4}$ **level teaspoon thyme**
1 **bay leaf**
**Salt and freshly ground black
   pepper**
4–6 **tablespoons dry white wine**
2 **tablespoons wine vinegar**
Olive oil
2 **level tablespoons coarsely chopped
   parsley**

1 Scrub mussels thoroughly under cold running water and remove 'beards'. Discard any that are cracked or still open at the end of this operation.

2 Place mussels in a large, heavy pan with a tight-fitting lid. Add finely chopped shallots, parsley, thyme and bay leaf; season very lightly with salt and freshly ground black pepper and moisten with dry white wine.

3 Cover pan tightly. Place over a high heat and cook for 5 to 7 minutes, or until mussels have opened. Discard any that remain closed – they, too, are suspect.

4 Remove pan from heat. As soon as mussels can be handled, scoop them out of their shells with a teaspoon into a bowl. You may, if you wish, pull off their dark little outer frills, but this is not necessary. Cover and keep warm.

5 Taste mussel liquor. If it is not too salty, boil it for a few minutes to reduce it and intensify the flavour. Pour a little mussel liquor through a sieve lined with double-thickness muslin or a piece of kitchen paper. If very salty, add a little more dry white wine.

6 Combine 2 tablespoons each mussel liquor and wine vinegar in a small bowl.

Beat in enough olive oil to make a good dressing. Stir in half the chopped parsley and season to taste with salt and freshly ground black pepper.

7 Pour dressing over warm mussels; toss lightly to coat them evenly and allow to cool. Then chill until ready to serve.

8 Just before serving, arrange mussels in a shallow serving dish and garnish with remaining parsley. Serve very cold.

Lamb Fried Rice

If you have only a little cooked lamb left over from your roast – about $\frac{1}{2}$ lb(225g), say – this is an excellent recipe for making a small amount of meat go a long way.

$\frac{1}{2}$ **lb(225g) cooked lamb, diced**
2 **eggs**
1 **level tablespoon butter**
Salt and freshly ground black pepper
4 **tablespoons oil**
1 **Spanish onion, finely chopped**
3 **cups cold cooked rice**
6 **mushrooms, diced**
2 **teaspoons soy sauce (or lemon juice)**
Finely chopped parsley

1 Make a thin omelette of eggs cooked in butter; season with salt and freshly ground black pepper; remove from pan and cut into strips.

2 Heat oil in a large frying pan and, when it is hot, add finely chopped onion and fry until transparent. Add diced lamb and continue to cook until meat and vegetables are golden. Season with salt and freshly ground black pepper. Add rice and diced mushrooms and fry gently, stirring from time to time, for 5 minutes.

3 Just before serving, stir in soy sauce (or lemon juice) and 2 teaspoons water; add salt and freshly ground black pepper to taste. Top with egg strips; sprinkle with a little parsley and serve immediately with **herbed buttered carrots** (see below).

Herbed Buttered Carrots

1 lb(450g) new carrots
2 tablespoons butter
2 tablespoons chicken stock
1 clove garlic, finely chopped
1 medium onion, finely chopped
1 tablespoon finely chopped parsley
Salt and freshly ground black pepper
$\frac{1}{2}$ level teaspoon rosemary
4 tablespoons cream

1 Wash carrots and cut diagonally into thin slices.

2 Melt butter in saucepan, and add chicken stock or water, sliced carrots, and finely chopped garlic, onion and parsley. Season to taste with salt, pepper and rosemary.

3 Cover and cook over a low heat for 10 to 15 minutes, or until carrots are just tender.

4 Just before serving, stir in cream and season to taste.

Apple Pie with Orange Juice

(illustrated on page 147)

$1\frac{1}{2}$ lb(675g) cooking apples
Juice of $\frac{1}{2}$ lemon
Pastry for shell and top
2 oz(50g) granulated sugar
2 oz(50g) dark brown sugar
1 tablespoon flour
$\frac{1}{8}$ level teaspoon grated nutmeg
$\frac{1}{4}$ level teaspoon powdered cinnamon
Grated peel of $\frac{1}{2}$ orange
Grated peel of $\frac{1}{2}$ lemon
2 oz(50g) chopped raisins and
    sultanas
1–2 tablespoons orange juice
1–2 tablespoons butter
Double cream or Cheddar cheese

1 Pare and core apples and slice thickly. Soak them in water to which you have added lemon juice to preserve their colour. Line a deep 9-inch(23-cm) pie dish with pastry, using your own favourite recipe or one of the new mixes.

2 Combine granulated sugar, brown sugar, flour, nutmeg and cinnamon, and rub a little of this mixture into pastry lining. Add grated peels to remaining sugar mixture. Cover bottom of pastry shell with sliced apples and sprinkle with a few chopped raisins and sultanas and some of the sugar mixture. Repeat layers until pie shell is richly filled.

3 Sprinkle with orange juice; dot with butter and fit top crust over apples, pressing the edges together or fluting them. Decorate pastry; cut slits in top crust to release steam and bake in a moderately hot oven (400°F/200°C/Mark 6) for 35 to 40 minutes, or until fruit is tender and pastry is golden brown. Serve warm, with cream or Cheddar cheese.

Fresh Spinach Soup

2 lb(900g) fresh spinach leaves
4 tablespoons butter
Salt and freshly ground black pepper
$\frac{1}{2}$ pint(3dl) double cream
$\frac{1}{2}$ pint(3dl) chicken stock

1 Wash the spinach leaves, changing water several times; drain thoroughly.

2 Put spinach in a thick-bottomed saucepan with butter and simmer gently, stirring continuously, until soft and tender.

3 Whisk in electric blender or put through a wire sieve. Season to taste with salt and freshly ground black pepper.

4 Combine with cream and chicken stock and heat through. Serve immediately.

Menu

Fresh Spinach
Soup

Italian Breaded
Lamb Chops
with
Harem Pilaff

Oranges with
Cream

Serves 4

*with this menu I suggest
the following Medium-
priced Red Wines*
**Brouilly
Morgon
Côte-Rôtie**

73

Italian Breaded Lamb Chops

8 baby lamb cutlets
Salt and freshly ground black pepper
Flour
Beaten egg
2 oz(50g) breadcrumbs
2 oz(50g) Parmesan cheese, grated
Oil, for deep-frying
Lemon wedges
Parsley

1 Season cutlets to taste with salt and freshly ground black pepper and dust with flour. Dip into beaten egg and coat with a mixture of breadcrumbs and grated Parmesan. Deep-fry until golden and tender. Drain on absorbent paper.

2 Serve garnished with lemon wedges and parsley. Decorate bones with cutlet frills.

Harem Pilaff
(illustrated on pages 70–71)

4–6 large, firm tomatoes
6 oz(175g) button mushrooms
½ Spanish onion, finely chopped
Butter
½ lb(225g) rice
4 tablespoons dry white wine (or cider)
1½ pints(8·5dl) chicken stock (made with 2 cubes)
Salt and freshly ground black pepper
1 clove garlic, finely chopped
2 tablespoons finely chopped parsley
¼ level teaspoon dried oregano
1 avocado pear, peeled and diced
3 oz(75g) raw chicken livers, diced

1 Drop tomatoes into boiling water for about 1 minute. Peel them at once, then seed and dice.

2 Slice or quarter button mushrooms.

3 Sauté finely chopped onion in 4 level tablespoons butter in a medium-sized heatproof casserole until golden; add rice and stir over heat for another minute or two. Then pour white wine (or cider) and chicken stock over rice. Season with salt and freshly ground black pepper, to taste. Bring to the boil; cover casserole and put it in a moderate oven (350°F/180°C/Mark 4) for 14–16 minutes. After about 10 minutes of cooking time, stir once with a fork.

4 Sauté sliced button mushrooms in 2 tablespoons butter for 3 minutes. Add finely chopped garlic, finely chopped parsley, dried oregano, diced tomatoes and season to taste with salt and freshly ground black pepper, and simmer for 2–3 minutes more. Scatter with peeled and diced avocado pear and keep warm.

5 In another pan sauté diced chicken livers in a little butter, then stir into the finished rice mixture with a fork.

6 Form rice into a ring and fill the centre with avocado and mushroom mixture.

Oranges with Cream

3 large oranges
¼ pint(1·5dl) fresh orange juice
Sugar
½ pint(3dl) double cream, whipped

1 Grate the rind of 1 orange and add to orange juice. Peel all the oranges and with a sharp knife cut off all the pith. Slice horizontally.

2 Place orange slices in overlapping rows in a shallow rectangular dish. Sprinkle with orange juice and sugar to taste.

3 Whip cream; sweeten to taste and spoon over orange slices. Chill until ready to serve.

Crème Elysées

1 small packet frozen peas
2 pints(1·1 litres) chicken consommé
4 tablespoons butter
½ cucumber, peeled and seeded
2 egg yolks
¼ pint(1·5dl) double cream
Salt and freshly ground black pepper

1 Defrost peas and simmer in 2 tablespoons each of chicken consommé and butter until cooked through. Drain and purée in an electric blender or through a fine sieve.

2 Cut cucumber into matchstick-size slivers and simmer in remaining butter until tender.

3 Beat eggs; add cream and purée of peas.

4 Heat consommé; stir in purée mixture and cook over gentle heat, stirring continuously, until liquid is smooth and thick. Do not let soup come to the boil or it will curdle.

5 Just before serving, stir in *julienne* of cucumber sticks and season with salt and freshly ground black pepper, to taste.

Kedgeree

(illustrated on pages 70–71)

½ lb(225g) rice
Salt
½ lb(225g) cooked smoked haddock
2 hard-boiled eggs
¼ lb(100g) butter
1 ¼-inch(0.5-cm) slice cooked ham, diced
2 level tablespoons tomato ketchup
4 level tablespoons watercress leaves, coarsely chopped
Freshly ground black pepper

1 Cook rice in boiling, salted water until just tender. Rinse well and drain.

2 Remove skin and bones from smoked haddock and flake the fish.

3 Chop whites of hard-boiled eggs.

4 Melt butter in a saucepan; toss rice in it. Then add flaked fish, chopped egg whites and diced ham. Stir in tomato ketchup and toss lightly over heat until hot. Stir in coarsely chopped watercress and season with salt and freshly ground black pepper.

5 Grate or sieve yolks of hard-boiled eggs over kedgeree and serve immediately.

Granita di Caffé (page 76)

Menu

Crème Elysées

Kedgeree
with
Spinach Salad
with Croûtons

Granita di Caffé
Serves 4

with this menu I suggest the following Inexpensive White Wines or Rosés
**Sancerre
Bourgogne Aligoté
Tavel Rosé**

Spinach Salad with Croûtons

(illustrated on page 148)

1 lb(450g) spinach leaves
6 tablespoons olive oil
Lemon juice
2 cloves garlic, finely chopped
Coarsely grated lemon rind
Salt and freshly ground black pepper
Sautéed croûtons (see page 178)

1 Wash spinach leaves, removing thick stalks, and gently dry with a clean tea towel.

2 Heat olive oil and 2 tablespoons lemon juice in a large saucepan; add garlic and coarsely grated rind of 1 lemon.

3 Add spinach and toss over moderate heat until it is hot and each leaf is thoroughly coated. Season to taste with salt and freshly ground black pepper.

4 Arrange leaves on a hot serving dish; garnish with *croûtons* and a little coarsely grated lemon rind.

Granita di Caffé

(illustrated on previous page)

4–6 level tablespoons instant coffee
1–1¼ pints(6–7dl) water
4–6 oz sugar
4–6 ice cubes
Whipped cream

1 Combine coffee and ½–¾ pint(3–4dl) water in a saucepan, adding sugar to taste. Bring to a boil, stirring constantly. Reduce heat and simmer for 5 minutes. Remove from heat. Add ½ pint(3dl) water and ice cubes; stir until ice is melted. Pour into refrigerator tray and freeze for 1½ to 1¾ hours, or until ice is firm around edges.

2 Turn ice into bowl of an electric mixer and mix at medium speed (or whisk with a rotary beater) until mixture is smooth.

3 Turn into 2 refrigerator trays and freeze until almost solid. This will take about 1 hour.

4 When ready to serve stir ice and spoon into parfait or sherbet glasses. Top with whipped cream and serve at once.

Stuffed Courgette Appetizer

8–12 courgettes 4 inches(10cm) long
Salt
1 Spanish onion, finely chopped
1 clove garlic, finely chopped
Well-flavoured French dressing
   (see page 100)
Lettuce
3 tomatoes, peeled and chopped
1 green pepper, finely chopped
1 tablespoon capers
1 tablespoon each parsley and basil
Freshly ground black pepper

1 Simmer courgettes, unpeeled, in salted water for about 5 minutes. Cut them in half lengthwise and carefully scoop out seeds. Lay courgettes, cut sides up, in a flat dish.

2 Combine half the chopped onion and garlic and cover courgettes with this mixture. Sprinkle half the French dressing over them, cover with aluminium foil and marinate in the refrigerator for at least 4 hours.

3 When ready to serve, remove onion and garlic and drain off marinade.

4 Arrange courgette halves on crisp lettuce leaves and fill the hollows with remaining French dressing combined with remaining onion and tomatoes, finely chopped green pepper, capers, parsley, basil, salt and freshly ground black pepper, to taste.

Menu

Stuffed Courgette
Appetizer

Spanish Pork and
Rice Casserole
with
Quick-fried
Asparagus

Strawberries
Romanoff

Serves 4–6

*with this menu I suggest
the following Inexpensive
Red Wines*
**Rioja Red
Serradayres
Cabernet Red
Gigondas**

Spanish Pork and Rice Casserole

(illustrated on pages 70–71)

4 large pork chops
Olive oil
Salt and freshly ground black pepper
1 green pepper, coarsely chopped
1 Spanish onion, coarsely chopped
½ lb(225g) rice, uncooked
¾ pint(4dl) chicken stock (made with a cube)
1 large can Italian peeled tomatoes
Paprika

1 Brown chops well on both sides in olive oil in a large frying pan. Remove from pan and trim off excess fat with a sharp knife. Arrange chops in a shallow heatproof baking dish or roasting pan. Season generously with salt and freshly ground black pepper.

2 Fry coarsely chopped green pepper and onion in fat remaining in frying pan until golden.

3 Add rice and continue to cook, stirring constantly, until rice is golden, adding a little olive oil to the pan if mixture gets too dry.

4 Moisten vegetables with chicken stock and tomatoes. Cover chops with this mixture; season with salt and freshly ground black pepper and sprinkle top with paprika.

5 Cover tightly with a piece of aluminium foil if baking dish has no cover and bake in a preheated moderate oven (350°F/180°C/Mark 4) for 40 to 50 minutes, or until rice tastes done and pork is tender.

A quick-fried vegetable in the Chinese manner – asparagus, broccoli or green beans – is one of the simplest vegetable accompaniments I know. Sauté the sliced vegetable for 2 to 3 minutes in a little seasoned oil; add 4 tablespoons of chicken stock and a dash of soy sauce or lemon juice; and steam until just tender.

Quick-fried Asparagus

1 bunch fresh asparagus
Vegetable oil
Salt and freshly ground black pepper
Monosodium glutamate
4 tablespoons chicken stock
Soy sauce or lemon juice

1 Cut stalks of asparagus diagonally, making thin, slant-edged slices about 1½ inches(4cm) long.

2 Heat oil in a large frying pan; add asparagus; sprinkle lightly with salt, freshly ground black pepper and monosodium glutamate to taste and cook over high heat, stirring, for 2 or 3 minutes.

3 Add chicken stock or water; cover pan and cook over medium heat for 3–5 minutes, shaking pan frequently.

4 Season to taste with soy sauce or lemon juice. Serve immediately.

Strawberries Romanoff

2 lb(900g) fresh strawberries
6 tablespoons icing sugar
3 tablespoons rum
3 tablespoons Cointreau
½ pint(3dl) double cream
3 tablespoons Kirsch

1 Wash, drain and hull strawberries, and place in a bowl.

2 Toss with 4 tablespoons icing sugar. Pour over rum and Cointreau and chill in refrigerator for at least 1 hour.

3 An hour before serving, whip cream until stiff; add remaining sugar, flavour with Kirsch and mix with the strawberries, tossing until every fruit is coated.

4 Keep cold until time to serve.

Breakfast and Brunch Parties

Doctors and nutritionists agree that the first meal of the day should provide from one-quarter to one-third of our daily intake of calories and proteins. Measure this against your cup of black coffee 'caught on the run' and you'll have a fair idea of why the mornings do not go as smoothly for you as they might. Breakfast should be as important – or almost as important – as the other two meals we normally eat every day – so why not make the most of it? All the time-worn excuses – 'in a hurry', 'not hungry', 'too sleepy', 'no time' – are worse than flimsy when the facts prove that non-breakfasters lag behind the big breakfast league in school, office and factory, not to mention house-work.

One of the main reasons for poor breakfasts is lack of planning. Far too many of us treat it as a slapdash affair, with the result that about half the nation starts the day inadequately fed, or so overstuffed with morning 'stodge' – fried bread, egg, tomato and greasy bangers – that they are more fit for a return to bed than for the morning's activities.

Make breakfast one of the most rewarding meals of the day by using individual recipes from the breakfast and brunch menus in this book to spark off your weekday mornings. And why not invite friends over to join the family for informal breakfast parties at weekends or during the holidays?

A good idea when planning a special breakfast party is to do everything possible the night before – even setting the table. In this way, when you get up all you have to do are the last-minute things like cooking the sausages and eggs and putting the coffee pot on to bubble.

The Sunday Breakfast Party

Sunday is the day of the week when your friends are most likely to be free for breakfast.

Why not take up the American habit of the breakfast party – late breakfast, of course – and invite friends around for an imaginative feast where sausages, bacon or kippers served on their own are absolutely banned? No traditional British 'stodge' allowed here – only the lightest, most sophisticated of fare.

Sunday breakfast should be an unhurried delight.

Make the invitation flexible. Invite your guests for 'about noon' or 'when you get up' – remember most people like to read the Sunday newspapers before they are ready to leave the house.

Plan to give guests simple things superbly served – grilled grapefruit with cinnamon, followed by a puffy bacon omelette with cheese sauce – or try that old familiar standby scrambled eggs, but brought up to scratch for the occasion with the addition of thin slivers of smoked salmon and snippets of chopped chives.

Paper-thin slices of hot toast spread with sweet butter, home-made *croissants* and a dollop of your own fresh fruit preserves, or piping hot baps or butter scones will add much to the occasion. If you are planning to serve hot breads for breakfast, make the dough the night before so that all you have to do is pop it into the oven as your family or guests sit down to the table. I have included several delicious recipes for delectable hot breads: American-style popovers, traditional Scottish baps, butter scones that melt in your mouth, and fabulous French *brioches* and *croissants*. It took me weeks to perfect my 'can't fail' *croissant* recipe and its foolproof method is described at length on pages 86–7.

Previous pages:
Stewed Apricots and
Prunes, Poached Salmon
or Turbot Kedgeree, and
Scottish Baps (pages 89,
90 & 91)

Some Breakfast Suggestions

For a really glamorous breakfast party, start off with a thick slice of chilled fresh melon topped with strawberries or raspberries, and follow with pan-fried trout, crisp and golden-crusted, hot from the frying pan, accompanied by tiny new potatoes.

Offer guests a choice of hot coffee or chilled white wine – and see which they choose!

A summer breakfast might begin with a compote of fresh fruits, or orange and grapefruit sections in lemon juice, followed by a simple little dish of eggs cooked *en cocotte* (cooked in cream in individual ramekins or soufflé dishes). Or try fried eggs with sausages and bacon, accompanied by popovers (the American breakfast variation on the Yorkshire pudding theme, but baked in the oven on their own so that they become crisp, golden puffs of flavour) – just right when served with home-made strawberry preserve and fresh unsalted butter.

For a winter breakfast, start off with a compote of dried fruits, particularly delicious when spiked with tangy lemon juice or a splash of port for late Sunday morning guests. Follow with a kedgeree made of chunks of poached salmon or turbot, rice and hard-boiled eggs in a creamy sauce, and devilled kidneys and bacon. Scottish baps are the breakfast hot breads here if you have the time to make them.

Why not sit down and plan a Sunday morning breakfast party right now? It's an original, easy way to entertain – and it's economical, too.

Grilled Grapefruit with Cinnamon

(illustrated overleaf)

5 **large grapefruit**
6 **tablespoons soft brown sugar**
2 **teaspoons ground cinnamon**
2 **tablespoons butter**

1 Cut all the grapefruit in half. With a sharp-pointed spoon scoop out each half-segment over a bowl to catch the juices, leaving behind the membranes dividing the segments. Take care not to crush the segments, so that pieces remain as large as possible.

2 Take 6 of the best half-shells and cut out all the pith and membranes from the centre.

3 Mix sugar and cinnamon together. Drain grapefruit segments, reserving juices; toss segments with cinnamon sugar and divide evenly among the 6 half-shells.

4 Arrange shells side by side in a grill pan, or a heatproof baking dish which will fit under your grill. Fill them to the brim with reserved grapefruit juice and dot with butter.

5 Have the grill preheated to hot. Slip the pan of grapefruit under the grill; reduce heat to moderate and grill steadily for 5 to 7 minutes, or until grapefruit are thoroughly hot and bubbling brown on top.

Puffy Bacon Omelettes with Cheese Sauce

(illustrated overleaf)

$\frac{1}{2}$ **lb(225g) bacon**
6 **eggs, separated**
Salt and freshly ground black pepper
2 **tablespoons butter**

CHEESE SAUCE:
1 **oz(25g) butter**
1 **oz(25g) flour**
1 **pint(6dl) milk**
4 **oz(100g) hard Cheshire or Cheddar cheese, grated**
2 **teaspoons Worcestershire sauce**
Salt and freshly ground black pepper

1 To make sauce: melt butter in a small, heavy pan; add flour and cook over very low heat for 2 minutes, stirring constantly. Add milk gradually, beating vigorously to

Menu

Grilled Grapefruit with Cinnamon

Puffy Bacon Omelettes with Cheese Sauce

Butter Scones

Serves 4–6

with this menu I suggest Coffee or Tea

81

avoid lumps; bring to the boil, stirring, and simmer for 8 to 10 minutes, stirring occasionally.

2 Remove from heat; stir in grated cheese and beat until smooth. Season to taste with Worcestershire sauce, salt and freshly ground black pepper.

3 Cover surface of sauce with a disc of greaseproof paper brushed with water to prevent a skin forming; keep hot.

4 **To make omelettes:** grill or fry bacon until crisp, then cut into $\frac{1}{2}$-inch (1·5-cm) strips.

5 Beat egg yolks with 2 tablespoons cold water until light and frothy. Season lightly with salt and freshly ground black pepper.

6 Preheat grill at highest temperature.

7 Whisk egg whites until stiff but not dry, and gently fold into egg yolk mixture.

8 Cook mixture in two batches one after another, using two 8- to 9-inch(20- to 21-cm) omelette pans simultaneously: melt 1 tablespoon butter in each pan; pour in half the omelette mixture and, swirling lightly with a fork, allow base to set over a steady heat. Slip omelettes under hot grill just long enough to puff and set tops and colour them slightly.

9 Scatter half the bacon strips over half of each omelette and carefully fold in two.

10 Remove omelettes to heated serving dishes, mask with hot cheese sauce and serve immediately.

Butter Scones
(for the recipe, see page 89)

Grilled Grapefruit with Cinnamon, Puffy Bacon Omelettes with Cheese Sauce, and Butter Scones (pages 81, 82 and 89)

*Summer Breakfast Compote, Fried Eggs
with Sausages and Bacon, and Whole
Strawberry Preserve (pages 84 and 85)*

Breakfast Apple Rings

6 tart eating apples
6 tablespoons sugar (white or brown)
1½ level teaspoons ground cinnamon
6 tablespoons melted butter

1 Wash and core apples, and slice them
crosswise into rings ½ inch(1·5cm) thick.
Mix sugar with cinnamon.

2 Place apple rings on a baking sheet; brush
with melted butter and dust with half the
cinnamon sugar.

3 Grill for about 5 minutes, or until rings
are golden brown on one side. Then turn
carefully with a spatula; brush with butter,
sprinkle with remaining cinnamon sugar
and grill for 5 minutes longer. Serve hot.

Scrambled Eggs with Mushrooms

6 oz(175g) button mushrooms
¼ lb(100g) butter
12 eggs
6 tablespoons cream, milk or water
6 3-inch(7·5-cm) pastry cases, prebaked
Salt and freshly ground black pepper

1 Wash or wipe mushrooms clean; trim
stems and slice mushrooms. Sauté in
1 oz(25g) butter for 5 minutes until softened.

2 Beat eggs lightly in a bowl with cream,
milk or water – just enough to mix them.
(Water will make extremely fluffy eggs;
cream gives a richer, smoother texture.)

3 Slip prebaked pastry cases into a
moderate oven (350°F/180°C/Mark 4) to
heat through.

4 Melt remaining butter in a large, heavy
saucepan (about 8 inches[20cm] in diameter). When butter is hot but not brown,
pour in eggs and cook over low heat,

Croissants (pages 86 and 87)

Menu

Breakfast Apple
Rings

Scrambled Eggs
with Mushrooms
or
Scrambled Eggs
with Smoked
Salmon and
Chives

Croissants

Serves 6

*with this menu I suggest
Coffee or Tea*

stirring constantly with a wooden spoon, until eggs are just on the point of setting. Add sautéed mushrooms and salt and freshly ground black pepper, to taste, at the halfway stage.

5 As soon as eggs are on the point of setting, remove pan from heat. Divide mixture between pastry cases and serve immediately.

Or

Scrambled Eggs with Smoked Salmon and Chives

1 Combine eggs with cream, milk or water as above.

2 Melt 3 oz(75g) butter in a large heavy saucepan. Add 6 oz(175g) smoked salmon, cut into thin strips. Sprinkle with 1 or 2 teaspoons lemon juice and heat through for a few seconds until strips change colour. Pour in eggs and scramble them as above.

3 Just before removing pan from heat, season mixture to taste with salt and freshly ground black pepper. Stir in 2–3 level tablespoons finely chopped chives (or spring onion tops or parsley), and serve immediately in hot pastry cases as above.

Croissants
(for the recipe, see pages 86–7)

Summer Breakfast Compote
(illustrated on previous page)

4 tablespoons lemon juice
2 tablespoons liquid honey
2 oranges
1 grapefruit
1 eating apple
1 banana
1 small punnet strawberries

1 Combine lemon juice and honey in a glass serving bowl.

2 Peel oranges and grapefruit and divide into segments, discarding pips and every scrap of pith and membrane. Toss with honey and lemon juice.

3 Quarter apple; remove core and cut (unpeeled) apple into dice.

4 Peel and slice banana.

5 Add apple and banana to the bowl and toss thoroughly until all surfaces are coated with juices to prevent them turning brown. Cover and chill until ready to serve.

6 Just before serving, hull strawberries and add them to the bowl.

Fried Eggs with Sausages and Bacon
(illustrated on previous page)

Fried Eggs
  Do not attempt to fry more than 4 eggs at a time in the average frying pan, and always make sure they are fresh – a stale egg has a 'watery' white which will run all over the frying pan instead of remaining firm and rounded. To test an egg for freshness, hold it upright between your thumb and forefinger and shake it gently up and down. If you can feel the yolk thudding lightly against the shell, the egg is stale.
  For 4 eggs, heat 2 tablespoons butter in a frying pan until sizzling but not coloured. Break 1 egg at a time into a cup; season with salt and freshly ground black pepper and slide into pan. Fry eggs very slowly until done to your liking; then lift out carefully with a spatula, drain and serve on hot plates.

Grilled Sausages
  Prick sausages lightly all over with a fork and lay them side by side in the bottom of the grill pan. Brush with melted lard, dripping or butter, and grill under a moderate heat for 6–8 minutes, turning sausages to colour them evenly.

Fried Sausages

Unless you are hooked on charred and burst sausages, try this method for keeping them whole and crisp, with a juicy centre: Melt about 1 tablespoon lard or dripping in a heavy frying pan; prick large sausages all over and arrange them in the pan in one layer.

Turn them over moderate heat until they just change colour. When sausages begin to sizzle, pour in 1 tablespoon water, clamp on a lid and continue to cook over moderate heat until water has been absorbed and sausages are crisp on the underside. Continue adding water and cooking sausages in this manner until they are brown and crisp all over. Drain and serve.

Bacon

Grill or fry rashers of bacon until done to your liking. Halved tomatoes, lightly seasoned, may be slipped into the grill pan a few minutes before bacon is ready, but do not let them reduce to a mush. Fried tomatoes should always be cooked in a separate pan.

Oeufs en Cocotte

Butter
8 fresh eggs
Salt and freshly ground black pepper
1–2 tablespoons single cream

1 Butter 4 heatproof ramekins (4–5 fl oz [100–150ml] capacity). Break 2 eggs into each ramekin; season with a pinch of salt and a few turns of the peppermill.

2 Arrange ramekins side by side in a wide pan with a lid. (Failing a large enough pan, use a roasting tin and cover it with a sheet of foil.) Pour in boiling water to come a third of the way up sides of ramekins. Cover pan tightly and simmer very gently for about 8 minutes for soft eggs, a minute or two longer if you prefer them on the firm side.

3 As soon as eggs are cooked to your liking, remove ramekins from water and swirl about 1 teaspoon cream round the top edge of each one. Serve immediately.

Hot Popovers
(for the recipe, see pages 88–9)

Whole Strawberry Preserve
(illustrated on page 83)

Makes about 1 lb(450g)
1 lb(450g) small, hard strawberries
¾–1 lb(350–450g) granulated sugar
Juice of 1 lemon

1 **The day before you intend to make preserve:** wash strawberries quickly, drain them thoroughly on absorbent paper and hull them. Pile strawberries up slightly on a wide, flat dish and cover completely with a layer of sugar taken from the total amount.

2 **The following day:** pour juices drawn from strawberries by the sugar into a pan. Add remaining sugar and set pan over very low heat. Allow sugar to melt, stirring and brushing down any sugar grains stuck to sides of pan with a little cold water. Then bring to the boil once and skim off any scum that collects on the surface.

3 Slide strawberries into pan; add lemon juice and simmer very gently for 5–8 minutes, or until strawberries are plump and soft but not disintegrating. They must not be stirred with a spoon while they are simmering. As flecks of white foam appear on the surface, shake the whole pan back and forth very gently so that foam collects in the centre; skim it off with a sterilized spoon.

4 When syrup just begins to set, remove pan from heat. Allow preserve to cool in the pan, swirling the latter gently from time to time so that strawberries remain suspended in syrup and do not sink to the bottom.

5 Pour into a dry sterilized jar and seal.

Menu

Summer Breakfast Compote

Fried Eggs with Sausages and Bacon
or
Oeufs en Cocotte
Hot Popovers

Whole Strawberry Preserve

Serves 4

with this menu I suggest Coffee or Tea

85

Breakfast Bakery

Croissants
(illustrated on page 83)

Makes 12

6 tablespoons lukewarm milk mixed with 3 tablespoons lukewarm water
3 level teaspoons (1 level tablespoon) castor sugar
1½ level teaspoons dried yeast
½ lb(225g) plain flour
1 level teaspoon salt
3 tablespoons melted butter
3 oz(75g) unsalted butter, chilled
Egg yolk beaten with a little water, to glaze

1 The day before you wish to serve croissants: put 3 tablespoons of the lukewarm milk and water mixture in a cup. Add 1 level teaspoon castor sugar and stir until dissolved. Sprinkle dried yeast over the surface; beat lightly with a fork and leave for about 10 minutes, or until liquid is frothy and yeast granules have completely dissolved.

2 Meanwhile, sift flour, salt and remaining castor sugar into a warmed bowl, and leave to warm gently.

3 Make a well in the centre of the flour; pour in dissolved yeast. Rinse cup out with remaining milk and water and add this to the flour, kneading to make a smooth dough which is quite soft, but firm enough to roll into a ball.

4 When dough is smooth and homogeneous, gradually add melted butter, kneading vigorously until dough is smooth and springy again.

5 Roll dough into a ball. Cover dough with a sheet of buttered greaseproof paper or foil; then cover bowl with a cloth and leave in a warm place to rise to 3 times its original bulk. This will take approximately 3½ hours.

6 When dough has risen, scoop it out on to a very lightly floured surface. Press it gently

with the palm of your hand to deflate it; then fold it over on to itself to make a ball again; return to the bowl, cover as before and leave to rise again. This time it should take about 2 hours to double its bulk.

7 Deflate dough once again. Pat it into a rectangle 8 × 4 inches(20 × 100cm) and seal in a parcel of foil. Chill for 30 minutes.

8 Towards the end of this time, take chilled butter and work it with your fingertips to make it malleable, but not oily. If your hands are warm, hold them under the cold tap for a minute or two to cool them.

9 Unwrap dough, place on a lightly floured surface and roll out into a rectangle 12 × 8 inches(30 × 20cm). Take small knobs of butter; pinch them out into paper-thin flakes between your fingertips and dot upper two-thirds of rectangle with them so that the entire surface is evenly covered, with just a $\frac{1}{4}$-inch(0·5-cm) border round the 3 outer sides unbuttered.

10 Fold unbuttered third of rectangle up over the centre; then fold the top (buttered) third down, making a neat packet composed of 3 layers of dough sandwiched with 2 layers of butter.

11 Dust board and rolling pin lightly with flour again if necessary, and roll packet out once more into a rectangle 12 × 8 inches(30 × 20cm). Use short, light strokes to avoid over-stretching the dough, or it will tear and allow butter to seep through. Fold in 3 as before; wrap in foil and chill for 15 minutes.

12 Unwrap foil and give packet a quarter-turn to the right, i.e. so that top now faces right. Repeat rolling and folding twice more, giving dough another quarter turn to the right each time and chilling it for 15 minutes in between. After the last rolling and folding, seal packet tightly in foil and chill overnight (or for at least 2 hours).

13 **To shape croissants:** on a lightly floured board, roll dough into a rectangle 15 × 5 inches(38 × 13cm). Cut in 3 to make three 5-inch(13-cm) squares, and return 2 of them to the refrigerator.

14 Roll remaining square into a rectangle 10 × 5 inches(26 × 13cm). Cut it in half to make two 5-inch(13-cm) squares again, and cut each square into 2 triangles.

15 Roll each triangle up quite tightly from the broadest end to the tip. Pull into a horse-shoe shape, twisting ends slightly, and lay on an ungreased baking sheet, with the tip underneath.

16 Repeat with the 2 remaining squares of pastry, taking them from the refrigerator one at a time.

17 Cover *croissants* with a cloth and leave to rise again until doubled in bulk, about 30 minutes.

18 Preheat oven to fairly hot (425°F/220°C/Mark 7).

19 When *croissants* are well risen, brush all over with beaten egg yolk. Bake for 8 to 10 minutes, or until light and crisp with a rich golden glaze.

20 Serve them lukewarm, or gently re-heated just before serving.

Brioches

(illustrated on page 93)

Makes 12
1 **level tablespoon dried yeast**
1¼ **lb(575g) plain flour**
4 **level tablespoons castor sugar**
½ **level teaspoon salt**
4 **eggs**
8 **tablespoons lukewarm milk**
1 **teaspoon vanilla essence**
¼ **lb(100g) softened butter**
Melted butter for moulds
1 **egg yolk beaten with a little water,
   to glaze**

1 **The day before you wish to serve
brioches:** dissolve dried yeast in a small
bowl with 8 tablespoons lukewarm water,
following directions on can or packet.

2 Sift flour, sugar and salt into a warmed
bowl, and make a well in the centre.

3 Beat eggs with lukewarm milk; stir in
vanilla and add to flour, together with
dissolved yeast. Mix well.

4 Add half the softened butter, diced, and
beat with a wooden spoon until dough is
smooth. It should be very soft at this stage.

5 Dot surface of dough with remaining
butter; cover bowl with a clean cloth and
leave in a warm place to rise until doubled in
bulk, about 1½ hours.

6 Punch dough down again and beat vigorously by hand for 5 minutes, or until it no
longer sticks to sides of bowl (flour your
hands from time to time while beating).

7 Cover bowl tightly with a sheet of foil
and refrigerate overnight. *Brioche* dough is
very rich and sticky, and chilling makes it
easier to handle.

8 **The following day:** brush 12 individual
brioche moulds with melted butter.

9 Turn dough out on to a lightly floured
surface and knead until smooth again.

10 Weigh dough and cut off a quarter,
making two balls. Divide each ball into 12
pieces of equal size. Roll the larger pieces
into balls and place them in prepared
moulds. Roll each of the smaller pieces into
a ball; snip top of each larger ball twice with
scissors to form a cross and set one of the
smaller balls on top.

11 Place moulds on a baking sheet and leave
brioches to rise again until doubled in bulk,
about 30 minutes.

12 Preheat oven to moderately hot
(400°F/200°C/Mark 6).

13 When *brioches* have risen, brush tops
with egg yolk beaten with a little water and
bake for 15 to 20 minutes, or until firm and a
rich golden colour.

14 Turn out and cool on a wire rack.

Hot Popovers

Makes 12
Melted butter (about 5 tablespoons)
2 **eggs**
7 **fl oz(200ml) milk**
Generous pinch of salt
¼ **lb(100g) plain flour, sifted**

1 Preheat oven to moderately hot (400°F/
200°C/Mark 6).

2 Put a teaspoon of melted butter at the
bottom of each of 12 turret moulds. Place
them on a baking sheet and slip into the oven
to heat through for 5–6 minutes.

3 Combine eggs with milk, salt and
1 tablespoon melted butter in a bowl, and
beat until well mixed. Add flour gradually,
beating vigorously until batter is smooth
and has the consistency of thick cream.

4 Divide batter between hot moulds and bake for 25–30 minutes, or until well puffed and golden brown.

5 Turn out and serve immediately.

Scottish Baps
(illustrated on pages 78–9)

Makes 12
¾ **pint(4dl) milk and water, mixed**
2 **oz(50g) lard**
2 **level teaspoons castor sugar**
1½ **level teapoons salt**
1 **level tablespoon dried yeast**
1¼ **lb(575g) plain flour**

1 Heat milk and water until lukewarm. Add lard, sugar and ½ level teaspoon salt; stir until dissolved.

2 Dissolve yeast according to instructions on can or packet, using some of the measured liquid.

3 Sift flour and remaining salt into a large, warmed bowl; make a well in the centre and pour in dissolved yeast. Work into flour by hand, adding enough of milk mixture to make a soft but manageable dough. Depending on quality of flour, you may need up to 4 tablespoons more or less liquid.

4 Knead dough vigorously until shiny and pliable. Roll into a ball; cover bowl with a damp cloth and leave in a warm place until dough has doubled in bulk, about 1½ hours.

5 Preheat oven to very hot (475°F/240°C/ Mark 9).

6 Punch dough down; knead lightly and divide into 12 even-sized balls. Arrange them, well spaced apart, on 2 or 3 baking sheets. Flour palms generously and flatten rolls into flat discs; then press a hole in the centre of each bap with your thumb – this is a characteristic feature of the Scottish bap.

7 Leave baps to rise again until puffy, about 20 minutes; then bake for about 10 minutes, so that they are just golden under their floury coating. Serve very fresh.

Butter Scones
(illustrated on page 82)

Makes 8
¾ **lb(350g) plain flour**
2 **level teaspoons baking powder**
½ **level teaspoon salt**
5 **oz(150g) butter**
2 **eggs, well beaten**
7 **tablespoons very cold milk**

1 Preheat oven to very hot (475°F/240°C/ Mark 9).

2 Sift flour, baking powder and salt into a bowl. Rub in butter with fingertips until mixture resembles very coarse breadcrumbs.

3 Make a well in the centre and pour in beaten eggs and cold milk. Combine lightly with a fork until dough holds together.

4 Turn dough out on to a board dusted with flour and roll lightly and quickly into a rectangle about ½ inch (1·5cm) thick. Fold in three as you would puff pastry and roll out again. Repeat procedure twice more, handling dough as little as possible and working very quickly.

5 After folding dough for the third time, roll it out just under ½ inch (1·5cm) thick and cut into 2½-inch(6·5-cm) rounds with a floured biscuit cutter.

6 Arrange scones on an ungreased baking sheet and bake for 10 to 15 minutes, or until well risen and a rich golden colour. Serve warm.

*with this menu I suggest
the following Inexpensive
Red Wines*
**Bourgueil
Pomerol
Beaujolais**

Dried Fruit Compote

¾ **lb(350g) mixed dried fruit:
apricots, peaches, apples, figs,
prunes, raisins or sultanas**
3 **tablespoons sugar**
2 **teaspoons grated orange rind**
Juice of 1 lemon
1 **orange, peeled and sliced**
1 **oz(25g) blanched almonds, slivered**

1 Preheat oven to moderate (350°F/180°C/
Mark 4).

2 Rinse fruit and place in a baking dish with
2 pints(1·1 litres) boiling water. Cover
tightly and bake for 1 to 1½ hours, or until
fruit is plump and soft.

3 Pour off cooking juices into a pan. Add
sugar, orange rind and lemon juice, to taste,
and simmer for 5 minutes.

4 Pour syrup over fruit in a serving dish.
Add orange slices and chill until ready to
serve.

5 Just before serving, sprinkle with slivered
almonds.

Stewed Apricots and Prunes
(illustrated on pages 78–9)

6 **oz(175g) plump prunes**
½–¾ **pint(3–4dl) strong hot tea**
6 **oz(175g) dried apricots**
3–4 **tablespoons sugar**

1 Cover prunes with hot tea, and apricots
with ½ to ¾ pint(3 to 4dl) hot water, in
separate bowls; leave to soak overnight, or
at least for several hours.

2 Slit prunes carefully and remove stones.

3 Transfer prunes and apricots to a pan,
together with their soaking liquids. Sweeten

to taste and simmer for 10 to 15 minutes, or
until fruits are tender and syrup slightly
thickened.

4 Cool; chill and serve, with a jug of chilled
pouring cream if liked.

Grilled Kippers

6 **plump kippers**
3 **tablespoons melted butter**

1 Preheat grill at maximum setting.

2 Remove heads, tails, fins and as many
large bones as possible from the kippers; lay
the fish flat in a large, deep dish (a roasting tin
is ideal). Pour over boiling water to cover;
leave for just 1 minute, then drain
thoroughly.

3 Grill kippers as follows, two or three at a
time, brush them liberally on both sides with
melted butter and arrange them, skin side
down, in the grilling pan. Slip under grill;
reduce heat to moderate and grill kippers for
3 minutes, or until thoroughly hot, without
turning them.

4 Remove each kipper to a heated plate and
serve immediately.

Devilled Kidneys and Bacon

18 **lambs' kidneys**
Milk and water
6 **oz(175g) softened butter**
1 **level tablespoon dry mustard**
1½ **level teaspoons curry powder**
1 **tablespoon lemon juice**
Tabasco sauce
Cayenne pepper
Salt and freshly ground black pepper
6 **tablespoons coarse stale
    breadcrumbs, toasted**
Grilled bacon, to garnish

1 Slice each kidney lengthwise through the core so that it lies flat, without separating halves. Remove thin outer skins. Soak kidneys in milk and water for 1 hour (or overnight).

2 When ready to cook kidneys: pound butter with mustard, curry powder, lemon juice, several drops of Tabasco, cayenne, salt and freshly ground black pepper to taste.

3 Drain kidneys and pat dry. Make small incisions on both sides of each one with the point of a sharp knife. Place them flat in a grill pan, cut sides uppermost; spread each with about 2 teaspoons devilled butter.

4 Place pan under a moderately hot, pre-heated grill. After 3 or 4 minutes, turn kidneys over, baste and grill for a further 3 minutes. Then turn kidneys again; baste once more and sprinkle with toasted bread-crumbs (1 teaspoon per kidney).

5 Turn grill up to maximum and grill for a final 3 to 4 minutes until kidneys are just cooked.

6 Serve immediately, sprinkled with pan juices and accompanied by crisp bacon rashers.

Poached Salmon or Turbot Kedgeree
(illustrated on pages 78–9)

6 oz(175g) long-grain rice
Salt
1½ lb(675g) poached salmon or turbot
3 hard-boiled eggs
6 tablespoons butter
1½ teaspoons curry powder or paste
Freshly ground black pepper
¾ pint(4dl) hot Béchamel sauce (see page 68)
6–8 tablespoons double cream

2 tablespoons lemon juice
3 tablespoons chopped parsley

1 Cook rice in plenty of boiling salted water until each grain is tender but still very firm. Drain thoroughly and keep warm.

2 Dice or flake fish coarsely, picking out any bones or pieces of skin.

3 Shell hard-boiled eggs; separate yolks from whites and chop the latter finely.

4 Melt butter in a wide, heavy pan; blend in curry powder or paste; add fish and toss over very gentle heat until hot and golden.

5 Add rice and finely chopped egg whites and toss lightly until well mixed, taking care not to crumble fish.

6 Season to taste with salt and freshly ground black pepper; remove from heat and keep hot.

7 Combine hot Béchamel sauce with double cream and lemon juice, to taste.

8 Fold sauce into rice mixture, together with chopped parsley.

9 Turn kedgeree into a heated serving dish. Sieve hard-boiled egg yolks over the top and serve very hot.

Scottish Baps
(for the recipe, see page 89, illustrated on pages 78–9)

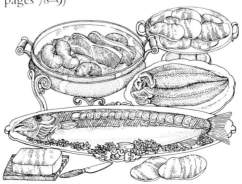

Strawberries in
Orange Juice
or
Fruit in a Melon
Ring

Fried Trout with
New Potatoes

Brioches

Apple Butter

Serves 6

*with this menu I suggest
Champagne Nature or the
following Inexpensive
White Wines*
**Muscadet
Sancerre
Chevalier d'Alsace**

Strawberries in Orange Juice

1½ lb(675g) strawberries
**Juice of 2 oranges, strained
Sifted icing sugar
Whipped cream (optional)**

1 Choose small strawberries – or wild ones if available. Toss with strained orange juice and sifted icing sugar to taste. Chill in the refrigerator for at least 1 hour.

2 Serve in individual cups or bowls, garnished with a little whipped cream if liked.

Fruit in a Melon Ring

**6 thick slices ripe melon
1 lb(450g) soft fruit: strawberries,
    raspberries, etc.
Sifted icing sugar
Lemon juice**

1 Cut thick slices across the widest part of a large, ripe melon, well chilled. Scoop out seeds to make neat rings.

2 Toss fruit with sugar and lemon juice, to taste, and pile in centre of melon rings. Serve immediately.

Fried Trout with New Potatoes

**6 trout, ½ lb(225g) each
Salt and freshly ground black pepper
Milk
Flour
2–3 tablespoons olive oil
4–6 tablespoons butter
6 slices lemon
Small bunch of parsley
1½ lb(675g) small new potatoes,
    cooked**

**PARSLEY BUTTER:
4 tablespoons softened butter**

**2–3 tablespoons finely chopped
    parsley
Lemon juice
Salt and freshly ground black pepper**

1 Wash and dry trout thoroughly both inside and out. Season with salt and freshly ground black pepper. Dip trout in milk; shake off excess, then coat with flour, patting it on gently so that it sticks to the skin.

2 Melt half the oil and butter in each of 2 large frying pans. When it is hot and sizzling, lay 3 trout side by side in each pan. Fry over moderate heat for 8 to 10 minutes, turning trout carefully with a spatula halfway through.

3 To make parsley butter: pound softened butter with finely chopped parsley. Season to taste with lemon juice, salt and freshly ground black pepper, and chill until firm again.

4 Transfer trout to a large heated serving dish. Garnish with lemon slices and tiny sprigs of parsley and serve accompanied by hot boiled new potatoes tossed with diced parsley butter.

Brioches
(for the recipe, see page 88)

Apple Butter

Makes about 1 lb(450g)
**2 lb(900g) crisp apples
1 pint(6dl) sweet cider
Juice of 1 lemon
½ lb(225g) sugar
¼ level teaspoon ground cloves
¼ level teaspoon ground cinnamon
¼ level teaspoon freshly grated
    nutmeg**

1 Wash apples; slice them without coring or peeling, and put them in a heavy saucepan. Moisten with ¼ pint(1·5dl) water; bring to

the boil and cover tightly. Simmer for 10 to 15 minutes, or until apples are soft and fluffy.

Above: Fried Trout with New Potatoes and Parsley Butter

2 Drain apples and rub them through a sieve.

Below: Brioches (page 88)

3 While apples are cooking, simmer cider in a heavy pan until reduced to about 6 tablespoons.

4 Combine sieved apples with reduced cider, lemon juice, sugar and spices; stir over low heat until sugar has dissolved, then leave to simmer, stirring occasionally, for about 20 minutes, or until purée is thick and glossy with the consistency of thick jam.

5 Pour into a hot, sterilized jar and seal.

Luncheon Parties are Fun

Try the recipe for *Salade de Moules au Kari* (a fresh-tasting salad of curried mussels) or Crab Louis with Cucumber (tomato, cucumber and crab salad) to start your luncheon feast off with a flourish.

The main dishes in this section–Sauté of Veal with Asparagus, little 'Tournedos' of Lamb, and *Omelette Arlésienne* – all bring a note of lightness to the menus.

As do the sweets and puddings – Pineapple Ambrosia, Cold Lemon Soufflé, Blackcurrant Sorbet, Angel Food Cake, and Glazed Apple Tart.

Get all the shopping done the day before – your three-course lunch will probably take up all of your time after clearing away breakfast, unless a sweet or some other advance preparation has been seen to the previous evening.

Lunchtime entertaining doesn't mean roughing it in the kitchen – so polish up the silver and let your best china see the light of day.

Finally, a word of warning: never make the mistake of inviting lunch guests too early in the day. For one thing, you'll horrify your bachelor friends, for whom a lunch party is the most delicious prospect imaginable to look forward to at the end of a long, relaxing weekend morning.

Right: Gratin Dauphinois (page 98)

Previous pages: A summer meal outdoors

96

Invite friends around for a meal and ten times out of ten they will assume that you mean dinner or supper. Lunches seem to have been relegated to the realms of expense account living, or a quick salad and coffee on a shopping trip to town.

True, with husbands away from dawn till dusk and wives shopping frantically among the office lunch-hour crowds or coping at home with endless snacks of baked beans, fish fingers or hamburgers as the children bundle in and out, there seems little place in our modern way of life for the leisurely late luncheon parties of our grandparents' day.

It helped, of course, in those days, to have a kitchenful of cooks and maids hard at work preparing the feast from the early morning.

You may think that weekday lunch parties in suburban deserts devoid of menfolk are a pleasure you can do without – but every week has its oasis, and it is then that the weekend luncheon with its comfortable pattern of unhurried food in a free-and-easy setting comes into its own.

What about those friends who live just that little bit too far away to make driving back after a late dinner party feasible? Ask them over for Sunday lunch instead. You can read the papers over coffee before you start putting the food together (especially if you've done some of the preparation the evening before), and they can still get back home in time to prepare themselves for the stark realities of Monday morning.

A weekend lunch party is a great idea for a group of friends who are planning to go on to some other activity together – be it a football match, a game of bridge, or just lazy chatter in the afternoon sun; for friends that you like well enough for you not to mind if they linger on into the evening (an occupational hazard for weekend lunch-party givers); or for friends with late-night baby-sitting problems (children are bright and relaxed enough early on in the day to enjoy you and your guests at the lunch table).

Some of my best lunch parties have been given in my house in the South of France. There we can sit fourteen around the huge farmhouse table, and it's a sort of cook-as-you-eat pattern where guests help to string the beans and carry away the dishes as I produce the next course. Great fun.

Lunch parties should be informal. That's really why they are such a pleasure to go to or to give.

Don't treat a lunch party like a poor relation of a dinner party. For, while the kind of food one serves is more or less elastic it is wise to keep it on the light side, and the drink as well: save your heavier, more full-bodied wines for leisurely evenings when you can give yourself up to them fully without fear of the consequences. Our menus for lunch parties are mainly three-course affairs – a light appetizer, a main course with a vegetable or salad, and an inspired sweet.

One of my favourite luncheon first courses – an avocado, tomato and onion appetizer – was created when I myself was a weekend guest in the country and was asked to make something out of what was in the larder. To make it, peel avocado pears; cut them crosswise into thickish rings and combine them with thick slices of tomato and thin rings of onion; then toss in French dressing for a deliciously light luncheon appetizer.

Menu

Pâté Liégeois

German Veal with Almonds with Quick Hollandaise Sauce and Gratin Dauphinois

Italian Bean Salad

Fresh Blackcurrant Sorbet

Serves 6

with this menu I suggest the following Inexpensive White Wines
Chablis
Muscadet

Pâté Liégeois

1 lb(450g) chicken livers
Salt
½ lb(225g) unsalted butter
4 tablespoons grated Spanish onion
2 teaspoons dry mustard
½ teaspoon freshly grated nutmeg
¼ teaspoon ground cloves
Freshly ground black pepper

1 Cover livers with salted water; bring to the boil; reduce heat and simmer, covered, for 20 minutes. Drain livers, pat dry and put twice through the finest blade of your mincer – or liquidize in an electric blender.

2 Return paste to pan and beat over a moderate heat for 1 minute to evaporate excess moisture.

3 Work butter with a wooden spoon until soft and creamy. Flavour with onion, mustard, nutmeg and cloves; then beat in minced livers. Season to taste with salt and freshly ground black pepper. If you prefer an absolutely smooth texture, rub *pâté* through a fine sieve.

4 Pack *pâté* firmly into one or two small earthenware pots or terrines and chill until ready to use. Serve with hot toast.

German Veal with Almonds

6 oz(175g) button mushrooms, thinly sliced
4 tablespoons butter
4 tablespoons olive oil
Salt and freshly ground black pepper
2 tablespoons Madeira
6 veal escalopes, about 4–5 oz (100–150g) each
6 oz(175g) cooked tongue
1–2 eggs
3 oz(75g) fine dry breadcrumbs
2 oz(50g) flaked almonds
Plain flour

1 Sauté mushrooms in 1 tablespoon each butter and olive oil until soft and golden. Add salt and freshly ground black pepper sprinkle with Madeira and allow to cool.

2 Beat escalopes out as thinly as possible.

3 Cut tongue into thin strips; divide into 6 bundles and pile each in the centre of an escalope. Spoon mushrooms on top and fold each escalope into an envelope.

4 Beat egg(s) lightly with a little water. Toss breadcrumbs with flaked almonds.

5 Dust veal envelopes with flour; dip into egg and coat with almond-breadcrumb mixture, patting it on firmly. Chill.

6 To cook veal: melt remaining butter and oil and fry envelopes slowly on both sides until golden brown, about 10 minutes. Serve immediately with a sauceboat of **quick hollandaise sauce** (see next page).

Gratin Dauphinois
(illustrated on page 96)

2 lb(900g) potatoes
1 pint(6dl) milk
Salt and freshly ground black pepper
4 tablespoons butter
½ pint(3dl) single cream
8 tablespoons grated Gruyère cheese
3 tablespoons grated Parmesan cheese

1 Preheat oven to moderate (375°F/190°C/Mark 5).

2 Peel and slice potatoes thinly into a bowl of cold water. Drain slices thoroughly and arrange in a 2-pint(1-litre) *gratin* dish.

3 Pour over milk; season to taste with salt and freshly ground black pepper.

4 Bake for 20 to 30 minutes, or until potatoes are half-cooked. Remove from oven and reduce temperature to 325°F/170°C/Mark 3.

5 Drain potatoes. Rinse and dry *gratin* dish, then grease it with 2 tablespoons butter.

6 Layer potato slices in buttered dish. Pour over cream, sprinkle with grated cheese and dot with remaining butter.

7 Return to the oven for a further 30 minutes, or until potatoes are tender, with a golden crust. (Cover dish with foil if they brown too quickly.) Serve very hot.

Quick Hollandaise Sauce

6 oz(175g) butter
6 egg yolks
Lemon juice
Salt and white pepper

1 Melt butter in a small pan, taking care that it does not bubble or sizzle.

2 Warm goblet of an electric blender and in it combine egg yolks with $1\frac{1}{2}$ teaspoons lemon juice, $1\frac{1}{2}$ tablespoons water and a pinch each of salt and white pepper.

3 Switch blender to moderate speed and, when yolks are well mixed, remove lid and pour in butter in a thin stream. If butter is poured in slowly enough, sauce will thicken into a genuine Hollandaise. However, if it remains too liquid, transfer to the top of a double saucepan and stir over hot water for a few seconds to thicken it; conversely, an over-stiff sauce may be thinned by beating in a tablespoon or two of very hot water.

4 Add more salt, pepper or lemon juice if necessary and keep sauce warm over warm water until needed.

Italian Bean Salad

(for the recipe see page 159, illustrated on page 148)

Fresh Blackcurrant Sorbet

$1\frac{1}{2}$ lb(675g) trimmed blackcurrants
9 oz(250g) sugar
1 tablespoon lemon juice
2 egg whites
Raspberry purée, to serve (see step 9)

1 Set refrigerator at lowest temperature.

2 Put blackcurrants in the top of a double saucepan with 9 tablespoons water. Cook over simmering water for 30 minutes, or until blackcurrants have released their juice. Strain through a fine sieve, pressing out as much juice as possible with the back of a spoon.

3 Dissolve sugar in $\frac{3}{4}$ pint(4dl) water and simmer for 10 minutes. Stir in lemon juice.

4 Combine sugar syrup with blackcurrant juice in a measuring jug. Make up to $1\frac{1}{2}$ pints (8·5dl) with water. Taste mixture: if it seems too sharp, add a little more water.

Note: Remember, however, that the addition of egg whites later will modify flavour, as will freezing itself.

5 Pour mixture into an oiled freezer tray or loaf tin and freeze until half set. This will take about 1 hour.

6 Remove from refrigerator and stir well with a fork to break up ice crystals.

7 Beat egg whites until stiff but not dry, and fold gently but thoroughly into sorbet.

8 Freeze until firm, stirring once or twice with a fork to ensure that sorbet does not separate.

9 Serve with a bowl of raspberry purée – fresh raspberries rubbed through a fine sieve and flavoured with a little icing sugar and lemon juice.

SALADS

Green Salad Variations

A crisp green salad, tossed at the table with a classic dressing of olive oil and wine vinegar or fresh lemon juice, can be one of the highlights of a meal.

The very word 'salad' evokes a vision of green lettuce leaves, carefully washed and dried, bathed with fruity olive oil and flavoured with a touch of wine vinegar, a hint of garlic and a dusting of salt and freshly ground black pepper. Sometimes, too, I add a little Dijon mustard and a sprinkling of finely chopped fresh herbs – basil, tarragon and chives. On second thoughts, not too finely chopped after all. We want to see them. And taste them.

Tossed Green Salad
Wash the leaves of 1 to 2 heads of lettuce well in a large quantity of water. They should be left whole, never cut. Drain well and dry thoroughly in a cloth or a salad basket so that there is no water on them to dilute the dressing.

To serve: pour French dressing (see below) into salad bowl; arrange prepared lettuce leaves on top. Check seasoning. Then, before serving at the table, give a final toss to the ingredients to ensure that every leaf is glistening with dressing. This salad will serve 4 to 6.

Variations
Add other salad greens in season – cos lettuce, endive, chicory, batavia, young spinach leaves, watercress and French *mâche* (corn salad).

Add finely chopped garlic or shallots, or a combination of the two, to salad dressing.

Add fresh green herbs – finely chopped chervil, basil, tarragon, chives or *eau-de-cologne* mint – to the dressing.

For crunch appeal, add diced celery, green pepper or fennel.

French Dressing

Vinaigrette Sauce
Mix together 1 tablespoon lemon juice, 1 to 2 tablespoons wine vinegar and $\frac{1}{4}$ to $\frac{1}{2}$ level teaspoon Dijon mustard, and season to taste with coarse salt and freshly ground black pepper. Add 6 to 8 table-spoons olive oil, and beat with a fork until mixture emulsifies

Special Vinaigrette Sauce
Make French dressing as directed. Add a little finely chopped parsley and onion or chives, finely chopped green olives, capers or gherkins, and the sieved yolk of a hard-boiled egg.

Salade Paysanne

Wash and dry leaves from 2 heads of lettuce. Chill. Sauté 6oz/175g diced fat salt pork in 2 tablespoons of olive oil until golden. Arrange lettuce in bowl; add diced pork and hot fat, 2 hard boiled eggs chopped, 3 table-spoons finely chopped chervil, tarragon or basil, and salt, freshly ground black pepper and wine vinegar, to taste.

Avocado, Tomato and Onion Appetizer

4–6 large slices Spanish onion
2 large ripe avocados
6 firm ripe tomatoes
1–2 tablespoons chopped parsley
Finely chopped fresh herbs: basil, tarragon or chives

VINAIGRETTE DRESSING:
3 tablespoons olive oil
1–2 tablespoons wine vinegar
Salt and freshly ground black pepper
Pinch of dry mustard
Pinch of sugar

1 To make vinaigrette: beat olive oil and vinegar with a fork; season generously with salt, freshly ground black pepper and a pinch each of mustard and sugar.

2 Take onion rings apart and use only the ones between 1½ inches and 2 inches (3·5 and 5cms) in diameter. Soak them in iced water for 15 minutes, then drain thoroughly.

3 Peel avocados and cut into rings cross-wise, slipping each ring off the stone as you slice it.

4 Toss avocados with vinaigrette, coating each ring thoroughly to prevent it dis-colouring. Arrange in a deep serving dish.

5 Slice tomatoes and add them to the avocados, together with onion slices. Toss lightly; sprinkle with chopped parsley and fresh basil, tarragon or chives, to taste, and toss again. Serve very cold.

Sauté of Veal with Asparagus

2 lb(900g) mature asparagus
Salt
2 lb(900g) boned loin of veal
3 oz(75g) butter

Freshly ground black pepper
4 spring onions or shallots, finely chopped
1½ oz(40g) flour
¼ pint(1·5dl) double cream
1 teaspoon lemon juice

1 Clean asparagus carefully, trimming root ends. Cut stalks in two, separating tips and stems. Cook tips and stems until tender in separate pans of simmering salted water: tips for about 8 minutes, stems 3 to 5 minutes longer. Drain well, reserving cooking liquors; keep hot.

2 Cut veal into 2-inch(5-cm) cubes.

3 Melt butter in a wide, heavy pan or casserole without letting it colour, and sauté veal gently until golden on all sides. Season to taste with salt and freshly ground black pepper.

4 Add chopped spring onions or shallots and sauté for a few minutes longer.

5 Sprinkle veal and onions with flour and simmer gently until flour is cooked, taking care as before not to let ingredients brown.

6 Stir in ¾ to 1 pint(4 to 6dl) reserved asparagus liquor; cover and simmer for 15 to 20 minutes, or until veal is tender.

7 Purée asparagus tips in a liquidizer or rub through a fine sieve. Stir purée into veal, together with cream and lemon juice. Taste for seasoning, adding more salt, freshly ground black pepper or lemon juice if necessary. (Asparagus liquor will already have contributed some salt.) Simmer for 7 to 8 minutes longer.

8 Heat a large, deep serving dish. Transfer veal to dish and pour over sauce. Arrange asparagus stems attractively in small bunches around sides of dish and serve immediately, accompanied by a bowl of **plain boiled rice** (see page 70)

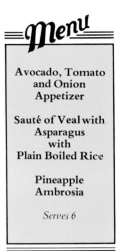

Menu

Avocado, Tomato
and Onion
Appetizer

Sauté of Veal with
Asparagus
with
Plain Boiled Rice

Pineapple
Ambrosia

Serves 6

with this menu I suggest the following Inexpensive White Wines or Rosés
**Vouvray
Saumur Blanc
Tavel Rosé**

Pineapple Ambrosia

3 small ripe pineapples, about
  1 lb(450g) each
2 oranges
2 bananas
Juice of $\frac{1}{2}$ large lemon
$\frac{1}{2}$ lb(225g) fresh strawberries
3 oz(75g) icing sugar
3 oz(75g) freshly grated or dessicated
  coconut

1 Using a very sharp knife, slice each pineapple in half vertically through the flesh and leafy stem. Carefully scoop out flesh, leaving a firm shell; cut flesh into small dice and place in a bowl.

2 Peel oranges and remove pith. Slice oranges into thin rounds, discarding pips.

3 Peel and slice bananas. Toss in lemon juice to prevent discolouring.

4 Hull strawberries.

5 Layer fruit in pineapple shells, sifting a little icing sugar to taste between each layer. Sprinkle with coconut and chill.

Salade de Moules au Kari

$\frac{1}{2}$ lb(225g) long-grain rice
Salt
3 pints(1·7 litres) mussels
$\frac{1}{2}$ pint(3dl) dry white wine
1 onion, finely chopped
2 level teaspoons curry powder
$\frac{1}{4}$ lb(100g) peeled shrimps
2 firm tomatoes, sliced
1–2 tablespoons chopped parsley
Vinaigrette dressing (see step 6)
Crisp lettuce leaves, to garnish

1 Boil rice in salted water until tender but still firm. Drain thoroughly; cool.

2 Scrub mussels clean and remove 'beards'.

Place them in a heavy pan with wine, chopped onion and curry powder; cover tightly and cook over high heat, shaking pan frequently, until mussels have all opened.

3 Shell mussels over pan to catch any liquor trapped inside. Filter liquor through muslin and return to rinsed-out pan; add shrimps and simmer for 15 minutes.

4 Drain shrimps, reserving liquor, and combine with rice and mussels in a bowl; add tomatoes and parsley.

5 Simmer shrimp liquor until reduced to about 3 tablespoons.

6 Make a highly seasoned vinaigrette, using 2 tablespoons wine vinegar, 5 tablespoons olive oil, 1 finely chopped shallot, salt and pepper, and beating with a fork until ingredients form an emulsion. Blend in reduced shrimp liquor and pour over salad; toss lightly and chill before serving piled in a lettuce-lined bowl.

Shepherd's Pie
(illustrated on page 105)

Butter
1 Spanish onion, finely chopped
2 tablespoons olive oil
1 lb(450g) cooked roast beef, coarsely
  minced
$\frac{1}{4}$ pint(3dl) rich beef gravy or Quick
  Brown Sauce (see below)
2 teaspoons Worcestershire sauce
1 tablespoon chopped parsley
$\frac{1}{4}$ teaspoon mixed herbs
Salt and freshly ground black pepper

POTATO TOPPING:
6 tablespoons double cream
3 tablespoons melted butter
2 eggs, lightly beaten
2 lb(900g) potatoes, peeled, boiled and
  mashed
Salt and freshly ground black pepper

1 Generously butter a deep, 3-pint(2-litre) baking dish.

2 Preheat oven to moderately hot (400°F/200°C/Mark 6).

3 Sauté chopped onion in olive oil until soft and transparent. Stir in minced cooked beef, gravy or **quick brown sauce** (see below), Worcestershire sauce, chopped parsley and herbs, and season to taste with salt and freshly ground black pepper. Remove from heat.

4 **To make potato topping:** beat cream, 2 tablespoons melted butter and lightly beaten eggs into hot mashed potatoes, and season to taste with salt and freshly ground black pepper.

5 Spread meat mixture evenly in baking dish. Top with mashed potatoes and brush with remaining melted butter.

6 Bake for 20 to 25 minutes, or until potatoes are puffed and golden brown.

7 Serve with **sautéed courgettes and tomatoes** (see page 43).

Quick Brown Sauce

2 tablespoons butter
1 Spanish onion, roughly chopped
1 carrot, roughly chopped
½ bay leaf
3 stalks parsley
Sprig of fresh thyme or pinch of dried thyme
2 tablespoons flour
1 teaspoon tomato purée
¾ pint(4dl) hot beef stock (made with a cube)
Freshly ground black pepper

1 Melt butter in a heavy pan. Add roughly chopped onion, carrot, bay leaf, parsley and fresh thyme or dried thyme. Brown vegetables thoroughly, stirring occasionally with a wooden spoon and scraping bottom of pan. Dust with flour and continue to cook until this has browned as well.

2 Stir in tomato purée and beef stock, scraping bottom of pan vigorously to dislodge crusty brown bits. Season lightly with freshly ground black pepper and simmer for 45 minutes, stirring occasionally.

3 Strain sauce through a fine sieve, pressing vegetables against sides of sieve to extract all their juices. Correct seasoning.

Note: The sauce can be used immediately, or stored for 2 days in an airtight container in the refrigerator.

Cold Lemon Soufflé

3 eggs, separated
5 oz(150g) castor sugar
Finely grated rind and strained juice of 3 large lemons
2 teaspoons powdered gelatine
½ pint(3dl) double cream
Whipped cream, to decorate (optional)

1 Tie a double thickness of greaseproof paper around the outside of a 5-inch(13-cm) soufflé dish to come at least 2 inches(5cm) above the rim.

2 Place egg yolks in a bowl; add sugar and whisk over hot water until very light, white and fluffy.

3 Gradually add grated lemon rind and strained juice, beating constantly, and whisk until mixture thickens; then remove from heat and whisk until cool.

4 In a small cup, soften gelatine in 3 to 4 tablespoons cold water; place cup in a pan of hot water and stir gently until gelatine has completely dissolved.

5 Whisk egg whites until stiff but not dry.

Menu

Salade de Moules au Kari

Shepherd's Pie with Quick Brown Sauce and Sautéed Courgettes and Tomatoes

Cold Lemon Soufflé with Langues de Chat

Serves 6

with this menu I suggest the following Inexpensive White Wines
Muscadet
Sancerre
or the following Inexpensive Red Wines
Côtes-du-Rhône
Bourgueil

6 Whisk cream until barely stiff enough to hold its shape.

7 Whisk dissolved gelatine into egg and lemon mixture (for a completely smooth texture, they should both ideally be at the same temperature). Carefully fold in cream, followed by beaten egg whites.

8 Pour mixture into prepared soufflé dish and chill until set.

9 **To serve:** carefully peel off paper collar from dish and serve soufflé decorated with more piped whipped cream if liked, and accompanied by a plate of crisp **langues de chat** (see below).

Langues de Chat

Makes about 24
Butter and flour for baking sheets
2 oz(50g) softened butter
2 oz(50g) castor sugar
2 egg whites
2 oz(50g) plain flour

1 Preheat oven to fairly hot (425°F/ 220°C/Mark 7). Butter and dust 2 or 3 baking sheets with flour, shaking off any excess.

2 In a small bowl, beat softened butter until creamy. Add sugar and beat vigorously with a wooden spoon until mixture is very pale and fluffy again. (This will take several minutes; the success of the biscuits largely depends on adequate beating.)

3 Put egg whites in a shallow dish. Then, with a teaspoon, add them (unbeaten) to the butter mixture a little at a time, beating vigorously after each addition.

4 Sift flour over mixture and fold in lightly but thoroughly with a metal spoon.

5 Spoon mixture into a piping bag fitted with a plain $\frac{1}{4}$-inch(0·5-cm) nozzle and pipe out in 3-inch (7·5-cm) lengths, spacing them about 2 inches(5cm) apart, as they spread considerably. If you do not have enough baking sheets to take all the biscuits at once, the mixture will come to no harm if piped out and baked in batches.

6 Bake for 5 minutes, or until biscuits are very thin and tinged with brown round the edges.

7 Quickly transfer to wire cooling racks with a spatula and allow to become quite cold and crisp before serving or storing in an airtight container.

Crab Louis with Cucumber

$\frac{1}{2}$ **pint(3dl) well-flavoured, home-made mayonnaise (see page 152)**
2 tablespoons tomato ketchup
3 tablespoons olive oil
1 tablespoon wine vinegar
2 tablespoons grated onion
2 tablespoons finely chopped parsley
6 tablespoons double cream, whipped
Tabasco or Worcestershire sauce (optional)
Salt and freshly ground black pepper
Cayenne pepper
1–2 tablespoons chopped, stuffed or ripe pitted olives
1 lb(450g) cooked crabmeat, flaked
Thinly sliced unpeeled cucumber, lettuce leaves and 2 tablespoons chopped chives, to garnish

1 Blend first 7 ingredients together. Season with Tabasco or Worcestershire sauce, if used, salt, freshly ground black pepper and a dash of cayenne, to taste.

2 Stir in chopped olives and chill for at least 1 hour, preferably 2, before serving.

3 When ready to serve, fold flaked crabmeat into sauce.

Menu

Crab Louis with Cucumber

'Tournedos' of Lamb with Potatoes O'Brien

Angel Food Cake with Orange Sauce

Serves 4–6

with this menu I suggest the following Medium-priced White Wine
Pouilly Fuissé
or the following Medium-priced Red Wines
Médoc
Beaune
Volnay
Nuits-St-Georges

4 Decorate outer edge of 4 or 6 individual plates with a ring of overlapping cucumber slices, and lay a large, crisp lettuce leaf in the centre. Pile with crabmeat mixture and serve, garnished with chopped chives.

'Tournedos' of Lamb

1 Spanish onion, finely chopped
1 clove garlic, finely chopped
2 tablespoons butter
2 tablespoons olive oil
2 oz(50g) soft white breadcrumbs
3–4 tablespoons cold milk
1¼ lb(575g) lean minced lamb

3 tablespoons chopped parsley
¼ teaspoon dried oregano
2 teaspoons Worcestershire sauce
1 egg
Salt and freshly ground black pepper
Flour
6–8 rashers fat bacon

1 Simmer onion and garlic in half the butter and oil until soft; cool. Soak breadcrumbs in milk; then squeeze out excess moisture.

2 Place lamb in a large bowl. Add onion and garlic, breadcrumbs, herbs, Worcestershire sauce and egg, and mix well. Season with salt and freshly ground black pepper.

Shepherd's Pie with Quick Brown Sauce and Sautéed Courgettes and Tomatoes (pages 43, 102 & 103)

3 Divide mixture into 6 portions. Shape into balls; roll in flour and flatten into patties 2 inches(5cm) in diameter.

4 Stretch each bacon rasher thinly with the back of a knife to meet round the middle of a patty, using an extra strip of bacon if necessary, and tie securely with string.

5 Heat remaining fats in a large frying pan, or 2 smaller pans, and fry patties slowly on all sides until cooked through, about 30 minutes.

6 Discard strings, transfer patties to a heated serving dish and serve very hot.

Potatoes O'Brien

2–2½ lb(0·9–1·1kg) potatoes, peeled and finely diced
1 large green pepper, cored, seeded and finely chopped
1 large Spanish onion, finely chopped
1 tablespoon flour
4 tablespoons chopped parsley
¼ lb(100g) freshly grated cheese
Pinch of cayenne
Salt and freshly ground black pepper
¼ pint(1·5dl) hot milk
¼ pint(1·5dl) double cream
2 tablespoons butter

1 Preheat oven to moderately hot (400°F/200°C/Mark 6).

2 Place potatoes, green pepper and onion in a bowl. Toss lightly.

3 Sprinkle vegetables with flour, chopped parsley and grated cheese and toss again. Then season to taste with a pinch of cayenne, salt and a little freshly ground black pepper, bearing in mind that the mixture may already be quite peppery because of the green pepper.

4 Spread potato mixture evenly in a

3-pint(2-litre) ovenproof dish; pour over milk and cream, dot with butter and bake for 1 hour, or until potatoes are soft, with a crisp, golden brown topping.

Angel Food Cake

3 oz(75g) plain flour
1 oz(25g) cornflour
½ level teaspoon salt
½ lb(225g) castor sugar
10 egg whites
1 tablespoon lemon juice
1 level teaspoon cream of tartar
½ teaspoon vanilla essence

1 Preheat oven to moderate (350°F/180°C/Mark 4).

2 Prepare a 9-inch(23-cm) tube cake tin, making sure that it is spotlessly clean, as otherwise the delicate cake will not rise properly.

3 Sift flour with cornflour and salt. Sift castor sugar separately, then resift flour mixture 3 times with 3 oz(75g) of the sugar.

4 Mix egg whites with lemon juice and 1 tablespoon water; beat until foamy. Add cream of tartar and continue to beat until stiff but not dry.

5 Beat in remaining 5oz(150g) castor sugar, a tablespoon at a time. **Note:** If you are using an electric mixer, start adding sugar a little earlier to avoid overbeating.

6 Flavour with vanilla.

7 Sift 2 to 3 tablespoons flour mixture over egg whites and fold in quickly and gently but thoroughly. Fold in remaining flour mixture gradually in the same way.

8 Turn mixture into prepared tin; bake for about 45 minutes, or until cake springs back when lightly pressed with a finger.

9 Remove cake from oven and immediately invert tin at an angle upside down, so that the cake hangs free – a milk bottle is good for this. Leave cake hanging for about 1½ hours, or until quite set and cold.

10 Then gently shake cake out of the tin on to a serving dish. Serve with **orange sauce** (see below).

Orange Sauce

Juice of 4 large oranges and ½ lemon
Finely grated rind of 2 oranges
2 tablespoons arrowroot
3 tablespoons castor sugar
2 tablespoons butter
2 egg yolks, lightly beaten
1–2 teaspoons Grand Marnier

1 Combine orange and lemon juice with grated orange rind in a measuring jug. There should be ½ pint (3dl) liquid. Make up to 1 pint (6dl) with water.

2 Mix arrowroot smoothly with some of juice, then combine with remaining juice and pour into pan.

3 Bring to the boil, stirring, and simmer for 2 to 3 minutes, until sauce is thick and translucent.

4 Beat in sugar and butter over low heat until dissolved.

5 Pour hot sauce over lightly beaten egg yolks, beating constantly.

6 Return to pan and stir over low heat for a minute or two longer until sauce thickens slightly, taking great care not to let it boil.

7 Strain sauce; cool slightly and flavour to taste with a little Grand Marnier.

8 Serve warm or cool.

Smoked Trout Appetizer

3 smoked trout
6 slices white bread
6 tablespoons double cream
1–2 tablespoons grated horseradish, or to taste
Finely chopped parsley

GARNISH:
6 crisp lettuce leaves
6 slices firm tomato
6 large black olives, pitted and halved
6 lemon wedges

1 Skin and fillet smoked trout, and cut each fillet in two.

2 Toast bread slices on both sides and remove crusts.

3 Whisk double cream; add 1–2 tablespoons iced water and whisk again until firm. Fold in grated horseradish, to taste.

4 Spread each slice of toast with horseradish chantilly cream and arrange pieces of trout on top. Sprinkle with a pinch of finely chopped parsley. Cut each slice of toast in half diagonally.

5 Serve 2 toast triangles per person on individual plates garnished with lettuce, tomato, black olives, and lemon wedges to squeeze over the trout.

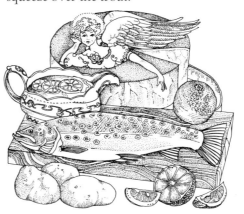

Smoked Trout Appetizer

Omelette Arlésienne

Glazed Apple Tart

Serves 4–6

with this menu I suggest the following Medium-priced White Wines and Rosés
Chablis
Tavel Rosé

Omelette Arlésienne

A rich, thick omelette which makes a substantial summer luncheon dish. Follow with a fresh green salad.

Omelette Arlésienne

3 ripe aubergines
Salt
8 tablespoons olive oil
1 Spanish onion, finely chopped
2 lb(900g) ripe tomatoes, peeled, seeded and diced
Freshly ground black pepper
1 clove garlic, finely chopped
4 tablespoons finely chopped parsley
8 eggs
1–2 tablespoons melted butter

1 Peel aubergines and cut flesh into dice. Leave them to soak in a bowl of salted water for at least half an hour.

2 Heat half the olive oil in a deep, heavy frying pan. Add finely chopped onion and diced tomatoes and sauté gently for a few minutes.

3 Drain aubergines thoroughly, squeezing out as much as possible of their bitter juices between the palms of your hands. Add aubergines to the simmering tomato mixture and mix well.

4 Season to taste with salt and freshly ground black pepper and cook gently for about 25 minutes, stirring occasionally with a wooden spoon.

5 Add finely chopped garlic and parsley, mix well and cook for a minute longer. Remove from heat and keep warm.

6 Beat eggs lightly with a fork. Season to taste with salt and freshly ground black pepper.

7 Heat remaining oil in a large omelette pan; pour in eggs and stir over a moderate heat until they begin to thicken and have set underneath.

8 Spoon aubergine mixture down centre, reserving 2 or 3 tablespoons for garnish.

9 Continue to cook omelette until firm and golden brown on the underside but still creamy on top; then slide it up one side of the pan and fold it over on itself.

10 Slip folded omelette out carefully on to a heated serving dish. Brush with melted butter and garnish with remaining aubergine mixture. Serve immediately.

Glazed Apple Tart

You will need: 1 pastry case, Crème Pâtissière filling, tart apples sliced thinly (enough to cover tart), lemon juice, and apricot glaze.

PASTRY CASE
8 oz (225g) plain flour
Pinch of salt
2 level tablespoons icing sugar

5 oz (150g) cold butter
1 egg yolk
2 teaspoons lemon juice
Iced water

1 Sieve the flour, salt and icing sugar into a large bowl.

2 Cut cold (not chilled butter) into $\frac{1}{4}$ inch (0.5cm) dice. Add to bowl.

3 Using a pastry blender (or two knives held scissor fashion, one in each hand) cut diced butter into flour mixture until it resembles coarse breadcrumbs.

4 Discard pastry blender or knives. Scoop up some of the mixture in the palms of both hands and let it shower back lightly

through your fingers, gently rubbing out the crumbs of fat between your fingertips. You should only need to do this six or seven times for the mixture to be reduced to fine breadcrumbs.

5 Beat egg yolk in a small bowl. Add 2 teaspoons lemon juice and 1 tablespoon iced water, and beat lightly until well mixed.

6 Sprinkle this over flour mixture, tossing and mixing with a fork. Rinse out bowl with another tablespoon of iced water and mix this into the pastry in the same way. Continue tossing and mixing with the fork until about three-quarters of the pastry is holding together. Then use your hand, cupped, to press the pastry

Glazed Apple Tart

lightly into one piece.

7 Shape pastry into a round. Wrap in a sheet of greaseproof paper, followed by a dampened tea towel, and chill for at least one hour before using.

8 If chilled dough is too firm for handling, let it stand at room temperature until it softens slightly. Then turn on to a floured board, knead or pat lightly into a round, roll out and use as required.

9 Bake 'blind' in a preheated, fairly hot oven (425°F/220°C/Mark 7) for fifteen minutes; lower heat to 350°F/180°C/Mark 4 and bake for thirty minutes.

CRÈME PÂTISSIÈRE FILLING
The magic trick of a French fruit tart is the sweet, creamy filling hidden underneath the fruit. Crème Pâtissière holds its shape when cold, yet is soft and never stiff in texture.

Makes ¾ pint (4dl)
¾ pint (4dl) milk
2-inch (5cm) piece of vanilla pod, split
5 egg yolks
4 oz (150g) castor sugar
2 level tablespoons plain flour
1 level tablespoon cornflour
1 level tablespoon butter
A few drops of vanilla essence and/or flavouring according to specific recipe.

1 Pour milk into a medium-sized pan and add vanilla pod, split to give out maximum flavour. Bring to boiling point over a low heat. Cover pan and put aside to infuse until needed.

2 In a bowl, whisk egg yolks with sugar until thick and light. Gradually whisk in flour and cornflour.

3 Fish out vanilla pod. Gradually pour milk into egg yolk mixture, beating with the whisk until well blended.

4 Pour mixture back into pan. Bring to the boil over a moderate heat, stirring constantly. Then simmer for three minutes longer, beating vigorously with a wooden spoon to disperse lumps. (These lumps invariably form, but they are easy to beat out as the cream thickens.)

5 Remove pan from heat. Beat in butter and continue to beat for a minute or two longer to cool the pastry cream slightly before adding flavourings called for in your recipe.

6 Pass cream through a sieve if necessary. Put it in a bowl and cover with a sheet of lightly buttered greaseproof paper to prevent a skin forming on top.

7 Allow to become quite cold; then chill until required.

8 To assemble tart: Half fill baked pastry shell with Crème Pâtissière; peel and slice apples thinly and brush with lemon juice to preserve colour. Arrange apple slices on Crème Pâtissière bed in overlapping rows (see illustration). Coat with apricot glaze.

TO MAKE APRICOT GLAZE
Makes enough for 1 tart
8 tablespoons apricot jam
4 tablespoons water
1–3 tablespoons rum, brandy or Kirsch (optional)

1 Heat apricot jam and water in a small saucepan, stirring constantly, until mixture melts. Strain.

2 If desired, stir in rum, brandy or Kirsch. Keep warm over hot water, until ready to use.

3 Brush surface of fruit to give a shiny glaze.

Come for a Quiche and a Salad

One of the most delicious dishes I know is *Quiche Lorraine*. This is a custard mixture of eggs and cream, sometimes thinned with a very little chicken, veal or beef stock. This savoury mixture is poured over sautéed green bacon bits and thin slices of Gruyère cheese. (I have often used Cheddar in the country, when Gruyère was unavailable – not quite as delicate perhaps, but absolutely delicious in its own right.) You will find that the variations on this masterly recipe are practically limitless once you have perfected the basic savoury custard mixture – and the pastry case.

From this basic – but delicious – *quiche* recipe, it is just a simple step to a host of variations on the *quiche* theme. Tiny ones serve as cocktail savouries; larger ones as the main course for luncheon or supper, with a crisp, lightly oiled salad as an accompaniment.

Quiches are a great boon to the busy host or hostess, as the pastry can be prepared the day before and chilled; the cases baked 'blind' before they are filled and then put into the oven just 30 minutes before the guests sit down to dinner.

Ideally, *quiches* should be served warm, not too hot. I like to bake them in special large pastry tins with loose bottoms to make the turning out operation simple and painless.

It took me just four days to perfect the foolproof 'fingertip' pastry that I use for all the *quiches*, savoury tarts, and flans that I serve daily in my restaurant, and that I have made for public demonstrations and parties all over the world.

Make the *quiche* your speciality. It's a wonderful 'secret weapon' in the cook's arsenal for using up leftovers discreetly and elegantly. For a pastry shell filled with a savoury custard mixture and your choice of garnish – bacon and cheese *(Quiche Lorraine)*; smoked salmon, prawns, crab or lobster (seafood *quiche*); sliced mushrooms or courgettes simmered in butter and oil (vegetable *quiche*); spinach, cottage cheese and Parmesan (cheese and spinach flan); or homely leeks and sausages – makes some of the best eating imaginable.

All you need to make the fabulous crumbly butter-rich pastry is $\frac{1}{2}$ lb(225g) plain flour, 1 level tablespoon icing sugar, a generous pinch of salt, 5 oz(150g) slightly softened butter, 1 beaten egg yolk and an equal amount of iced water.

The savoury custard mixture is easier still: 4 eggs, $\frac{3}{4}$ pint(4dl) milk or cream (or a combination of the two) and salt, pepper and nutmeg or cayenne to taste.

A Lesson in Making Perfect Pastry

Make pastry in as cool a place as possible; the colder it is kept during the making, the lighter it will be.

See that all utensils used – pastry board, basin, rolling pin, etc. – are clean and cool. The board or marble should be smooth and perfectly flat. Use it for pastry-making only.

Clean, dry hands are a must for pastry-making. In the summer, when hands are apt to be warm, mix the pastry as much as possible with a knife or a pastry cutter to keep it cool.

Liquids should be added to the flour as quickly and lightly as possible. Some cooks do this on the board or slab by making a well in the centre of the flour and pouring the water into the centre as they mix. I find that mixing it in a large mixing bowl is much easier.

When handling pastry, never rub little pieces off the fingers on to the pastry or the pastry board as these tend to form hard lumps when cooked.

Pastry should always be wrapped in foil or a damp cloth and allowed to 'repose' in the refrigerator for at least half an hour before it is used.

TO ROLL OUT DOUGH

Sprinkle the pastry board with flour; lay the dough on it and work lightly with the hands until free from cracks. Flour a rolling pin; press down the pastry and then with sharp quick strokes roll pastry out to the thickness required.

Roll lightly and try to press equally with both hands.

Never allow pastry to stick to the board; lift it occasionally on the rolling pin and dust some flour underneath. If any has stuck to the board, scrape it off carefully with a knife before beginning to roll again.

Always sprinkle flour over board and pastry through a flour sifter to make it finer and lighter, using as little flour as possible for this, as too much tends to make the pastry hard.

If the rolling pin sticks to the pastry, dust with a little flour and brush it off again lightly with a small brush kept for this purpose.

TO BAKE PASTRY

A fairly hot oven is required for pastry, for if it is not hot enough the butter will melt and run out before the starch grains in the flour have had time to burst and absorb it. If the oven is too hot, however, the pastry will burn before it has risen properly.

Pastry should never be baked in an oven in which meat is being roasted, or with any other dish that generates steam, as moist heat is apt to destroy its crispness. When baking pastry, open and close the door as gently as possible and never more often than is absolutely necessary.

If pastry becomes too brown before it has cooked sufficiently, cover it over with a piece of aluminium foil. If the pastry is not to be used at once when taken from the oven, allow it to cool slowly in the warm kitchen. Light pastry tends to become heavy when cooled too quickly.

TO BAKE BLIND

Pastry that is going to be cooked with its filling should be pre-baked in a hot oven for a while just to keep it from going soggy. To protect pastry during this process, professional cooks bake it 'blind' in the following manner.

Line a pastry tin with pastry, fluting the edges; chill. Prick bottom with a fork; cover bottom of pastry with a piece of waxed paper or aluminium foil, and cover this in turn with dried beans; then bake in a hot oven (450°F/230°C/Mark 8) for about 15 minutes, just long enough to set the crust without browning it. Remove beans and paper or foil and allow to cool. Then fill as desired and bake in a slow oven (325°F/170°C/Mark 3) until done. The beans can be reserved in a storage jar and used again.

However, if your tart or flan case is to be filled with a filling that is already cooked, it is imperative to continue cooking it as below.

TO BAKE PASTRY SHELL ONLY

Bake 'blind' as above for 15 minutes; remove beans and foil; lower heat to 375°F/190°C/Mark 5 and bake for 10–15 minutes more. If crust becomes too brown at edges, cover rim with a little crumpled foil.

FINGERTIP PASTRY

Enough for 9–10 inch(25cm) tart shell

1 Sieve $\frac{1}{2}$ lb(225g) plain flour and 1 level tablespoon icing sugar into a large mixing bowl. Add a generous pinch ($\frac{1}{4}$ level teaspoon) salt and 5 oz(150g) diced, slightly softened butter to the ingredients in the bowl. Lift flour gently over the butter cubes with your hands and then rub in the butter gradually with the tips of your fingers – lifting flour and butter out of bowl each time – until the mixture resembles fine breadcrumbs. Do this very gently and lightly or the mixture will become greasy and heavy. (More pastry has been ruined by over-handling than by under-handling.)

2 Place 1 egg yolk in a measuring jug or small bowl and add 4 tablespoons iced water. Mix well, sprinkle over pastry mixture and work in lightly with your fingers.

3 Shape moist dough lightly into a slightly flattened round; wrap in aluminium foil, a clean tea towel or a plastic wrap and put it in the refrigerator for at least 1 hour to 'ripen' and become firm.

If chilled dough becomes too firm for easy handling, let it stand at room temperature until it softens slightly. Then turn out on to a floured board and roll as required.

4 Press into a pastry tin (or individual tins) with your fingers and prick with a fork.

Italian Antipasto Salad

(illustrated on the previous page)

1 head lettuce
4 heads chicory, sliced lengthwise
2 roots fennel, cut into sections
1 green pepper, sliced in rings
1 red pepper, sliced in rings
**1 large Spanish onion, very
  coarsely diced**
4 anchovy fillets, coarsely chopped
2 tablespoons capers
Parsley sprigs, to garnish

ITALIAN DRESSING:
6 tablespoons olive oil
2 tablespoons lemon juice
$\frac{1}{2}$ clove garlic, finely chopped
2 tablespoons finely chopped parsley
Salt and freshly ground black pepper

1 Wash and dry the lettuce leaves, and arrange them in the bottom of a large shallow salad bowl.

2 Arrange chicory, fennel, peppers and diced onion in groups on the lettuce.

3 Mix the chopped anchovies with capers and place in the centre of the salad.

4 To make dressing: mix the first four ingredients together and season to taste with salt and freshly ground pepper.

5 Sprinkle salad with well-flavoured Italian dressing and garnish with sprigs of parsley.

Smoked Haddock Quiche

$\frac{1}{2}$ lb(225g) fingertip pastry (see above)
$\frac{1}{2}$ lb(225g) smoked haddock
Milk
4 eggs
$\frac{1}{4}$ pint(1·5dl) cream
Salt and freshly ground black pepper
Freshly grated nutmeg
Butter

1 Soak smoked haddock in water for 1 hour. Drain, place in a small saucepan, cover with equal amounts of milk and water and bring to a fast boil. Remove from heat and allow to stand for 15 minutes. Drain again, reserving stock. Remove skin and bones and break fish into pieces.

2 Whisk eggs together with cream, $\frac{1}{4}$ pint(1·5dl) milk and $\frac{1}{4}$ pint(1·5dl) reserved haddock stock. When well mixed, flavour to taste with salt, freshly ground black pepper and freshly grated nutmeg.

Menu

Italian Antipasto
Salad

Smoked Haddock
Quiche

Baked Apple
Compote

Serves 4–6

*with this menu I suggest
the following Inexpensive
White Wines*
**Chianti Ruffino
White
Macon-Vire
Bourgogne Aligoté**

3 Line a large pastry tin (or 6–8 individual tins) with pastry; prick bottom with a fork and bake 'blind' in a hot oven (450°F/230°C/Mark 8) for 10–15 minutes, or just long enough to set pastry without browning it. Allow to cool.

4 Arrange flaked cooked haddock in bottom of pastry case (or cases) and fill with custard mixture. Dot with butter. Bake in a slow oven (325°F/170°C/Mark 3) for 30–40 minutes and serve immediately.

Note: Unless you use a very large pastry tin (one of those with a removable bottom), you will have surplus custard mixture. Use for baked fish custard with any leftover fish.

Baked Apple Compote

2 lb(900g) cooking apples
Rind and juice of 1 lemon
6 oz(175g) brown sugar
2 oz(50g) butter
Double cream

1 Slice peeled and cored cooking apples into a buttered baking dish.

2 Sprinkle the slices with lemon juice, grated lemon rind and brown sugar and dot with butter.

3 Bake, uncovered, in a moderate oven (375°F/190°C/Mark 5) for 30 minutes, or until tender. Serve with double cream.

Quiche Lorraine

Fingertip pastry for 8-inch(20-cm) pie (see previous page)
Beaten egg
4 egg yolks
½ pint(3dl) single cream
Salt and freshly ground black pepper
Freshly grated nutmeg
¼ lb(100g) green bacon (or fat salt pork) cut in 1 piece
2 tablespoons butter
¼ lb(100g) Gruyère cheese, diced

1 Line pastry tin with shortcrust pastry. Prick bottom with a fork; brush with a little beaten egg and bake 'blind' at 450°F/230°C/Mark 8 for 15 minutes.

2 Whisk egg yolks in a bowl; add cream and whisk until thick and lemon-coloured. Flavour to taste with salt, freshly ground black pepper and freshly grated nutmeg.

3 Cut bacon or fat salt pork into thin strips; remove rind and blanch in boiling water for 3 minutes; sauté strips in butter until golden.

4 Arrange strips with diced cheese in pastry case. Pour over cream and egg mixture and bake in a moderate oven (375°F/190°C/Mark 5) for about 30 minutes. Serve hot.

Tossed Green Salad with Herbs

(for the recipe, see **green salad and variations** page 100)

Fresh Pineapple with Kirsch

8–12 thin slices fresh pineapple
Sugar
Kirsch

1 Cut 8–12 thin slices fresh pineapple. Trim cores and rinds and arrange slices in overlapping circles in a flat serving dish.

2 Sprinkle with sugar and Kirsch to taste.

Quiche Lorraine

Tossed Green Salad with Herbs

Fresh Pineapple with Kirsch

Serves 4–6

with this menu I suggest the following Inexpensive White Wines and Rosés
Sylvaner d'Alsace
Touraine Sauvignon
Chablis
Tavel Rosé

Tagliatelle alla Crema

Four Summer Meals from the Continent Summer Food – Italian Style

Menu

Tagliatelle alla Crema

Breaded Lamb Cutlets

Watercress and Radish Salad

Orange Ice

Serves 4–6

One of the most delicious pasta dishes I know – and one of the quickest and easiest to prepare – is *Tagliatelle alla Crema*, egg noodles in a creamy, cheese-flavoured sauce. The noodles are cooked in boiling, well-salted water until they are tender, but not mushy, drained and then tossed in a sauce made of double cream and egg yolks, well seasoned with salt and freshly ground black pepper. You will find that the heat of the *tagliatelle* cooks the delicate sauce as you toss it. But make sure that the serving bowl, dishes and *tagliatelle* are piping hot before you start operations. To finish the dish, add a lump of butter and some freshly grated Parmesan cheese and serve immediately. Our second course – Breaded Lamb Cutlets – is an Italian innovation which might have come right out of an eighteenth-century English cookbook. The lamb cutlets should be tiny – they're no bigger than your finger in Italy. They are dipped in egg yolk and then in grated breadcrumbs before being deep-fried. The crisp, golden casing and the moist, pink-tinted meat within make a perfect combination of taste and texture. Italians often serve them after a pasta dish. I like them with well-drained fresh spinach simmered in butter or, for an even better contrast, a peppery watercress and radish salad tossed in a mustard-flavoured vinaigrette sauce. Orange Ice, with a touch of lemon, ends this light summer meal with a clean, sharp flavour.

with this menu I suggest the following Inexpensive White Wines
Soave
Verdicchio
Lachryma Christi

Tagliatelle alla Crema

1 lb(450g) tagliatelle
Salt
Butter
4 egg yolks
¼ pint(1·5dl) double cream
Pinch nutmeg
Freshly grated Parmesan cheese

1 Bring 3–4 quarts (3–4 litres) well-salted water to the boil in a large saucepan. Add *tagliatelle* and cook until tender but still firm.

2 Melt 2 oz(50g) butter in a large saucepan. Drain the pasta and, while it is still very hot, toss in the butter.

3 Pour the egg yolks beaten with cream over the pasta; add a grating of nutmeg. Stir for a minute; remove from heat and add 2 oz(50g) more butter. The sauce and eggs should not begin to solidify. Serve with freshly grated Parmesan cheese and additional butter.

Tortellini in Brodo (page 122)

Breaded Lamb Cutlets

4–6 tender lamb cutlets
Salt and freshly ground black pepper
Flour
2 eggs, well beaten
Fresh breadcrumbs
4–6 tablespoons clarified butter
Béarnaise sauce (see page 153)

1 Trim lamb cutlets and flatten with the side of a cleaver. Season with salt and freshly ground black pepper to taste. Roll cutlets in flour; dip in beaten eggs and then roll in breadcrumbs.

2 Heat clarified butter in a thick-bottomed frying pan and sauté cutlets for 5 minutes on each side, or until golden brown and tender.

3 Serve with a Béarnaise sauce.

Watercress and Radish Salad

1 head lettuce
1 bunch watercress
1 bunch radishes

1 Wash and trim lettuce and watercress. Dry thoroughly.

2 Wash and trim radishes, then slice paper-thin. Chill lettuce, watercress and radishes.

3 To assemble salad: arrange lettuce leaves in a salad bowl and spread watercress on top. Scatter thinly sliced radishes over this.

4 Make **French dressing** (see page 100) and just before serving add dressing and toss until every ingredient glistens.

Orange Ice
(illustrated on page 120)

$\frac{3}{4}$ lb(350g) sugar
$\frac{3}{4}$ pint(4dl) orange juice
$\frac{1}{4}$ pint(1·5dl) lemon juice
Finely grated rind of 1 orange and
 1 lemon
Orange segments
Slivered orange rind

1 Bring sugar and $1\frac{1}{2}$ pints(8·5dl) water to the boil; boil for 5 minutes.

2 Cool slightly and add orange juice, lemon juice and grated orange and lemon rind.

3 Cool, strain through a sieve and freeze.

4 Serve in individual dishes, garnished with orange segments and slivered orange rind simmered in a little syrup.

Butter Cookies

$\frac{3}{4}$ lb(350g) sifted flour
2 level teaspoons baking powder
1 level teaspoon salt
6 oz(175g) butter
8 oz(225g) granulated sugar
2 eggs
1 teaspoon vanilla or almond essence

1 Sift flour with baking powder and salt into a bowl. Beat butter, sugar and eggs until creamy. Add vanilla or almond essence and continue to beat until well mixed. Blend in flour mixture. Divide dough into two parts and chill until it can be easily handled.

2 Preheat oven to moderately hot (400°F/200°C/Mark 6).

3 Roll out half the dough on a lightly floured surface, about $\frac{1}{8}$-inch(0·3-cm) thick. Cut into desired shapes with floured cookie cutters.

4 Place cookies on ungreased baking sheets about 1 inch(2·5cms) apart. Bake for 6 to 8 minutes, or until firm and slightly browned. Repeat steps **3** and **4** with remaining dough.

Summer Luncheon in Provence

The easiest way to take yourself back to some well remembered holiday place is to recreate at home the dishes you enjoyed there. This menu takes us to Provence, where you can eat in some of the most famous restaurants in the world or have a three-course meal in a charming back-street eating house for a very modest sum – with the wine and service thrown in. No matter where you choose to eat, you will find the cuisine is based on the fresh vegetables (often dressed in olive oil) and fruit which are one of the blessings of Provençal markets, on the region's specialities, such as black olives, and on recipes designed to bring out the subtle flavours of the ingredients.

One of the best ways to reproduce a Provençal meal in Britain is to start off with a typical selection of hors-d'oeuvres: roasted pepper and fresh tomato salads, tuna fish, anchovies and a cold *ratatouille* served in individual *terrines*, bowls or *raviers* (those oblong, porcelain hors-d'oeuvre dishes used by French restaurants the world over).

The main course is an earthy *daube* of beef, flavoured with finely chopped Spanish onions, green bacon, garlic and herbs. The secret here is the long, slow cooking which brings unexpected tenderness and flavour to one of our most inexpensive cuts, shin of beef.

You'll find that this recipe uses no liquids. It is the juices of the vegetables and meat, slowly simmered in an iron or enamelled iron *cocotte* or casserole, that give richness to the dish. For extra flavour, I sometimes boil a quarter of a bottle of red wine to a quarter of its original quantity and stir it into the juices just before serving.

Serve the *daube* with boiled new potatoes or rice. Follow with a green salad and then end the meal with a tart, mouth-freshening lemon sorbet.

Provençal Hors-d'Oeuvres

1 PEPPERS
Choose sweet peppers – both yellow and green – and brush with olive oil. Drain and put them under the grill until they begin to change colour. Then slice them and dress with a well-flavoured vinaigrette sauce (see page 100) to which you have added a little finely chopped garlic and parsley.

2 ANCHOVY SALAD
Wash ½–¾ lb(225–350g) salted anchovies in water until liquid is clear; dry them with a clean cloth and remove heads, tails and fins. Strip fillets from bones and place in a bowl. Add 1 medium-sized onion, finely chopped, 2 tablespoons finely chopped parsley and 4 thin lemon slices. Combine 4 tablespoons olive oil and 4 tablespoons red wine and pour over fillets. Add freshly ground black pepper to taste and marinate for at least 2 hours before serving.

3 TOMATOES
Choose large, ripe tomatoes; slice them in half and arrange in an hors-d'oeuvre dish. Top with thinly sliced shallots or raw leeks and finely chopped parsley. Dress with a well-flavoured vinaigrette sauce (see page 100).

4 GREEN AND BLACK OLIVES

5 TUNA FISH
Slice tinned tuna fish and arrange in an hors-d'oeuvre dish. Top with slices of hard-boiled egg, thinly sliced spring onions and finely chopped parsley. Dress with a well-flavoured vinaigrette sauce (see page 100).

Menu

Provençal
Hors-d'Oeuvres

Boeuf en Daube

Lemon Sorbet

Serves 4–6

with this menu I suggest the following Medium-priced White Wines and Rosés
Quincy
Chablis
Rosé de Provence
or the following Medium-priced Red Wines
Médoc
Pommard
Moulin-à-Vent

Orange Ice (page 118)

Boeuf en Daube

3 lb(1·4kg) shin of beef, cut into
    2-inch(5-cm) cubes
1 lb(450g) green bacon (1 piece)
3 Spanish onions, sliced
3 tablespoons olive oil
3 tablespoons butter
Flour
Coarse salt and freshly ground black
    pepper
1–2 cloves garlic
1 strip dried orange peel
2 cloves
Bouquet garni:
    (2 sprigs thyme, 4 sprigs parsley,
    2 bay leaves)

1 Cut green bacon into large cubes; combine with sliced onions, olive oil and butter and sauté until onions are transparent.

2 Sprinkle beef cubes with flour; add to casserole and continue to cook, stirring constantly, until brown.

3 Then add coarse salt, black pepper, garlic, dried orange peel, cloves and *bouquet garni*. Place casserole in a preheated very slow oven (275°F/140°C/Mark 1 to 300°F/150°C/Mark 2) and cook for $2\frac{1}{2}$–3 hours.

Lemon Sorbet

$\frac{1}{2}$ lb (225g) sugar
$\frac{1}{2}$ pint(3dl) lemon juice
Finely grated rind of 1 large lemon

1 Bring sugar and $1\frac{1}{4}$ pints(7dl) water to the boil; boil for 5 minutes. Cool slightly and add lemon juice and grated lemon rind.

2 When cold, strain through a fine sieve and freeze in a rectangular aluminium loaf tin in the freezer or in the ice tray of the freezing compartment of your refrigerator. Stir it from time to time. It will take 2–3 hours to freeze.

A Continental Summer Luncheon for Four

Summer meals should be comparatively easy to fix. The French and Italians often solve the problem of warm weather food with casseroles, which save standing at a hot stove. This summer lunch begins with a simple, satisfying dish made of tomatoes and aubergines – substantial enough to stand alone as a main course, yet just right as a prelude to the super-light rolls of veal and *prosciutto* which follow.

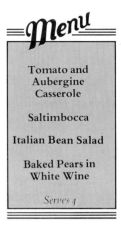

Menu

Tomato and
Aubergine
Casserole

Saltimbocca

Italian Bean Salad

Baked Pears in
White Wine

Serves 4

*with this menu I suggest
the following Inexpensive
White Wines*
**Soave
Verdicchio
Lachryma Christi**

Tomato and Aubergine Casserole

A bubbling casserole of sliced tomatoes and golden-fried aubergines in alternate layers, the whole flavoured with cheese and cream. Served right from the cooking pot, it has a melting texture and smooth, rich flavour.

4–6 aubergines
Salt
2 tablespoons olive oil
Butter
Freshly ground black pepper
8 tablespoons freshly grated
   Parmesan cheese
¼ pint (1·5dl) fresh cream
4–6 tomatoes, thickly sliced
4 tablespoons breadcrumbs

1 Peel the aubergines; cut in thin slices; sprinkle with salt and let them 'sweat' in a dish for 2 hours. Drain slices, wipe and fry lightly in olive oil until soft and golden, but not quite cooked. Drain again.

2 Butter a deep ovenproof casserole; place a layer of aubergine slices in the bottom; season with freshly ground black pepper and sprinkle generously with grated Parmesan cheese and fresh cream.

3 Add a layer of sliced raw tomatoes; add ground black pepper and a little more cream and cheese, then another layer of aubergine slices and so on until the dish is full.

4 Finish with cream on top, cover with breadcrumbs and grated Parmesan, dot with butter and cook in a moderate oven (375°F/190°C/Mark 5) for 45 minutes.

Saltimbocca

Wine-glazed rolls of veal and Parma ham – as easy to make as they are to serve. They are sautéed in butter before guests arrive and then simmered gently on top of the stove until ready to serve. Accompany them with a chilled **Italian bean salad** – cooked green beans flavoured with a French dressing and a little finely chopped garlic and fresh parsley (see page 159).

4 thin slices of veal
8–12 small fresh sage leaves or ½–1 level
   teaspoon rubbed sage
Freshly ground black pepper
4 thin slices prosciutto (Parma ham)
Flour
Melted butter
2 tablespoons Marsala or dry white
   wine

1 Flatten veal into thin pieces, cut each slice into 2 or 3 pieces. Place 1 sage leaf (or pinch of rubbed sage) on each slice, and add freshly ground black pepper, to taste (no salt, the *prosciutto* will flavour meat). Cover each slice of veal with *prosciutto* cut to the same shape; make each into a small roll and secure with a toothpick.

2 Dust rolls with flour and cook in melted butter until golden all over; then add Marsala or white wine.

3 Cook over a high heat for a moment; then reduce heat; cover the pan and simmer gently until the veal and ham rolls are quite tender. Remove toothpicks from each roll and transfer to a hot serving dish. Serve immediately.

Baked Pears in White Wine

4 pears
White wine, to cover
Sugar
2 tablespoons chilled Kirsch (optional)
Whipped cream

1 Peel pears and place in an ovenproof baking dish with dry white wine and sugar.

2 Cover and bake in a moderate oven (375°F/190°C/Mark 5) for 45 minutes.

3 Serve warm with chilled Kirsch and/or whipped cream.

A Simple Italian Dinner

Tortellini in Brodo

1 lb(450g) shin of beef with bone
1 beef stock cube
2 stalks celery, roughly chopped
1 Spanish onion, roughly chopped
6 carrots, peeled and chopped
3 tomatoes, chopped
Salt and freshly ground black pepper
7 oz(200g) tortellini noodles
Finely chopped parsley

1 Ask your butcher to cut through the shin bone in 2 or 3 places.

2 Place the meat and bones in 3 pints(1·7 litres) water; add the stock cube and bring to the boil. Remove surface scum; add the vegetables; cover with a lid and simmer for 1 hour.

3 Remove the meat and strain the broth. Season to taste with salt and freshly ground black pepper.

4 Add the *tortellini* to the broth and cook for a further 20 minutes.

5 Serve in a heated soup tureen, garnished with a little chopped parsley.

Liver and Onions, Italian Style

The Italians are past masters at cooking liver. Their secret is to cut it almost paper-thin and then sear the slices in butter and oil over high heat so that they remain meltingly pink and tender inside. It is overcooking that causes liver to toughen and lose its flavour.

1 lb(450g) lambs' or calves' liver
½–¾ level teaspoon crumbled sage
Salt and freshly ground black pepper
2 oz(50g) butter
2 tablespoons olive oil
1 lb(450g) Spanish onions, thinly sliced
Lemon juice
2 level tablespoons finely chopped parsley

1 Cut the liver into very thin slices, or have this done by your butcher.

2 Dust slices with crumbled sage and season with salt and freshly ground black pepper.

3 In a large frying pan, melt butter with olive oil. Add thinly sliced onions and sauté over moderate heat until soft and a rich golden colour. Remove onions with a slotted spoon and keep hot.

3 Add a little more butter and oil to the pan if necessary. Raise the heat and fry liver slices quickly for just 1 or 2 minutes on each side. Then return onions to the pan and toss together with liver for a few seconds longer.

4 Sprinkle a few drops of lemon juice over the entire pan; garnish with finely chopped parsley and serve immediately with **buttered spinach** (see pages 182–3).

Menu

Tortellini in Brodo

Liver and Onions, Italian Style with Buttered Spinach

Cold Orange Soufflé or Peach Water Ice

Serves 4–6

with this menu I suggest the following Inexpensive Red Wines
Chianti Ruffino Red Valpolicella
or a Medium-priced Red Wine
Barolo

Cold Orange Soufflé

3 eggs
Juice of 5 medium oranges
2 level teaspoons gelatine
3 level tablespoons sugar
1 level teaspoon cornflour
Juice of 1–2 lemons
Vanilla essence
2 tablespoons orange-flavoured
   liqueur (optional)
$\frac{1}{4}$ pint(1·5dl) double cream

TO DECORATE:
Orange segments
Whipped cream

1 Separate the eggs. Place the egg yolks in the top of a double saucepan and beat well. Place the whites in a round-bottomed bowl.

2 Squeeze the oranges and strain the juice into an enamelled saucepan. Add gelatine and allow to soak for 30 minutes. Then add sugar and cornflour and cook over gentle heat, stirring constantly, until mixture comes to the boil. As soon as it starts to boil, remove from heat and pour through a fine sieve over well-beaten egg yolks. Beat well and place the top of the double saucepan over hot, but *not* boiling water. Cook the orange mixture, whisking constantly, until the sauce coats the back of a spoon. (**Note:** Do not allow the sauce to come to the boil, or it will curdle.) Add lemon juice to taste, $\frac{1}{2}$ teaspoon vanilla essence and orange-flavoured liqueur, if desired.

3 Whip the cream until stiff; beat the egg whites until stiff; fold both gently into the orange cream. Spoon into 4 ramekins or individual soufflé dishes around which you have tied a piece of aluminium foil to make a 'lip' about 2 inches(5cm) high – or use 1 large soufflé dish. Leave in the refrigerator to set.

4 **When ready to serve:** remove the foil and decorate the tops of the soufflés with orange segments and a swirl of whipped cream.

Or

Peach Water Ice

$\frac{1}{2}$ pint(3dl) peach purée
$\frac{1}{2}$ pint(3dl) syrup for ices (see below)
Juice of 1 lemon
2–3 drops almond extract
2–3 drops red food colouring

1 Rub peaches through a fine nylon sieve or strainer until a sufficient quantity of purée is obtained.

2 Add syrup to the fruit purée and flavour to taste with strained lemon juice and almond extract. Tint mixture slightly with red food colouring. Cool and then freeze, stirring the mixture up vigorously with a fork every half hour, until half frozen, then leaving it for a further 2 or 3 hours until frozen hard. Transfer water ice to main cabinet of refrigerator about 1 hour before serving.

A water ice should not be served when it is still hard. It is best served scooped into glass coupes, just one stage harder than slushy – i.e., firm enough to hold a shape in scoop.

Note: It is the absence of any fat in the syrup that permits large ice crystals to form in the ice. In order to break these down, the mixture must be beaten vigorously with a fork at regular intervals before being allowed to freeze hard.

Syrup for Water Ices

Makes $1\frac{1}{4}$ pints(7dl)
$\frac{1}{2}$ lb(225g) sugar
1 pint(6dl) water
Juice of $\frac{1}{2}$ lemon

Combine sugar and water in an enamelled saucepan; bring to the boil and boil for 10 minutes, removing any scum that rises. Add lemon juice and strain through a muslin-lined sieve.

123

Three for the Pot

Pot Roast of Pork with Grapes (page 127)

If you like long, slow, even cooking – the kind you don't have to watch – you will find that pot roasting is the easiest way to cook the Sunday joint that you've ever come across.

And it's economical too. For by pot roasting your meat over the lowest of heats or in the lowest of ovens – up to 4 hours for a 5–lb(2·3-kg) roast – you can make the most inexpensive joint so tender that you can cut it with a fork. And it's extra delicious if you add a few carrots, onions, turnips and just enough beef stock, water or wine to moisten the meat, not stew it.

Pot roasts are most successful in a heavy, tightly covered casserole, kettle or deep frying pan that is only slightly bigger than the cut of meat to be cooked. Inexpensive cuts of brisket, chuck, top rump, round, top ribs and shin of beef respond well to this slow, moist method of cooking. Select cuts that are well marbled with fat or ask your butcher to lard some fat through the joint for you.

Sliced Egg Appetizer

Sliced Egg Appetizer

4–6 hard-boiled eggs
½ cucumber, seeded and diced
4–6 tomatoes, peeled, seeded and diced
1–2 tablespoons finely chopped parsley
Mayonnaise
Vinaigrette sauce (see below)

1 Make mayonnaise, using quantities given on page 152.

2 Make a vinaigrette sauce, using 2 tablespoons wine vinegar, 6–8 tablespoons olive oil, coarse salt and freshly ground black pepper.

3 Shell eggs and cut into even slices. Place a bed of mayonnaise on a flat hors-d'oeuvre dish. Cover with 2 rows of overlapping slices of egg.

4 Garnish with a ring of diced cucumber and a ring of diced tomato. Sprinkle vegetables only with a little finely chopped parsley and vinaigrette sauce.

Menu

**Sliced Egg
Appetizer**

**Beef Pot Roast
with
Greek Lemon
Potatoes
and
Haricots Verts**

**Soused
Camembert**

Serves 4–6

*with this menu I suggest
the following Inexpensive
Red Wines*
**Macon Rouge
Beaujolais
Valpolicella**

Beef Pot Roast

(illustrated on pages 10–11)

4–6 lb(1·8–2·7kg) lean brisket,
    top rump, shin or round steak,
    in one piece
Salt and freshly ground black pepper
½ **level teaspoon dried thyme**
4 **tablespoons bacon fat or olive oil**
½ **pint(3dl) well-flavoured beef stock**
4 **large carrots,**
    cut into 1-inch(2·5-cm) lengths
2 **Spanish onions, quartered**
2 **turnips, quartered**
2 **cloves garlic, crushed**
8 **peppercorns**
4 **whole cloves**
2 **whole allspice**
2 **bay leaves**
1 **tablespoon softened butter**
1 **tablespoon flour**
Finely chopped parsley

1 Rub meat with salt, freshly ground black pepper and dried thyme.

2 Melt bacon fat or heat olive oil in a thick-bottomed, heavy iron heatproof casserole. Add meat and brown well on all sides. Pour in half of the beef stock and bring to the boil; reduce heat until liquid barely simmers.

3 Add carrots, onions, turnips, garlic, peppercorns, whole cloves, allspice and bay leaves. Cover casserole and simmer for 3½–4 hours, or until meat is tender, turning roast once or twice during cooking time. Add remaining stock if necessary.

4 Remove roast to a heated serving platter and surround with vegetables. Keep warm.

5 Allow sauce to cool and skim off fat. Thicken by adding 1 tablespoon each softened butter and flour mashed to a smooth paste. Cook over high heat, stirring continuously, until sauce is smooth. Season to taste with salt and freshly ground black pepper.

6 Pour sauce over meat and vegetables, and sprinkle with parsley. Serve with **Greek lemon potatoes** and **haricots verts** (see below).

Greek Lemon Potatoes

2 **lb(900g) potatoes**
4 **tablespoons butter**
Juice of ½ **lemon**
½ **beef stock cube**
Salt and freshly ground black pepper

1 Peel potatoes and cut in quarters lengthwise. Place in a *gratin* dish or shallow casserole with butter, half the lemon juice and ½ crumbled beef stock cube. Season to taste with salt and freshly ground black pepper.

2 Cook in a moderately hot oven (400°F/200°C/Mark 6) for 15 minutes. Turn potatoes over and return to oven for 15 minutes more.

3 Remove excess fat from dish; add remaining lemon juice and return to oven for 5 minutes more, or until tender.

Haricots Verts

1 **lb(450g) green beans**
Salt and freshly ground black pepper
2 **tablespoons butter**
1 **tablespoon finely chopped parsley**

1 Cook beans in boiling salted water until tender, about 20 minutes. Drain; place in a heated serving dish.

2 Season with salt and pepper; toss with butter and parsley.

Soused Camembert

(illustrated on page 188)

2 **ripe Camembert cheeses**

¼ pint(1·5dl) dry white wine
¼ lb(100g) softened butter
Salt
Cayenne pepper
Brandy
6 oz(175g) fresh white breadcrumbs, toasted
6 tablespoons finely chopped parsley

1 Scrape crust from cheeses; cut them in quarters and soak overnight in white wine.

2 Remove cheeses from wine; dry gently and cream thoroughly with softened butter and a little of the marinating liquid, if desired. Add a little salt and cayenne pepper if necessary, and flavour with a little brandy.

3 Press the cheese mixture into a 5-inch (13-cm) plain round flan ring on a foil-lined baking tin. Chill until firm.

4 Turn the cheese upside down on to very fine toasted breadcrumbs and remove the flan ring and foil. Coat bottom with toasted breadcrumbs and sides with finely chopped parsley. Serve with bread or biscuits.

French Onion Soup

(illustrated overleaf)

4 large Spanish onions
4 tablespoons butter
1 tablespoon sugar
2½ pints(1·4 litres) beef stock or water
Salt and freshly ground black pepper
Toasted rounds of French bread
Butter
Freshly grated Gruyère cheese

1 Peel onions and slice thinly. Separate the rings. Heat butter in a large saucepan with a little sugar; add the onion rings and cook them very, very gently over low heat, stirring constantly with a wooden spoon, until the rings are an even golden brown.

2 Add stock gradually, stirring constantly until the soup begins to boil. Then lower heat, cover pan and simmer gently for 30 minutes.

3 Just before serving, correct seasoning and serve in a heated soup tureen or in individual serving bowls, each one containing toasted buttered rounds of French bread heaped with grated Gruyère cheese.

4 French onion soup may also be served *gratinée*. When ready to serve, place thin rounds of toasted and buttered French bread in an ovenproof casserole or *marmite*; cover with freshly grated Gruyère cheese and pour onion soup over toast. Sprinkle top with more Gruyère and place casserole or *marmite* under the grill or in a hot oven until cheese is browned and sizzling.

Pot Roast of Pork with Grapes

(illustrated on page 125)

4 lb(1·8kg) lean loin of pork
Salt and freshly ground black pepper
3 tablespoons gin
¼ pint(1·5dl) unsweetened grape juice
¼ pint(1·5dl) dry white wine
2 level tablespoons butter
2 level tablespoons flour

MARINADE:
8 juniper berries, crushed
2 cloves, crushed
1 clove garlic, crushed
3 tablespoons olive oil
6 tablespoons dry white wine

GARNISH:
2 level tablespoons butter
1 lb(450g) seedless white grapes

1 Ask your butcher to skin, bone and roll a lean loin of pork. The rolled joint should weigh just under 3lb(1·4kg) after being prepared.

2 Combine marinade ingredients. Pour

Menu

French Onion
Soup

Pot Roast of Pork
with Grapes
with
Gratin Dauphinois
and
Crisp-fried
Courgettes

Floating Islands

Serves 4–6

*with this menu I suggest
the following Inexpensive
Red Wines*
**Bordeaux Supérieur
Côtes-du-Rhône
Châteauneuf-du-
Pape**

127

over joint in a deep dish, cover and leave to marinate, at the bottom of the refrigerator for 24 hours. Turn pork several times to keep it thoroughly coated with marinade.

3 When ready to cook pork, preheat oven to moderate (375°F/190°C/Mark 5).

4 Drain pork, reserving marinade, and put it in a roasting tin. Sprinkle pork with salt and freshly ground black pepper. Pour about $\frac{1}{4}$ pint(1·5dl) cold water around it and roast, basting occasionally until cooked through but still moist. It will take about $1\frac{3}{4}$ hours, or 35 minutes per lb/450g.

5 Ten minutes before taking pork out of the oven, **prepare garnish:** melt butter in a large, deep frying pan and sauté grapes for

French Onion Soup
(page 127)

4–5 minutes until golden brown. Reserve.

6 When pork is cooked, transfer to a deep, hot, flameproof serving dish. Pour 3 tablespoons gin over it, stand well back and set alight with a match. (Or, if you find it easier, pour gin into a heated metal ladle, set it alight and quickly pour all over the meat.)

7 Skim fat from juices left in roasting tin. Pour back into the tin any juices that have collected around the pork on the serving dish and return pork to the turned-off oven to keep hot while you finish sauce.

8 To finish sauce: add grape juice, white wine and reserved marinade to the roasting tin and bring to the boil on top of the stove, scraping bottom and sides of tin with a wooden spoon to dislodge any crusty morsels stuck there. Allow to simmer for 2–3 minutes longer.

9 Meanwhile, work butter and flour to a smooth paste in a small cup to make a *beurre manié*.

10 Strain sauce into the frying pan over sautéed grapes and, over low heat, stir in *beurre manié* in small pieces. Continue to stir until sauce comes to the boil and simmer for 3–4 minutes longer to cook the flour. Season with salt and freshly ground black pepper.

11 To serve: spoon sauce and grapes over and around pork. Any excess sauce and grapes should be served with the meat in a heated sauce boat or bowl. Serve pork very hot, cut into thick slices with **gratin dauphinois** (see page 98) and **crisp-fried courgettes** (see below).

Crisp-fried Courgettes

8–12 courgettes
2 level tablespoons butter
2 tablespoons olive oil
Salt and freshly ground black pepper

1 Slice courgettes thinly.

2 Melt butter and olive oil in a frying pan. Add courgettes and sauté in combined fats over a medium heat until just tender, stirring from time to time to keep courgettes from browning. Season generously with salt and freshly ground black pepper.

Floating Islands

¾ pint(4dl) milk
2 tablespoons sugar
1-inch(2·5-cm) piece vanilla bean
    (or 1 scant teaspoon vanilla essence)
6 egg whites
Salt
½ lb(225g) castor sugar
6 egg yolks
Caramel garnish (see below)

1 **To make poached meringues:** combine the milk, sugar and vanilla bean in a shallow saucepan. (If vanilla essence is used, add it after milk has been scalded.) Bring to the boil, stirring well to dissolve sugar. Beat egg whites until stiff with a few grains of salt, gradually adding castor sugar at the same time and beating well after each addition. Test for stiffness by placing an egg on top of the beaten whites. If the egg doesn't sink, the whites are sufficiently beaten.

2 Shape the beaten egg whites with a tablespoon into small egg shapes and drop them into the scalded milk. After 1 or 2 minutes turn them carefully with a fork. Leave them in the hot milk for exactly 2 minutes more – no longer, or the meringues will collapse. Remove from the milk with a perforated spoon and drain on a dry cloth spread over a sieve.

3 **To make sauce:** strain the milk through a fine sieve into the top of a double saucepan. Beat 6 egg yolks well and gradually add the warm milk to them. Return to heat and cook over water, stirring constantly, until the mixture just begins to thicken. Remove from heat and cool. Chill until ready to use.

4 **To serve:** pour the custard sauce into a bowl and float the meringues on it.

Caramel garnish: If desired, an attractive garnish can be made for the 'floating islands' by dissolving 6 oz(175g) castor sugar in 4 tablespoons water and boiling rapidly until the caramel is a rich golden brown. Pour immediately over the meringues.

Variations on a theme: Ring the changes on this recipe by adding orange zest. Prepare sauce as above, and while still warm, add 2 thinly pared strips of orange or mandarin peel and flavour with 4 teaspoons Grand Marnier.

Floating Islands

*with this menu I suggest
the following Inexpensive
Red Wines*
**Chianti Ruffino Red
Valpolicella**

Italian Pizza
(illustrated on page 132)

PIZZA DOUGH:
$\frac{1}{2}$ **lb(225g) plain flour**
$\frac{1}{2}$ **level teaspoon salt**
1 level tablespoon dried yeast
Olive oil

TOPPING:
**2 lb(900g) canned Italian peeled
   tomatoes, coarsely chopped**
Salt and freshly ground black pepper
**3 oz(75g) Mozzarella cheese, thinly
   sliced**
6 anchovy fillets, cut in pieces
$\frac{1}{4}$ **level teaspoon oregano**
$\frac{1}{4}$ **level teaspoon basil**
Black olives, to garnish

1 To make pizza dough: sift flour and
salt into a warm mixing bowl. Measure
dried yeast into a small bowl. Add 8
tablespoons warm water and stir once.
Leave for 5 minutes and then stir with a
wooden spoon until smooth. Pour into
sifted flour with 1 tablespoon olive oil and
work flour into yeast mixture with your
hands to make a stiff dough. Knead with
your hands, pressing the dough out and
away from you with your palms. When it
feels light and elastic, roll it into a ball and
put it in an oiled bowl. Turn ball over to oil
entire surface; cover with 2 thicknesses of
clean tea towel and leave in a warm place
until it doubles in bulk (about 2 hours).

2 When ready to use, roll dough out on a
floured board into a large circle about
$\frac{1}{4}$ inch(0·5cm) thick, or divide it into 2 or 6
pieces to make smaller pizzas. Brush with a
little olive oil.

3 Finally, place circle of dough on an oiled
baking tin big enough to let pizza expand in
cooking. Spread dough with chopped
peeled tomatoes; season with salt and freshly
ground black pepper and arrange thin slices
of Mozzarella and cut anchovies over the

surface. Sprinkle with oregano and basil;
garnish with black olives and bake in a hot
oven (450°F/230°C/Mark 8) for about 25
minutes, or until pizza browns. Serve immediately.

Italian Pot Roast

**4–6 lb(1.8- 2.7kg) lean brisket, top
   rump, shin or round steak,
   in one piece**
Salt and freshly ground black pepper
$\frac{1}{2}$ **level teaspoon dried thyme**
4 tablespoons bacon fat or olive oil
$\frac{1}{2}$ **pint(3dl) well-flavoured beef stock**
**4 large carrots, cut into 1-inch
   (2·5-cm) lengths**
2 Spanish onions, quartered
2 turnips, quartered
2 cloves garlic, crushed
8 peppercorns
4 whole cloves
2 whole allspice
2 bay leaves
1 small can Italian peeled tomatoes
$\frac{1}{4}$ **pint(1·5dl) dry white wine**
2 tablespoons tomato concentrate
1 level teaspoon dried basil
Butter and flour (optional)
Finely chopped anchovies
Finely chopped parsley

1 Rub meat with generous amounts of salt,
pepper and dried thyme.

2 Melt bacon fat or heat olive oil in a thick-
bottomed, heavy iron heatproof casserole.
Add meat and brown well on all sides. Pour
in half the beef stock and bring to the boil;
reduce heat until liquid barely simmers.

3 Add carrots, onions, turnips, garlic, peppercorns, cloves, allspice, bay leaves, peeled
tomatoes, white wine, tomato concentrate
and dried basil. Cover casserole and simmer
for $3\frac{1}{2}$–4 hours, or until meat is tender,
turning roast once or twice during cooking
time. Add remaining stock if necessary.

4 Remove roast to a heated serving platter and surround with vegetables. Keep warm.

5 Allow sauce to cool for 5 minutes; then skim off fat. Thicken, if desired, by adding 1 tablespoon each softened butter and flour mashed to a smooth paste. Cook over high heat, stirring continuously, until sauce is smooth. Season to taste with salt and freshly ground black pepper.

6 Pour sauce over meat and vegetables. Sprinkle with equal amounts of finely chopped anchovies and finely chopped parsley.

Sautéed New Potatoes with Herbs
(illustrated on page 136)

2 lb(900g) small new potatoes
4 tablespoons olive oil
1 tablespoon each finely chopped
 parsley, chervil and chives
4 shallots, finely chopped
1 clove garlic, finely chopped
Salt and freshly ground black pepper
Lemon juice

1 Peel potatoes and cook whole in a frying pan with olive oil and finely chopped herbs, shallots and garlic.

2 Season potatoes to taste with salt, freshly ground black pepper and lemon juice and sauté until cooked through and golden. Serve immediately.

Orange and Onion Salad
(illustrated on page 133)

¼ head curly endive
1 head lettuce
4 oranges
1 large mild white onion

DRESSING:
4 tablespoons olive oil

2 tablespoons vinegar
1 clove garlic, crushed
¾ level teaspoon salt
½ level teaspoon dry mustard
1 level teaspoon sugar
Freshly ground black pepper

1 Wash endive and lettuce leaves carefully. Dry them and arrange them in a salad bowl.

2 With a sharp knife, peel the oranges. Slice thinly. Peel the onion and slice it into thin rings. Arrange the orange and onion slices in the salad bowl.

3 Mix all the ingredients for the dressing; just before serving, pour it over the salad.

Italian Cheeses
(see page 241)

Italian Pizza (page 130)

Orange and Onion Salad (page 131)

Cooking with Yoghourt

If you want to live long, stay healthy and have a good digestion until the day you die – *eat yoghourt*. That's the lesson I learned on a trip through the Middle East. Returning to England after a three-week lecture tour in Australia, I stopped off on the way home to enjoy the many varied flavours of the cities of the Lebanon. There in the hill villages behind the major towns I was astounded to see men and women of 70 and 80 with all the vitality and mental agility of people half their age.

The answer, I was assured time and time again, was yoghourt. Ever since the time of Abraham, the peoples of the Eastern Mediterranean have relied on this lightly fermented and delicious natural food as a basic necessity for good health.

I first fell in love with yoghourt – combined with diced cucumber, garlic, lemon juice and finely chopped fresh mint leaves – as a cooling summer appetizer in a small tiled restaurant in the Old Quarter of Beirut. I later found it equally delicious as a refreshing summer soup. In this case, the basic yoghourt-garlic-lemon juice mixture is thinned down with chilled chicken stock and the cucumber – peeled and seeded – is grated coarsely into it. A Balkan version of yoghourt soup is served hot with diced cooked meats and a little cooked rice in it.

Today, I make home-made fresh yoghourt often and use it in its natural state to add a tangy, fresh flavour to hot and cold soups and sauces. With a hint of vanilla and sugar added, it makes a fresh tasting 'carry all' for diced fresh fruits and berries.

SUMMER SALAD DRESSING

Use yoghourt as a dressing for a summer salad of sliced cucumbers, sliced green onions and red and white radishes. Just add a little oil, lemon juice and salt and freshly ground black pepper to taste and beat well before pouring over salad.

A LIGHT TASTING MAYONNAISE WITH YOGHOURT

Whisk equal parts yoghourt and home-made mayonnaise (see page 152) until well blended. Stir in 1 level teaspoon Dijon mustard, 1 tablespoon lemon juice and 2 level tablespoons each finely chopped parsley, chives and fresh tarragon. Excellent for poached fish or chicken, hard boiled eggs, tomato and cucumber salad, or coleslaw (shredded raw cabbage: dress with yoghourt mayonnaise dressing and let stand several hours before serving).

SAUCE FOR POACHED OR GRILLED FISH

Blend equal parts of yoghourt and well-flavoured mayonnaise. Season with a dash of lemon juice and cayenne pepper for a piquant sauce to serve with hot or cold cooked fish.

MAKE YOUR OWN YOGHOURT–IT'S EASY

To make your own yoghourt: bring 1 pint(6dl) of milk to the boil in a saucepan. Remove pan from heat and allow milk to cool until you can put your finger in it comfortably.

Place 1 heaped tablespoon of plain yoghourt in a warmed mixing bowl and beat with a fork until creamy. Beat in 1 tablespoon warm milk; then add 2 tablespoons warm milk and beat until well blended. Then add remaining warm milk gradually, beating continually until mixture is well blended. Cover mixing bowl with a plate; wrap covered bowl in a clean blanket and keep in a warm place – away from draughts – for 8 hours or until yoghourt is as creamy as a custard. It will keep perfectly in the refrigerator for 4 days. Then you will be able to make a new batch of fresh home-made yoghourt, using a tablespoon of your home-made mixture.

Cold Cucumber Soup with Yoghourt

½ clove garlic
1 level teaspoon salt
1 tablespoon olive oil
3 cartons plain yoghourt
Juice of ½ lemon
¾ pint(4dl) chicken stock
   (made with a cube)
1 cucumber
Chopped mint or chives

1 Mash garlic in the bottom of a large mixing bowl or soup tureen with salt, using the back of a wooden spoon. Add olive oil and continue to mash until garlic paste is completely smooth.

2 Add yoghourt and lemon juice and beat until smooth.

3 Add cool chicken stock to yoghourt mixture.

4 Peel cucumber; slice it in half lengthwise and remove seeds with the point of a teaspoon. Grate cucumber coarsely and stir into soup. Chill until ready to serve.

5 Just before serving sprinkle with chopped mint or chives.

Foil-baked Bass

(illustrated overleaf)

1 sea bass, 3 lb(1·4kg)
4–6 tablespoons softened butter
Salt and freshly ground black pepper
Lemon juice
½ teaspoon freshly grated nutmeg

GARNISH:
2 tablespoons finely chopped parsley
   or onion tops
Grilled tomatoes
Sautéed new potatoes
Lemon wedges

1 Clean the fish, removing the head if desired, and place in the centre of a piece of aluminium foil. Spread fish liberally with softened butter on both sides. Season with salt, freshly ground black pepper, lemon juice and the freshly grated nutmeg. Fold over foil to seal in fish. Cook under the grill for 15–20 minutes. Turn over and cook for a further 15–20 minutes. Turn back, open the foil and cook under the grill for 10 minutes longer.

2 Serve garnished with freshly chopped parsley or onion tops, grilled tomatoes, sautéed new potatoes with herbs (see page 131) and lemon wedges.

═Or═

Flamed Sea Bass with Fresh Herbs

2 sea bass, 3 lb(1·4kg) each
2–3 tablespoons flour
2–3 tablespoons olive oil
Salt
Freshly ground black pepper
4–6 sprigs each rosemary, fennel and
   thyme
2–3 tablespoons hot cognac

1 Flour cleaned fish lightly; brush with olive oil, and season to taste with salt and freshly ground black pepper.

2 Grill for 3 to 5 minutes on each side, or until fish flakes easily with a fork. Baste fish with olive oil from time to time.

3 Remove fish to a heated serving dish which has been covered with dried sprigs of rosemary, fennel and thyme. Top the fish with additional herbs; pour hot cognac over them and ignite. The burning herbs give the fish a delightful flavour.

═Or═

Menu

Cold Cucumber
Soup with
Yoghourt

Foil-baked Bass
or
Flamed Sea Bass
with
Fresh Herbs
or
Grilled Sea Bass
with
Fresh Herbs

Summer Pudding

Serves 4–6

with this menu I suggest the following Inexpensive White Wines
Muscadet
Sancerre

Grilled Sea Bass with Fresh Herbs

2 sea bass, 3 lb(1·4kg) each
2–3 tablespoons flour
2–3 tablespoons olive oil
Salt and freshly ground black pepper
2–3 sprigs each fennel, parsley and
    thyme

1 Flour cleaned fish lightly; brush with olive oil, and season to taste with salt and freshly ground black pepper.

2 Stuff cavities of fish with herbs and grill for 3 to 5 minutes on each side, or until fish flakes easily with a fork. Baste fish with olive oil from time to time.

Summer Pudding

(illustrated on page 146)

$\frac{1}{2}$ lb(225g) red or black currants
$\frac{3}{4}$ lb(350g) cherries
$\frac{1}{2}$ lb(225g) raspberries
4–6 oz(100–175g) sugar
Thin slices white bread
Whipped cream

1 Strip all stalks from currants and pit cherries; combine with raspberries and wash if necessary. Place fruits with $\frac{1}{4}$ pint(1·5dl) water and sugar in a saucepan and simmer until sugar melts.

2 Trim crusts from bread; cut each slice in half lengthwise and line sides of bowl or soufflé dish. Cover bottom of dish with triangles of bread, and trim off slices at rim of dish.

3 Fill dish with fruit mixture. Cut additional bread triangles to cover pudding. Place a flat plate on pudding; weight it and chill in refrigerator overnight.

4 When ready to serve, invert on to a serving dish and serve with whipped cream.

Paprika Chicken with Yoghourt

1 tender roasting chicken, about $3\frac{1}{2}$
    lb(1·5kg), cut into 8 serving pieces
Salt and freshly ground black pepper
4 level tablespoons butter
2 tablespoons olive oil
1 Spanish onion, chopped
1 green pepper, chopped
1 level tablespoon paprika
$\frac{1}{2}$ pint(3dl) chicken stock
2 level tablespoons cornflour
$\frac{1}{4}$ pint(1·5dl) yoghourt
    (1 small carton)

1 Season chicken pieces well and cook in butter and olive oil until golden brown on all sides.

2 Remove from pan; add chopped onion and chopped green pepper and sauté in remaining fats until the vegetables just start to turn colour. Stir in paprika, then add chicken stock.

3 Return chicken pieces to the pan; cover and simmer chicken and vegetables gently over very low heat for 45 minutes, or until chicken is tender.

4 Transfer chicken pieces to a heated serving dish. Add enough cold water to cornflour to make a smooth paste; combine with juices in pan and bring to the boil, stirring until sauce is thick. Then add yoghourt and stir over low heat until sauce is well blended.

5 Return chicken pieces to pan and warm through in hot, pungent sauce. Delicious served with **noodles sprinkled with almonds** (see overleaf) or **plain boiled rice** (see page 70).

**Paprika Chicken
with Yoghourt
with
Noodles with
Grated Almonds
or
Plain Boiled Rice**

Delmonico Salad

Cherries Jubilee

Serves 4–6

*with this menu I suggest
the following Inexpensive
White Wines*
**Muscadet
Chablis
Vinho Verde**

Noodles with Grated Almonds

1 lb(450g) noodles
Salt
¼ lb(100g) butter
Freshly ground black pepper
4–6 level tablespoons grated toasted
    almonds

1 Bring 3–4 quarts(3–4 litres) of well salted water to a boil in a large saucepan.

2 Add noodles and cook until *al dente* – tender but still firm 'to the bite'. Test by picking out a strand of noodle with a fork from time to time.

3 When noodles are tender, drain; add butter, salt and freshly ground black pepper. Mix well.

4 Sprinkle with grated almonds and serve immediately.

Delmonico Salad

2 heads lettuce

DRESSING:
6–8 tablespoons olive oil
2 tablespoons wine vinegar
2 tablespoons cream
2 tablespoons Roquefort cheese,
    crumbled
Freshly ground black pepper
Dash of Tabasco
1 hard-boiled egg, finely chopped
1 rasher cooked bacon, finely
    chopped

1 Wash and prepare lettuce. Shake dry in a salad basket, or dry each leaf carefully in a clean tea towel. Wrap in tea towel and allow to crisp in refrigerator until ready to use.

2 **To make dressing:** combine olive oil, wine vinegar, cream and crumbled Roquefort in a small bowl, and whisk until smooth. Season to taste with freshly ground black pepper and Tabasco and stir in finely chopped hard-boiled egg and chopped bacon.

3 Arrange lettuce in salad bowl. Pour over dressing; toss and serve.

Cherries Jubilee

1 large can pitted dark cherries
2 level tablespoons sugar
1 stick cinnamon
Juice and grated rind of ½ orange
1 teaspoon cornflour
4 tablespoons cognac
4 tablespoons cherry brandy
Vanilla ice cream

1 Drain cherries and measure out ½ pint(3dl) of the juice.

2 Combine sugar, cinnamon, orange juice, grated orange rind, cornflour and cherry juice, and bring slowly to the boil in bottom of chafing dish. Allow to bubble for 5 minutes, stirring from time to time, until sauce is reduced to a syrup.

3 Add cherries and heat through.

4 Heat cognac and cherry brandy and pour over cherries. Ignite, and when flames die down pour hot mixture over individual portions of vanilla ice cream.

Food After a Cocktail Party

If, like me, you are daunted by the terrors of a cocktail party at which no food is served, you might like to terminate your rout with something a little more substantial – perhaps a baked ham or a roast turkey, with a choice of salads and assorted breads. Or try a party idea from Alsace Lorraine: Cold Roast Loin of Pork with Potato and Sauerkraut Salads.

For both informality and comfort, make it a buffet-cum-sit-down-dinner, where guests serve themselves from a candlelit sideboard, then move along to a set table. There is no first course, and Raspberry and Redcurrant Tarts and coffee are arranged on a separate side table.

The main dish of Cold Roast Loin of Pork, flavoured with thyme, bay leaf and mustard, is cooked on the day preceding the party. Cut it into chops and serve it on a bed of fresh watercress; and for additional effect garnish it with hollowed-out apples filled with home-made Apple Sauce spiked with a little grated horseradish or mayonnaise. Make sure you brush the interiors of the apples with lemon juice to keep their colour fresh.

Serve this meal country-style – on thick white plates with red checked tablecloths and napkins – and accompany it with great steins of beer or a wine.

Cold Roast Loin of Pork

1 loin of pork (7–8 cutlets)
4 tablespoons softened butter
Crumbled thyme and bay leaf
Dijon mustard
Salt and freshly ground black pepper
Sprigs of watercress
Horseradish Apple Sauce or
    mayonnaise (see page 152)

1 Have your butcher remove rind but not fat from pork. Mix butter, crumbled thyme, bay leaf and Dijon mustard to a smooth paste and rub well into pork several hours before roasting. Sprinkle to taste with salt and freshly ground black pepper and let stand at room temperature to absorb flavours. Brown in a hot oven (450°F/230°C/Mark 8) for 15 minutes, fat side up. Reduce heat to moderate (350°F/180°C/Mark 4) and continue to roast until meat is done, about $1\frac{1}{4}$–$1\frac{1}{2}$ hours. Cool.

2 Cut cold loin of pork into chops.

3 Serve on a bed of watercress with choice of salads and horseradish apple sauce or mayonnaise.

Potato Salad

3 lb(1·4kg) new potatoes
Salt
1–2 tablespoons sugar
3 tablespoons wine vinegar
6 thin slices bacon
Olive oil
1 green pepper, finely chopped
3 tablespoons finely chopped onion
3 tablespoons finely chopped parsley
Lemon juice
Cayenne pepper

1 Scrub new potatoes; cook in boiling salted water until just tender, 15–20 minutes; drain, peel and slice. Place potatoes in a bowl and sprinkle with sugar and wine vinegar. Toss gently.

2 Sauté bacon in a little oil until crisp. Drain well, pouring fat over potatoes. Crumble or chop finely and add to potatoes with chopped green pepper. Toss gently.

3 Combine 6–8 tablespoons olive oil with finely chopped onion and parsley and season with lemon juice, salt and cayenne pepper, to taste. Pour over salad.

Menu

Cold Roast Loin
of Pork

Potato Salad
and
Choucroute Salad

Raspberry and
Redcurrant Tarts

Serves 6–8

*with this menu I suggest
the following Inexpensive
Rosés*
Tavel
Rosé de Provence

Choucroute Salad

1 Spanish onion, finely chopped
8 tablespoons olive oil
2 large cans sauerkraut
¾ pint (4dl) chicken stock
   (made with a cube)
Dry white wine (optional)
Salt and coarsely ground black pepper
1–2 cloves garlic, finely chopped
2–3 tablespoons vinegar
2–3 hard-boiled eggs, quartered
1 beetroot, cooked and sliced

1 Sauté finely chopped onion in 2 table-spoons olive oil until golden but not brown.

2 Place sauerkraut in a heavy saucepan with onion and pour over chicken stock. Simmer for three-quarters of an hour, adding a little more stock or dry white wine if necessary.

3 Cool sauerkraut; drain and season with salt and coarsely ground black pepper, to taste, finely chopped garlic and remaining olive oil and vinegar.

4 Serve garnished with quartered hard-boiled eggs and thin slices of cooked beet-root.

Raspberry and Redcurrant Tarts

6–8 baked tart shells
3–4 punnets raspberries
1 punnet redcurrants
5 oz (150g) sugar
Lemon juice
1–2 tablespoons redcurrant jelly
Kirsch (optional)

1 Combine raspberries, redcurrants and sugar in an enamelled saucepan and cook over low heat, stirring gently, until the sugar melts. Add lemon juice to taste and drain fruit, reserving juices.

2 Fill tart shells with fruit and bake in a moderate oven (350°F/180°C/Mark 4) for 10 minutes.

3 Meanwhile add redcurrant jelly to juices and boil until syrup is thick, adding a little Kirsch if desired. Cool tarts and strain syrup over fruit.

COCKTAILS

Drinks – the right kind – can float a party. Of course, there is always champagne or gin and tonic, whisky and soda, or the ubiquitous Bloody Mary. But for my money nothing beats one or two specially prepared cocktails for getting people quickly into a party mood.

The quantities given below are for 1 drink.

Bacardi Cocktail Combine the juice of half a large lime, or one small lime, with half a teaspoon granulated sugar and $1\frac{1}{2}$ fl oz/40ml Bacardi rum. Mix thoroughly and then strain through crushed ice.

Pernod Daiquiri Combine the juice of half a large lime, or one small lime, with $1\frac{1}{2}$ fl oz/40ml white rum and add a dash of Pernod and icing sugar, to taste. Strain through crushed ice.

Rye Snifter Crush 1 small lump of sugar with a dash of Angostura bitters and 2 tablespoons water in bottom of brandy snifter. Add ice cubes, $1\frac{1}{2}$ fl oz/40ml rye whiskey and 1 piece lemon peel. Finish with a generous squirt of soda water and top with 1 slice of orange or lemon and 1 maraschino cherry.

Orange Gin Fling Combine $1\frac{1}{2}$ fl oz/40ml gin with 1 tablespoon each Italian vermouth and French vermouth. Add 3 fl oz/80ml fresh orange juice and strain through crushed ice.

Manhattan Cocktail Put 2 or 3 ice cubes into an old-fashioned glass. Add $1\frac{1}{2}$ fl oz/40ml Bourbon whiskey, 1 tablespoon Italian sweet vermouth and a dash of Angostura bitters and stir. Top with 1 slice of orange and 1 maraschino cherry.

White Lady Combine $1\frac{1}{2}$ fl oz/40ml gin with 1 tablespoon each lemon juice and Cointreau. Strain through crushed ice.

Spanish Bloody Mary Combine $1\frac{1}{2}$ fl oz/40ml vodka with tomato juice, a little Tabasco and Worcestershire sauce, celery salt and freshly ground black pepper, to taste, and add a dash of La Ina sherry.

Champagne Cocktail Rub half a sugar cube with Angostura bitters; add a shot of cognac and a slice of orange and top with chilled champagne.

Champagne Orange Cut the peel from 1 orange in a long spiral. Arrange the strip of peel in a balloon glass and fill with ice cubes. Add $1\frac{1}{2}$ fl oz/40ml gin and enough chilled champagne almost to fill glass. Gently spoon in 2 tablespoons cognac.

CANAPÉS

Unusual canapés – fingers of toast spread with steak tartare, or bacon and chutney and cream cheese – can make your reputation as the best party giver in town. Try one, or more, at your next drinks party.

Steak Tartare Canapés

Grind 1 lb/450g lean beef twice and combine with 1 egg yolk, 4 tablespoons finely chopped onion, 2 cloves garlic, finely chopped, salt, freshly ground black pepper, 1 tablespoon Worcestershire sauce, 2 tablespoons finely chopped parsley and 4 tablespoons cognac in a mixing bowl. Mix thoroughly and chill until ready to serve.

Spread on rounds of rye or fingers of pumpernickel bread. Top with chopped onion and hard-boiled egg, parsley, capers or caviar.

Soused Camembert Canapés

Remove outer skin from ½ lb/225g Camembert cheese, cut in quarters and marinate in ½ pint/3dl dry white wine at room temperature for at least 6 hours, turning cheese several times. Drain cheese, discarding wine, and press through a coarse sieve; blend in ¼ lb/100g softened butter; add cayenne pepper to taste and chill. Spread rounds of bread or toast with cheese mixture and dust generously with finely chopped almonds.

Bacon and Chutney Canapés

Dice 8 rashers lean bacon finely and fry until crisp. Pour off fat and stir in 1 small jar mango chutney, finely chopped. Spread bread fingers with cream cheese and top with chutney mixture.

Provençal Canapés

Combine 4–6 level tablespoons of mayonnaise with 2 tablespoons olive oil and 1 level tablespoon French mustard and beat until smooth. Add 1 Spanish onion, 10 anchovies and 2 hard-boiled eggs, all finely chopped. Season with juice and grated rind of 1 lemon and freshly ground black pepper. Spread on buttered rounds of French bread.

DIPS & SPREADS

The same basic mixtures can serve for both spreads and dips. Just add a little more cream, sour cream or lemon juice to thin the spreads to a dippable consistency.

Use spreads with thin fingers or rounds of toasted white or dark bread, rye bread, *brioches* or pumpernickel.

Serve dips in small bowls with a

platter of crisp crackers, toasted fingers of white or dark bread, rye, *brioches* or pumpernickel. Greek *pita* bread and Mexican *tortillas* make good 'dippers', as do potato crisps, or crisp raw vegetables – slim fingers of carrot, green or red pepper, celery, cucumber, trimmed radishes and cauliflowerets – kept ice-cold in bowls of ice.

Olive Cheese Mix

Combine 1 cup cottage cheese, 6 level tablespoons chopped ripe olives and 6 level tablespoons chopped walnuts. Add just enough double cream or sour cream – or a combination of the two – to make a smooth spread for *canapés*. Add a few tablespoons more cream to make a smooth dip. Season with salt, pepper, lemon juice or cayenne pepper.

Curried Cheese Mix

Combine 1 cup cottage cheese, 2 level tablespoons chopped Indian chutney and 1 level teaspoon curry powder. Add enough double cream or sour cream – or a combination of the two – to make a smooth spread. Add more cream to make a dip. Season as above.

Mexican Cheese Mix

Combine 1 cup cottage cheese, 2 level tablespoons each chopped green pepper, chopped pimento and chopped onion. Add enough double cream or sour cream – or a combination of the two – to make a smooth spread. Add more cream for dip. Season as above.

Roquefort Cheese Mix

Combine 1 cup cottage cheese, 4 level tablespoons crumbled Roquefort cheese and $\frac{1}{2}$ level teaspoon dry mustard. Add enough double cream or sour cream – or a combination of the two – to make a smooth spread. Add more cream for dip. Season as above.

Provençal Herb and Garlic Mix

Combine 1 cup cottage cheese, 4 level tablespoons finely chopped fresh basil or tarragon, 2 level tablespoons finely chopped chives, 1 level tablespoon finely chopped parsley and 1 mashed garlic clove. Add double cream and lemon juice to taste. Add more cream and lemon juice for dip. Season as above.

Provençal Anchovy Mix (Anchoiade)

Combine in a mortar and pound to a smooth paste 1 tin of anchovy fillets in oil, 1 large clove garlic, 1 tablespoon olive oil and 1 tablespoon softened butter. Season to taste with a few drops of lemon juice or cognac and a little freshly ground black pepper.

Provençal Oil Mix (Tapénade)

Pound 36 stoned ripe olives, 12 anchovy fillets and 1 small can tuna fish in a mortar with 1 level tablespoon Dijon mustard and 4 level tablespoons chopped capers. When the mixture has been blended to a smooth paste, put it through a fine sieve and whisk in 12 tablespoons olive oil a little at a time. Add 2 tablespoons cognac and 2 hard-boiled eggs, sieved; blend well and season with freshly ground black pepper.

Mexican Avocado Mix (Guacamole)

Peel 2 ripe avocados and mash them lightly with a wooden spoon. Add the juice of 1 lemon, 1 crushed clove garlic, 4 tomatoes, peeled, seeded and coarsely chopped, $\frac{1}{2}$ Spanish onion, finely chopped, and 4 tablespoons finely chopped celery or green pepper. Stir in 1 tablespoon finely chopped coriander leaves or parsley, 2 to 4 tablespoons olive oil and salt and freshly ground black pepper to taste. Leave the avocado stones in the mixture until ready to serve to keep it from browning.

Let's Make it a Fondue Party

A good bet for informal entertaining for young parties is a Fondue Party, or Dip-in Dinner, which comes to us from France via America. It is easy and fun. 'Dip-ins' range from traditional Swiss fondue to *Fondue Bourguignonne*, where each guest is given a small bowl of marinated steak cubes, a variety of sauces – Béarnaise (see page 153). Mustard and Herbs, Garlic Mayonnaise and Spicy Tomato Béarnaise – and a long-handled fork with which to cook his own meat piece by piece in a central pot of simmering butter and oil.

Guests spear cubes of beef with their fondue forks; hold each cube in the simmering butter and oil until done to their taste – a matter of seconds – and then dip it into one of the accompanying sauces. Serve *Fondue Bourguignonne* with a good red Burgundy (Nuits-St-Georges or Moulin à Vent) and French bread. Follow with a tossed green salad.

Swiss Fondue is an easily prepared communal dip-in that combines good Swiss cheese, fine wine and good cheer. The ideal setting is a roaring fire and a long table big enough to seat several people. Make sure all ingredients are at hand before starting as the actual cooking time is brief.

Equip each guest with a long fork, cubes of crusty French bread, a glass of dry white wine (I like a Sylvaner or a Niersteiner) and a napkin. Each person in turn spears a cube of bread from his plate, dips it in the creamy fondue mixture, and scoops out the bread, now coated with the creamy cheese mixture. Swiss tradition has it that if a man drops his bread into the pot he will have to pay for the meal; if a woman drops hers in she will have to kiss each man at the table.

So here I have given you two basic fondue recipes together with my suggestions for variations. First decide your fondue, and then choose a starter and dessert to accompany it.

Swiss Fondue

$\frac{3}{4}$ **lb(350g) Gruyère cheese, coarsely grated**
$\frac{3}{4}$ **lb(350g) Emmenthal cheese, coarsely grated**
1 teaspoon cornflour
1 cut clove garlic
$\frac{1}{2}$–$\frac{3}{4}$ **pint(3–4dl) dry white wine**
2–4 tablespoons Kirsch
Nutmeg, salt and pepper
French bread, cut into crusty squares

1 Toss grated cheese with cornflour.

2 Rub inside of an earthenware casserole or fondue cooker with cut surface of garlic.

3 Pour in dry white wine and heat over very low heat until wine starts to bubble.

Add cheese gradually, stirring continuously, until blended. When cheese and wine mixture is smooth and well-blended, add Kirsch and nutmeg, salt and pepper to taste.

Note: Fondue should be kept warm, but not too hot. If fondue becomes too thick in cooking, add a little more dry white wine or, Kirsch.

4 **At the table:** each guest spears a cube of bread, dips it in the creamy fondue mixture, and scoops out the bread, now coated with the mixture. Serve with a **tossed green salad** (see page 100).

Fondue Bourguignonne
with sauces and garnishes
(page 149)

Fondue Bourguignonne

2 lb(900g) fillet steak
½ lb(225g) butter
¼ pint(1·5dl) corn or peanut oil

1 Dice meat in small bite-size cubes, cutting off all bits of fat or gristle. Marinate for at least 2 hours before serving (see below).

2 Combine butter and oil in fondue cooker or chafing dish and keep it simmering gently in the middle of the table.

3 **Garnish for each guest:** individual bowls of 3 or more of the following; Mustard and Herb Sauce; Garlic Mayonnaise; finely chopped garlic; finely chopped parsley and capers; Spicy Tomato Béarnaise; Béarnaise sauce (see page 153).

4 **At the table:** Each guest spears a cube of beef with his fondue fork; holds it in the simmering butter and oil until done to his taste; and then dips it into one of 3 accompanying sauces or garnishes. Serve with a **tossed green salad.**

MARINADE FOR FONDUE BOURGUIGNONNE:

6 **tablespoons olive oil**
6 **tablespoons dry white wine**
2 **bay leaves, crumbled**
2 **level tablespoons finely chopped parsley**
Salt and freshly ground black pepper

Combine first 4 ingredients and pour into a flat serving bowl or gratin dish. Add cubed meat and toss well. Season generously with salt and freshly ground black pepper, and toss again. Leave meat to marinate in the mixture for at least 2 hours before using.

Previous page right: Apple Pie With Orange Juice (page 73), left: Summer Pudding (page 137)

Above left: Tomato Aspic (page 155)
Below, far left: Italian Bean Salad (page 159)
Below, left: Spinach Salad with Croûtons (page 76)

MUSTARD AND HERB SAUCE:

2 **tablespoons wine vinegar**
1 **level tablespoon Dijon mustard**
8 **tablespoons olive oil**
1–2 **level tablespoons finely chopped onion**
1 **level tablespoon finely chopped parsley**
1 **level tablespoon finely chopped chives**
Salt
Freshly ground black pepper

Combine wine vinegar and Dijon mustard in a small bowl and blend well. Whisk in olive oil gradually and then add finely chopped onion, parsley and chives, and salt and freshly ground black pepper, to taste.

GARLIC MAYONNAISE:

4 **fat cloves of garlic per person**
Salt
1 **egg yolk for each two persons**
Olive oil
Freshly ground black pepper
Lemon juice

1 Crush garlic to a smooth paste in a mortar with a little salt; blend in egg yolks until the mixture forms a smooth homogeneous mass.

2 Now take olive oil and proceed (drop by drop at first, a thin fine trickle later) to whisk the mixture. The mayonnaise will thicken gradually until it reaches the proper stiff, firm consistency. The exact quantity of oil is, of course, determined by the number of egg yolks used.

3 Season to taste with additional salt, a little pepper and lemon juice. This sauce is served chilled in a bowl. Guests help themselves.

SPICY TOMATO BÉARNAISE:

Make Béarnaise (see page 153) and add tomato ketchup, lemon juice and cayenne pepper, to taste. Sauce should be highly flavoured.

149

*with this menu I suggest
the following Inexpensive
Red Wines*
**Macon Rouge
Beaujolais
Valpolicella**
*or the following Inexpensive
White Wines*
**Muscadet
Sancerre
Riesling**

Egg and Anchovy Barrels

4 hard-boiled eggs
8 anchovy fillets
2 tablespoons mayonnaise (see page
   152)
¼ teaspoon paprika
Freshly ground black pepper
Watercress
Capers

1 Shell eggs and cut tops and bottoms off
with a sharp knife dipped in cold water.
Carefully remove yolks from broad end of
eggs, being careful not to split whites.

2 Mash yolks to a smooth paste with 4
anchovy fillets, mayonnaise and paprika.
Season to taste with a little freshly ground
black pepper and stuff eggs with this mixture. If mixture is too stiff, add more
mayonnaise.

3 **To serve:** place eggs, broad end up, on a
bed of watercress. Split remaining anchovy
fillets and wrap around centre of each egg.
Top each barrel with capers.

Asparagus Appetizer Salad

1 **bunch fresh asparagus, or
   2 small packets frozen asparagus**
1 **head lettuce**
1 **canned pimento, cut in strips**
2 **hard-boiled eggs, sliced**
Chopped white of 1 hard-boiled egg
Paprika (optional)

SOUR CREAM DRESSING:
¼ **pint (1·5dl) sour cream (1 carton)**
Lemon juice
Salt and freshly ground black pepper
1 **tablespoon each finely chopped
   fresh parsley, chives and tarragon**
Tabasco or paprika

1 **To prepare fresh asparagus:** wash
stalks thoroughly and, if sandy, scrub them

gently with a vegetable brush. Remove any
isolated leaf points below the head. To
remove the woody base, break the stalks
rather than cut them. You will find that they
snap off easily at the point where the tender
part begins. Put the stalks in cold water as
you clean and trim them.

2 Select a deep, narrow pan in which the
asparagus stalks can stand upright and pour
in boiling water to come halfway up the
asparagus; in this way, the tough stalks will
cook in water while the tender heads cook in
steam. Simmer gently – for about 15
minutes from the time the water comes to
the boil again is just about right. Remove
asparagus from pan and drain.

Note: If you have no deep, narrow pan,
stand the asparagus upright in the bottom of
a double saucepan. Add boiling water and
cover asparagus with the inverted top of the
double saucepan. Or, crumple some aluminium foil into one side of a large, flat
casserole with cover. Place asparagus in
casserole, with heads supported on foil, add
enough boiling water to cover stalks only.
Cover casserole. Cook for about 15
minutes, as above.

3 Wash and dry the lettuce leaves and line a
serving dish with them. Divide the cooked
asparagus into 2 bunches and arrange them
on the lettuce leaves. Garnish with strips of
pimento and sliced hard-boiled eggs, reserving the end slices of each egg to chop for
added garnish. Dust lightly with paprika if
desired. Serve the dressing separately.

4 **To make sour cream dressing:** combine sour cream with lemon juice, salt and
freshly ground black pepper, to taste. Stir in
the finely chopped fresh herbs with a dash of
Tabasco sauce or paprika.

Tossed Green Salad

(for the recipe, see **green salad and variations,** page 100)

Fruits in Port Wine

2 lb(900g) ripe pears
Juice and rind of ½ lemon
Rind of 1 orange
½ pint(3dl) port wine
½ lb(225g) sugar
1 jar (about ½ lb/225g)
brandied cherries

1 Peel the pears and place them in a bowl of water to which you have added the lemon juice to keep them from browning. Reserve the lemon rind.

2 With a sharp knife remove the outer rind of the orange and half-lemon – just the rind, not the white pith. Cut the rinds into thin slivers.

3 Bring wine, 1½ pints(8·5dl) water, sugar, lemon rind and the orange rind to the boil in an enamelled saucepan. Simmer until the sugar has dissolved. Remove the pears from lemon water and add them to the syrup; simmer until tender. Add brandied cherries and chill. Serve fruit in syrup with a little slivered orange rind scattered over fruits.

Swiss Apple Flan

1 baked pastry shell
1½ lb(675g) cooking apples
2 tablespoons butter

SWISS APPLE SAUCE FILLING:
(Makes about 1 pint[6dl])
2 lb(900g) cooking apples
4–6 level tablespoons butter
2–3 lemon slices
2 level tablespoons sugar
1 clove
½ teaspoon vanilla essence
Cinnamon

1 **To make Swiss apple sauce filling:** Wipe, quarter and core 2 lb(900g) apples.

2 Cut quartered apples into thick slices and put them in a large saucepan together with butter, lemon slices, sugar, clove and 4 tablespoons water. Bring gently to the boil; cover pan and simmer gently for about 10 minutes, stirring once or twice during cooking time to prevent sauce from scorching.

3 When sauce is thick and smooth, remove lemon slices and clove and purée through a fine sieve.

4 Flavour with vanilla essence and cinnamon, to taste, adding a little more sugar, if desired. Allow to cool before using. Half-fill baked pastry shell with this mixture.

APRICOT GLAZE:
6 tablespoons apricot jam
1 tablespoon rum, brandy or Kirsch

5 **To prepare glaze:** heat apricot jam and 3 tablespoons water in small saucepan, stirring constantly, until mixture melts. Strain and if desired stir in rum, brandy or Kirsch. Keep warm until ready for use.

6 **To prepare apples:** peel, core and slice apples as thinly as possible. Arrange in overlapping concentric circles on top of Swiss apple sauce filling. Dot with knobs of butter and bake under pre-heated grill for 3–5 minutes, or until apple slices are nicely browned. Coat with apricot glaze.

Emulsion

SAUCES

How to Make Perfect Mayonnaise

Place 2 egg yolks (without gelatinous thread of egg) in a small mixing bowl or pudding basin with $\frac{1}{2}$ level teaspoon Dijon mustard and salt and freshly ground black pepper to taste. Twist a cloth wrung out in very cold water round the bottom of the bowl to keep it steady and cool. Use a wire whisk, fork, wooden spoon or rotary whisk, and beat the yolks to a smooth paste. Add a little lemon juice (the acid helps the emulsion) and, drop by drop, beat in about 2 fl oz/50ml of the oil. Add a little more lemon juice; then, rather faster now, add more oil, beating the while. Continue adding oil and beating until the sauce is of a good thick consistency (you will need about 1 pint/6dl oil in all). Then correct the seasoning, adding more salt, pepper, and lemon to taste.

If mayonnaise curdles, break another egg yolk into a clean bowl and gradually beat curdled mixture into it.

When mayonnaise is to be used to dress a fish or potato salad, thin it down considerably with dry white wine, champagne, vinegar or lemon juice. If it is to be used for coating meat, poultry or fish, add a little liquid aspic to stiffen it.

If you are keeping mayonnaise a day before using, stir in 1 tablespoon boiling water. This will prevent it turning or separating. Cover the bowl with a cloth wrung out in very cold water to prevent skin forming.

Blender mayonnaise: combine in electric blender 2 whole eggs, $\frac{1}{4}$ pint/1·5dl olive oil, 4 tablespoons lemon juice or vinegar, $\frac{1}{2}$ level teaspoon each dry mustard and salt, with freshly ground black pepper to taste. Cover the container and turn the motor to high. When blended, remove cover and add $\frac{1}{2}$ pint/3dl olive oil in a thin steady trickle, as you blend continuously. Correct seasoning and use as desired.

Horseradish mayonnaise: add juice of $\frac{1}{2}$ lemon and salt to taste to $\frac{3}{4}$ pint/4dl mayonnaise. Just before serving, stir in 2 to 3 tablespoons freshly grated horseradish. (For eggs, egg salads or seafood.)

Russian mayonnaise dressing: add 3 tablespoons tomato ketchup, a dash of Tabasco or Worcestershire sauce and 1 level teaspoon each chopped tinned pimentos and chives. (For eggs, cooked vegetable salads and seafood.)

Cucumber mayonnaise: add $\frac{1}{4}$ cucumber, finely chopped, and 2 tablespoons finely chopped parsley to $\frac{1}{4}$ pint/1·5dl mayonnaise.

Mustard mayonnaise: add more Dijon or powdered mustard to taste.

Sauce Tartare: add 1–2 teaspoons each chopped parsley, tarragon, chervil, capers and gherkins to mayonnaise.

Béarnaise, Hollandaise and Variations

The two great French 'emulsion' sauces – Béarnaise and Hollandaise – are served hot to add a fillip to dishes of grilled meats and grilled or poached fish. Hollandaise is used, too, to add interest to cooked egg and vegetable dishes – and as a delicious golden sauce for those aristocratic vegetables, artichokes and asparagus.

Professional chefs also use Hollandaise to add body and richness to *gratin* sauces. It helps them 'stand up' under the heat.

Both sauces are quite easy to achieve in minutes if you are careful with the heat over which they are cooked.

Sauce Béarnaise

1 Chop leaves and stems of 2 sprigs tarragon and 3 sprigs chervil coarsely and combine with 1 tablespoon chopped shallots, 2 crushed peppercorns, 2 tablespoons tarragon vinegar and $\frac{1}{4}$ pint/1·5dl dry white wine in the top of a double saucepan. Cook over a high flame until liquid is reduced to about 1 tablespoon. Reducing the sauce in this way to almost a glaze on the bottom of the pan seems to make the following steps easier.

2 Add 3 egg yolks and 1 tablespoon water to the herb and wine mixture in the top of double saucepan, and place it over hot, but not boiling water. Whisk until light and fluffy. **Never let water in bottom of saucepan begin to boil, or sauce will not 'take'.** Add $\frac{1}{4}$ lb/100g soft butter gradually to egg mixture, whisking briskly all the time as sauce begins to thicken. Continue adding butter gradually (about $\frac{1}{4}$ lb/100g more), whisking continuously until sauce is thick. Season to taste with salt and cayenne pepper. Strain through a fine sieve and serve.

Sauce Choron

Make a Béarnaise sauce as above, and flavour to taste with tomato concentrate.

Sauce Hollandaise

1 Combine 1 teaspoon lemon juice, 1 tablespoon cold water, salt and white pepper in the top of a double saucepan or *bain-marie*. Divide $\frac{1}{2}$ lb/225g soft butter into 4 equal pieces. Add 4 egg yolks and a quarter of the butter to the liquid in the saucepan and whisk the mixture over hot, but not boiling, water until the butter is melted and the mixture begins to thicken. Add the second piece of butter and continue whisking. As the mixture thickens and the second piece of butter melts, add the third piece of butter, stirring from the bottom of the pan until it is melted. **Be careful not to allow the water over which the sauce is cooking to boil at any time.** Add rest of butter, beating until it melts and is incorporated in the sauce.

2 Remove top part of the saucepan from the heat and whisk sauce for 2 to 3 minutes longer. Replace saucepan over hot, but not boiling, water for 2 minutes more, beating constantly. By this time the emulsion should have formed and your sauce will be rich and creamy. Finish sauce with a few drops of lemon juice, strain and reserve.

If at any time in the operation the mixture should curdle, beat in 1 or 2 tablespoons cold water to rebind the emulsion.

Mustard Hollandaise

Make a Hollandaise sauce as above, and flavour to taste with Dijon mustard.

Sauce Mousseline

Make in the same way as Hollandaise sauce, adding 4 to 6 tablespoons whipped cream just before serving.

You Can be a Pasta Master

It's a new Italian renaissance. Italian restaurants are booming. Italian speciality stores are springing up in towns and cities across the country. Italian products were featured on the shelves of every supermarket I visited this week.

The reason for this great new revival is simply **Pasta.** Britain is potty about pasta – so inexpensive, so easy to cook, so wonderfully easy to eat and enjoy, whether you serve it with a hamburger, make it the main dish of a company dinner, or serve it as a first course as the Italians do.

There are hundreds of types of pasta in Italy, and almost as many sauces. And each type of pasta – believe it or not – tastes quite different because of its shape, thickness or thinness and the way it takes up the sauce. Try it and see with one of the four most popular types below.

Tubular pasta: macaroni, spaghetti, vermicelli, etc.

Flat or ribbon pasta: noodles, fettucine, tagliatelle, lasagne.

Envelope pasta: ravioli, manicotti, canneloni – usually stuffed first, then cooked with a sauce.

Fancy-shaped pastina: innumerable types including bows, stars, shells, alphabet letters, etc. The very tiny ones – almost like confetti – are used only in soups.

To Cook Pasta Perfectly

All you need is a big pot, a *very* big pot.

You fill the pot with water; season generously with salt and bring the water to a fast boil. Then you put in the pasta. Don't break it, just push it in gently with your hand. For, as the pasta at the bottom of the pot softens in the hot water, it will gradually bend. Then stir the pasta so it will not stick to the bottom of the pot.

Now comes the all-important direction. No one can say exactly how long to cook pasta. The time varies with the type of pasta used. So it is useless to depend on the clock. You have to stand over the pot and taste.

To be perfect, pasta should be neither too hard nor too mushy, but at the beginning point of softness when it is just tender and a little resistant to the teeth. To test this, just fish out a piece of pasta with a fork and bite it, then decide on the perfect moment for yourself.

And take a tip from a pasta lover who knows: add plenty of butter before saucing. With a fork in each hand, lift the long strands a few times, almost tossing – spaghetti or noodles must be very hot so the butter will melt all through and separate the strands. Now on with the spicy sauce and a liberal helping of grated Parmesan cheese, freshly grated if you can get it – it tastes so much better – packaged, if you cannot.

For four persons, use a little less than 1 lb(450g) pasta if it is to be a first course. If it is the main dish of the meal, use more, depending on the appetites of your friends.

Tomato Aspic

(illustrated on page 148)

2¼ pints(1·3 litres) cooked or canned
    tomatoes
1 celery stalk, chopped
1 onion, chopped
½ lemon, chopped
2 level teaspoons sugar
1 level teaspoon salt
2 bay leaves
2 cloves
1 clove garlic, chopped
1 oz(25g) powdered gelatine
¼ pint(1·5dl) cider vinegar
Worcestershire or Tabasco sauce

GARNISH:
Small tomatoes
Cauliflowerets
Curly endive leaves
Radishes
Sliced green pepper
Sprig of parsley
Lemon slices

1 Combine the first nine ingredients in a saucepan and simmer for 20 minutes. Strain the tomato mixture through a sieve, pressing the vegetables well to extract juices.

2 Soften the gelatine in the cider vinegar. Stir into the sieved tomato mixture until dissolved. Add Worcestershire sauce or Tabasco to taste.

3 Pour the mixture into a 2½-pint(1·4-litre) mould. Refrigerate until firm.

4 **To serve:** unmould and garnish the aspic with small tomatoes, cauliflowerets, endive, radishes, green pepper and a sprig of parsley, and serve with lemon slices.

Note: The above recipe is quite delicious, too, if you fold diced green pepper, celery and defrosted Norwegian prawns into the 'syrupy' aspic mixture before you refrigerate it. Garnish the mould as above.

Cheese and Macaroni Loaf

½ lb(225g) macaroni
Salt
Butter
2 level tablespoons flour
Freshly ground black pepper
½ level teaspoon paprika
¾ pint(4dl) milk
6 oz(175g) grated cheese
3 eggs

1 Cook macaroni in boiling, salted water until tender but not mushy.

2 Melt 2 level tablespoons butter in the top of a double saucepan; stir in flour and season generously with salt, black pepper and paprika. Add milk and stir over low heat until sauce is smooth and thick. Add cheese and stir until cheese has melted. Stir in macaroni.

3 Separate eggs. Beat yolks until smooth and add to mixture. Heat through. Be careful not to let mixture boil at this stage, or your eggs will curdle.

4 Beat egg whites until stiff. Fold into mixture. Correct seasoning, adding a little more salt and pepper if necessary, and then turn mixture into a well-buttered loaf pan 9 × 3 × 5 inches(23 × 7·5 × 13cm) and set in a roasting pan of hot water. Place pan over high heat until water starts to bubble, then place in a preheated moderate oven (350°F/180°C/Mark 4) for 50 minutes or until the loaf is firm. When ready to serve, turn out and serve hot.

Variations on a theme: Ring the changes on this basic recipe by adding 2 level tablespoons finely chopped cooked bacon; 2 level tablespoons finely chopped fried onions; or 2 level tablespoons finely chopped parsley and chives to the above. Or, wrap tomato wedges in a half slice of partially cooked bacon and bury in the cheese and macaroni loaf.

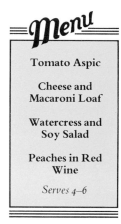

menu

Tomato Aspic

Cheese and
Macaroni Loaf

Watercress and
Soy Salad

Peaches in Red
Wine

Serves 4–6

*with this menu I suggest
the following inexpensive
White Wines or Rosés*
**Sancerre
Bourgogne Aligoté
Tavel Rosé**

155

Pasta Shells with Broccoli

Vitello al Herbe

Chocolate Refrigerator Cake

Serves 4–6

with this menu I suggest the following Inexpensive White Wines
Muscadet
Sancerre
Verdicchio

Watercress and Soy Salad

2 bunches watercress
1 bunch radishes
4–6 stalks celery

SOY DRESSING:
6–8 tablespoons olive oil
1 teaspoon sugar
1 tablespoon lemon juice
1 teaspoon soy sauce
Freshly ground black pepper
Monosodium glutamate

1 Prepare watercress and chill in a damp towel. Trim and slice radishes; slice celery.

2 **To make dressing:** combine olive oil, sugar, lemon juice and soy sauce, seasoning to taste with pepper and monosodium glutamate.

3 **Just before serving:** place watercress in a salad bowl; arrange sliced radishes and celery in centre. Add dressing and toss until every ingredient glistens.

Peaches in Red Wine

2–2½ lb(900g) small peaches
½ lb(225g) sugar
Cinnamon
¼ pint(1·5dl) red Burgundy
Whipped cream

1 Peel peaches but do not remove the stones. Put them in a saucepan with the sugar and ¼ pint(1·5dl) water and cinnamon to taste. Simmer them, covered, for about 15 minutes. Add Burgundy and continue to cook, uncovered, over a low heat for 15 minutes.

2 Put peaches in a deep serving dish. Cook the liquid until reduced to the consistency of a light syrup. Pour syrup over the peaches and put in the refrigerator to chill. Serve very cold with whipped cream.

Pasta Shells with Broccoli

1 lb(450g) fresh or 2 packets frozen broccoli
Salt
¾ lb(350g) pasta shells
¼ Spanish onion, finely chopped
2 level tablespoons finely chopped parsley
2–4 anchovy fillets, finely chopped
Finely chopped garlic
2 tablespoons olive oil
2 tablespoons butter
Freshly ground black pepper
2–4 tablespoons freshly grated Parmesan cheese

1 Cook broccoli in boiling salted water until just tender. Drain well and chop coarsely.

2 Cook pasta shells in boiling salted water until just tender. Drain.

3 Sauté finely chopped onion, parsley, anchovies and a little garlic in olive oil and butter until onion just begins to turn golden; add drained, chopped broccoli, season generously with salt and freshly ground black pepper, and continue cooking until broccoli begins to turn golden.

4 Place hot pasta shells in a heated serving dish, add broccoli and toss until well mixed.

5 Correct seasoning; sprinkle with a little freshly grated Parmesan cheese and serve immediately.

Vitello al Herbe

1½ lb(675g) fillet of veal, cut into thin slices
Salt and freshly ground black pepper
3 oz(75g) butter
Rosemary leaves
Juice of 1 lemon
Rings of lemon

Vitello al Herbe

Pasta Shells with Broccoli 157

1 Season veal to taste with salt and pepper.

2 Melt butter in a thick-bottomed frying pan; add veal with rosemary leaves to taste and sauté until golden. Add lemon juice and cook until tender (3–5 minutes more). Serve garnished with rings of lemon.

Menu

Appetizer Salad

Spaghetti
Bolognese

Italian Bean Salad

Cold Zabaglione

Serves 4–6

with this menu I suggest the following Inexpensive White Wines
**Soave
Verdicchio
Lachryma Christi**

Chocolate Refrigerator Cake

8 egg yolks
6 oz(175g) sugar
$\frac{3}{4}$ pint(4dl) milk
$\frac{1}{2}$–1 teaspoon vanilla extract
2 level tablespoons gelatine
$1\frac{1}{2}$ oz(40g) bitter chocolate, melted
2 tablespoons melted butter
4 tablespoons rum or Kirsch
$\frac{3}{4}$ pint(4dl) double cream
Sponge fingers
Kirsch and water
Whipped cream
Walnuts

1 Combine egg yolks and sugar in the top of a double saucepan and work the mixture with a wooden spoon until smooth. Bring the milk to a boil and add vanilla extract; then add milk gradually to the yolk mixture, stirring rapidly with a wire whisk. Cook over boiling water until the mixture becomes smooth and thick. Do not allow mixture to boil, or it will curdle.

2 Soften the gelatine in 4 tablespoons cold water and add it to the hot custard, stirring until it dissolves. Cool the custard.

3 Divide the custard into two portions and add melted chocolate, melted butter and rum or Kirsch to one portion. Whip cream until stiff and fold half of it into each of the two mixtures.

4 Line the sides of a medium spring-form cake tin with sponge fingers dipped in equal quantities of Kirsch and water. Fill the mould with alternating layers of chocolate

and vanilla cream, allowing each layer to set in refrigerator for about 30 minutes before adding the next. Set the cake (still in its pan) in the refrigerator to chill for at least 12 hours, or overnight.

5 When ready to serve, remove pan sides, leaving cake in the bottom of the pan. Top with whipped cream and walnuts.

Appetizer Salad

4 ripe tomatoes, peeled
4 new potatoes, boiled
1 avocado pear
Juice of 1 lemon
1 green pepper, seeded and boiled
1 head lettuce
French dressing (see below)
1 small onion, cut into thin rings

1 Peel tomatoes in the following manner: place a tomato on the end of a kitchen fork and hold in boiling water for a minute or two, until skin begins to crack. Remove from water and with a sharp knife gently peel skin from tomato. Cut in thick wedges. Peel potatoes and slice thickly. Peel and stone avocado pear and cut crosswise in thick slices. Brush slices with lemon juice to preserve colour. Cut boiled pepper into thick strips.

2 Wash lettuce leaves well in a large quantity of water. They should be left whole, never cut. Drain well and dry thoroughly in a cloth or a salad basket.

3 Make French dressing with 1 tablespoon wine vinegar and 3 tablespoons olive oil, generously seasoned with salt and freshly ground black pepper.

4 Line a salad bowl with lettuce leaves. Toss prepared vegetables lightly in French dressing and arrange in lettuce-lined bowl. Pour remaining dressing over salad and garnish with thinly sliced onion rings.

Spaghetti Bolognese

1 lb(450g) spaghetti
Butter, margarine or olive oil
$\frac{1}{4}$ lb(100g) fat salt pork or
   green bacon, finely chopped
1 Spanish onion, finely chopped
4 carrots, finely chopped
1 stalk celery, finely chopped
$\frac{1}{2}$ lb(225g) raw minced beef
1 strip of lemon peel
1 bay leaf
6 level tablespoons tomato purée
$\frac{1}{4}$ pint(4dl) beef stock
   (made with a cube)
Salt and freshly ground black pepper
Freshly grated nutmeg
Freshly grated Parmesan cheese

1 Heat 4 level tablespoons butter, margarine or olive oil in a large thick-bottomed frying pan; add finely chopped fat salt pork or green bacon, onion, carrots and celery and sauté over moderate heat, stirring occasionally, until meat browns.

2 Add minced beef and brown evenly, stirring continuously. Add lemon peel, bay leaf, tomato purée, beef stock, salt, freshly ground black pepper and nutmeg to taste. Cover pan and simmer very gently for half an hour, stirring occasionally.

3 Remove lemon peel and bay leaf and simmer, uncovered, for half an hour, or until sauce has slightly thickened.

4 Cook spaghetti in boiling water until tender. Drain. Dot with butter and serve with Bolognese sauce and freshly grated Parmesan cheese.

5 Another version of this famous dish tosses cooked spaghetti with Bolognese sauce; spoons it into an ovenproof baking dish; sprinkles it with grated Parmesan cheese; dots it with butter and bakes it in a moderate oven (375°F/190°C/Mark 5) until golden.

Italian Bean Salad

(illustrated on page 148)

$\frac{3}{4}$ lb(350g) fresh green beans
Lettuce leaves
2 tablespoons chopped parsley

GARLIC DRESSING:
6 tablespoons olive oil
Juice of 1 lemon
Salt and freshly ground black pepper
1–3 large cloves garlic, chopped

1 **To make dressing:** combine oil and lemon juice, adding salt, pepper and garlic.

2 Cook the beans in boiling salted water until just tender. Drain and toss with garlic dressing while still warm.

3 Line a bowl with lettuce leaves and arrange the green beans in the centre. Sprinkle with parsley and serve.

Cold Zabaglione

6 egg yolks
2 oz(50g) granulated sugar
6–8 tablespoons Marsala or sherry
1 level teaspoon gelatine
3 tablespoons brandy
$\frac{1}{4}$ teaspoon vanilla essence
$\frac{3}{8}$ pint(2dl) double cream, whipped
Grated lemon rind

1 In the top of a double saucepan, combine egg yolks with sugar and Marsala or sherry, and whip the mixture over hot but not boiling water until it thickens.

2 Stir in gelatine, softened in 2 tablespoons cold water and dissolved over hot water.

3 Put the pan in a bowl of ice and stir the *zabaglione* well until it is thick. When it is almost cold, fold in brandy, vanilla essence and whipped cream, and pour into glasses. Chill. Decorate with grated lemon rind.

Giving a Dinner Party

'As they eat,' goes an old Roman saying, 'so will your guests love and remember you.' This is as true today as it was over two thousand years ago. And yet, how easy it is to entertain today – thanks to modern cooking equipment, modern refrigeration and conveniently wrapped or packaged foods.

Now is the time to enliven meals at home with new foods, new wines and new table settings; to try out the party ideas in this section on the family, or on one or two close friends; to share with your loved one the small luxury of a superb new dish cooked just for the two of you.

Giving a dinner party for two, for four, or for more, can be wonderfully rewarding. Yet too many cooks seem to have too small a repertoire of favourite recipes. As a result, they repeat the same ones again and again.

Too many mothers allow themselves to be ruled by their children's lack of interest in trying out new dishes. How many times on my visits around the world have I met women who profess to be 'real gourmets', but who restrict their daily cooking to chops, steaks and hamburgers because 'that's what the children like'.

Every member of the household – from father to the youngest child – should be made to devote a little time to gastronomic exploration and innovation.

It's a dull diet indeed if every day, week in and week out, we sit down to the same things, varying this regular monotony perhaps with a few seasonal delicacies – strawberries, asparagus, summer fruits, game – as they first appear, and then falling back into the same old weary routine of daily eating.

We can get so much pleasure and excitement from ringing the changes in our daily menu; God knows, the shops are full of possibilities well within our reach, both gastronomically and economically. Whether you are feeding the family or special guests, just one new dish each week will make a dramatic difference to your culinary vocabulary and give them the pleasure of voting on your latest creations.

A word of caution, though: don't go overboard with too many completely new dishes at a time. One surprise is a conversation piece, but if you have a number of them, some will be ignored – and so will you, if any of them go wrong.

Let Perfect Coffee be the Perfect Finale to Every Dinner Party

'Black as night, sweet as love, hot as Hell' was the ancient Turk's recipe for coffee – the finale to every dinner party. No matter how you make it – drip, percolated, filter, expresso, or infused in an earthenware jug, the golden rules for perfect coffee remain the same: use freshly roasted or vacuum-packed coffee beans; grind them just before you're ready to use them, selecting the degree of fineness suitable for your method; never let coffee boil, or it will turn cloudy and lose its flavour; always serve coffee with hot, not boiling milk; and match blend and roast to the occasion, using milder coffee for the morning, strong black blends for after dinner.

Red Caviar Roll
(illustrated overleaf)

ROLL:
**Foil, olive oil and flour, for
    baking tin**
4 tablespoons butter
8 tablespoons plain flour
½ pint(3dl) hot milk
Salt
2 teaspoons castor sugar
Pinch of grated nutmeg
4 eggs, separated

FILLING:
6 oz(175g) cream cheese
1 tablespoon lemon juice
2 tablespoons sour cream
Freshly ground black pepper
¼ pint(1·5dl) double cream
3–4 tablespoons red caviar

GARNISH:
Sour cream
Red caviar

1 Preheat oven to moderately hot (400°F/200°C/Mark 6). Line a swiss roll tin 13 × 8 inches(33 × 20cm) with foil; brush with olive oil and dust with flour, shaking out excess.

2 To make roll: melt butter in a small pan; add 4 tablespoons flour and stir over a low heat to form a *roux*. Gradually stir in hot milk and cook gently, stirring constantly, until sauce thickens. Bring to the boil and simmer, stirring, for 3 to 4 minutes.

3 Pour sauce into a bowl. Beat in a pinch of salt, the sugar and small pinch of grated nutmeg.

4 Beat egg yolks lightly; pour into sauce in a thin stream, beating constantly. Cool.

5 Whisk egg whites with a pinch of salt until stiff but not dry. Fold a quarter into tepid sauce.

6 Fold in half of remaining flour, sifted, followed by a third of remaining whites, the rest of the flour, and finally all the remaining egg whites.

7 Pour mixture into prepared tin; level out with a spatula.

8 Bake for 5 minutes; lower oven temperature to 300°F/150°C/Mark 2 and continue to bake for 50 to 55 minutes, or until golden brown and springy.

9 Turn cake out on to a damp cloth lined with greaseproof paper. Remove foil and trim crusty edges. Roll cake loosely with cloth and paper. Cool.

10 To make filling: Blend cream cheese, lemon juice and sour cream together. Season to taste with freshly ground black pepper. Whip cream until light and fluffy; fold into cheese mixture, followed by red caviar. (Remember to reserve a little sour cream and red caviar as garnish.) Correct seasoning and chill until firm.

11 Unroll baked sponge, spread with filling and roll up like a swiss roll.

12 Serve cut in slices, each portion garnished with a little soured cream and a teaspoon of red caviar. Allow 2 thin slices per person as this is an extremely rich dish.

Boeuf à la Ficelle
(illustrated on page 165)

**6 tournedos steaks, about 6 oz(175g)
    each**
1½ lb(675g) carrots
1½ lb(675g) small, sweet turnips
**3 pints(1·7 litres) well-flavoured beef
    stock**
¾ lb(350g) button mushrooms
6 thin strips pork fat
Freshly ground black pepper
6 teaspoons brandy

> *menu*
>
> **Red Caviar Roll**
>
> **Boeuf à la Ficelle
> with
> Potatoes in Butter**
>
> **Nègre en Chemise**
>
> *Serves 6*

*with this menu I suggest
the following Medium-
priced White Wines*
Quincy
Chablis
**Pouilly Blanc
Fumé**
*or the following
Expensive Red Wines*
Moulin-à-Vent
Savigny-les-Beaune
Chambolle-Musigny

1 Peel carrots and cut them lengthwise into $\frac{1}{4}$-inch(0·5-cm) slices; then cut into thin strips $1\frac{1}{2}$ inches(4cm) long. Peel turnips and cut them into strips of the same size.

2 Select a wide, deep saucepan or casserole. Pour in stock, add carrot strips, bring to the boil and simmer for 10 minutes. Then add turnips and simmer for 5 minutes longer.

3 Clean and trim mushrooms; add to pan and continue to cook gently for another 5 minutes, or until all vegetables are tender.

4 Remove vegetables from stock with a spoon. Keep aside with a little of the stock.

5 Wrap a thin strip of pork fat round the middle of each tournedos. Cut 6 pieces of string long enough to go round each tournedos and hang over side of pan when meat is submerged in stock. Tie one end of each string quite firmly round each tournedos to keep pork fat in place.

6 **Just before serving:** bring stock to the boil and lower in tournedos side by side. Simmer for 5 minutes if you like them rare, 8 for medium, and 12 minutes for well done.

7 When tournedos are ready, remove from stock. Reheat vegetables in simmering stock.

8 Remove strings and strips of pork fat from tournedos and transfer steaks to a heated serving dish. Season with freshly ground black pepper and sprinkle with brandy. Garnish dish with vegetables; moisten with a little stock and serve immediately, accompanied by potatoes in butter and coarse salt.

Potatoes in Butter

$1\frac{1}{2}$–2 lb(675–900g) potatoes
2 oz(50g) clarified butter
2 tablespoons olive oil
Salt and freshly ground black pepper

Red Caviar Roll (page 163)

1 Peel and slice potatoes paper-thin. Rinse off excess starch under cold running water. Dry thoroughly.

2 Combine clarified butter with corn oil, and divide half between two 6-inch(15-cm) frying pans.

3 Arrange potato slices in pans in tight, overlapping circles, seasoning each layer generously with salt and freshly ground black pepper. Each cake should be $\frac{3}{4}$ inch(2cm) thick.

4 Pour remaining butter and oil over the top.

5 Cool potato 'cakes' over low heat for 15 minutes, or until crisp and golden brown underneath. Then turn out on to a plate; slip back into pans and cook for 10 to 15 minutes longer until cakes are golden brown all over and feel soft when pierced with a skewer.

6 Serve hot, cut in wedges.

Nègre en Chemise

6 oz(175g) trimmed white bread
$\frac{3}{4}$ pint(4dl) double cream
Softened butter
4 eggs
2 egg yolks
2 oz(50g) ground almonds
Castor sugar
6 oz(175g) bitter chocolate, melted

1 Shred and soak bread in half the cream for five minutes.

2 In a large bowl, beat 2 oz(50g) butter with a wooden spoon until fluffy. Work in soaked bread until completely blended. Add eggs, egg yolks, ground almonds and 1 oz(25g) sugar, beating vigorously between each addition. (Mixture may curdle when eggs are added, but this does not matter as chocolate will bind it again.)

3 Add half of egg mixture to melted chocolate and beat well; then combine with remaining egg mixture and continue to beat vigorously until thoroughly blended.

4 Butter a tall, tapering, $1\frac{1}{2}$-pint(8·5-dl) mould – a metal measuring jug will do – and line base with a circle of buttered greaseproof paper. Pour in chocolate mixture and make a slight hollow in the centre with the back of a spoon. Cover top of mould tightly with foil or a pudding cloth.

5 Place mould in a pan with water to come halfway up sides. Bring to the boil; cover pan and steam for $1\frac{1}{2}$ hours, topping up water in the pan as necessary.

6 To serve: whip remaining cream and sweeten lightly with castor sugar. Turn mould out; pipe generous swirls of cream around base and serve immediately before cream melts from heat of pudding.

Boeuf à la Ficelle

WINES

To Judge a Wine

Wine has a great appeal to the eye – we are all accustomed to judging and appreciating the colour and clarity of a wine – but it is your nose that gives the first intimation of how great a wine can be. All those loving expressions of a wine's quality – 'aroma', 'bouquet', 'nose', or its 'fruitiness' – are first picked up by that most elusive of our senses, the sense of smell. Then the sense of taste comes into play. Many wines have a lingering after-taste that is quite distinct in its impact on our taste buds from its 'original' taste. These, then, are the traits to look for in a wine: colour, clarity, 'nose', taste and after-taste. This is why drinking wine is such a rewarding experience; a good wine is not just an accompaniment to a good meal – it is something to inhale, to sip, to savour, and then to remember as a fabulous flavour-sensation to store in your memory so that you can judge and compare future wines at meals to come.

Red wines are almost always at their best with red meats, game and even some of the richer fish dishes such as salmon and carp. And in the summer – when the weather is at its hottest – I like to drink a light red Beaujolais or Fleurie 'on the rocks' as a refreshing accompaniment for any meal.

Wine is a living thing with its own distinctive character. Wine knowledge comes from drinking. The more wines you taste, the more you will enjoy them, the more you will know about them. White wines, except the sweet ones which can live for a generation, should be drunk when young. Red wines such as Beaujolais and the lighter Burgundies are almost always drunk when young. Red wines of quality need a little time to be at their best.

Choosing the right wine for the right dish is not as difficult as you may think. First of all, a fresh, dry white wine served slightly chilled – a flinty Chablis, a light Muscadet or Sancerre, a fuller flavoured Pouilly-Fuissé, Pouilly-Fumé or Puligny Montrachet – provides the perfect accompaniment to most first courses, *quiches,* flans, and all fish and chicken dishes. Serve a chilled dry white wine or rosé, too, in the hot summer months to accompany cold or grilled meats and veal and lamb dishes. You'll find the cooling light freshness of dry whites and rosés the perfect foil for summer dining.

Low-Priced White Wines

Bourgogne Aligoté
Cabernet Blanc
Chablis
Chaud Soleil Blanc
Chevalier d'Alsace
Chianti Ruffino White
Coquillages
Lachryma Christi
Mâcon Blanc
Mâcon-Vire
Médoc
Muscadet
Oustalet Blanc
Pouilly Blanc Fumé
Quincy
Retsina

Riesling
Sancerre
Saumur Blanc
Soave
Sylvaner d'Alsace
Touraine Sauvignon
Verdicchio
Vinho Verde
Vouvray

Medium-Priced White Wines
Chablis
Meursault
Pouilly Blanc Fumé
Pouilly Fuissé
Puligny Montrachet
Quincy
Riesling d'Alsace
Sancerre
Felstar
Adgerstone
Hambledon

Moulin-à-Vent
Nuits-St-Georges
Pomerol
Pommard
St Emilion

Expensive White Wines
Cheval Blanc
Corton-Charlemagne
Montrachet
Petrus

Low-Priced Rosé Wines
Rosé d'Anjou
Rosé de Provence
Tavel

Low-Priced Red Wines
Barolo
Beaujolais
Beaujolais Fleurie
Beaujolais Villages
Bordeaux Supérieur
Bourgueil
Cabernet Red
Châteauneuf-du-Pape
Chianti Ruffino Red
Chinon
Côtes-du-Rhône
Fleurie
Gigondas
Mâcon Rouge
Médoc
Pomerol
Pommard
Rioja Red
Serradayres
Valpolicella

Medium-Priced Rosé Wines
Rosé de Provence
Tavel

Medium-Priced Red Wines
Aloxe Corton
Barolo
Beaune
Brouilly
Côtes de Bourg
Côtes-du-Rhône
Côte-Rôtie
Médoc
Mercurey
Morgon

Expensive Red Wines
Bonnes Mares
Chambertin
Chambolle-Musigny
Clos de Vougeot
La Tache
Moulin-à-Vent
Musigny
Richebourg
Savigny-les-Beaune

	Muscadet	Sancerre	Chablis/Pouilly	Mâconnais	Champagne Nature	Alsace	Graves Secs	Bourgognes Blancs	Entre-Deux-Mers	Graves Doux	Vouvray	Saumur	Côtes-du-Rhône	Bourgueil/Chinon	Beaujolais-Fleurie	Côtes de Bordeaux	Médoc	St-Emilion	Côtes de Beaune	Bourgognes Rouges	Côtes-Rôties	Rosés Doux	Rosés Secs	Sauternes and Dessert Wines	Champagnes
Cold Hors-d'Oeuvres	X	X	X	X	X	X		X															X		
Hot Hors-d'Oeuvres			X		X			X																	
Oysters, Mussels, etc.	X	X	X	X	X	X		X																	
Caviar			X		X																				X
Smoked Salmon	X	X	X		X																				
Foie Gras, Pâtés, etc.			X		X																				
Cooked Egg Dishes and Omelettes	X	X	X		X	X					X	X											X		
Cooked Fish, Shellfish-Hot	X	X	X	X	X	X	X	X	X														X		
Cooked Fish and Shellfish-Cold	X	X	X			X	X																X		
Tripe, Sweetbreads, Offal	X	X	X	X	X	X		X					X	X				X					X		
Roast Chicken, Turkey, etc.			X					X					X	X	X	X	X	X							
Roast Duck and Game Birds													X	X	X	X		X	X	X	X				
Roast Game													X	X	X	X		X	X	X	X				
Beef-Grilled and Roast													X	X	X	X	X	X	X	X	X				
Beef-Sauced													X	X	X	X	X								
Veal-Grilled and Roast			X	X	X								X					X					X		
Lamb-Grilled and Roast													X	X		X	X	X							
Veal and Lamb-Sauced													X			X		X							
Pork													X	X		X	X	X		X					
Ham													X	X		X	X						X		
Cheese, Fermented													X	X	X	X	X	X	X	X					
Cheese, Fresh	X	X	X		X			X										X							
Sweets, Puddings, Cakes, etc.				X						X	X	X						X				X	X	X	X

167

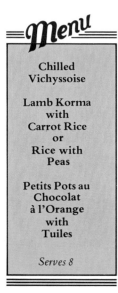

*with this menu I suggest
the following Inexpensive
White Wines or Rosés*
**Sancerre
Bourgogne Aligoté
Tavel Rosé**

Chilled Vichyssoise

9 large leeks, white parts only
Salt
6 tablespoons butter
6 medium-sized potatoes
2½ pints (1·4 litres) chicken stock
Freshly ground black pepper
Freshly grated nutmeg
¾ pint(4dl) double cream
Finely chopped chives

1 Wash leeks carefully and cut into 1-inch(2·5-cm) lengths. Melt butter in a large pan; add leeks and sauté gently until soft, taking great care not to let them colour.

2 Peel and slice potatoes and add to leeks, together with chicken stock. Simmer gently until vegetables are soft, adding salt, freshly ground black pepper and freshly grated nutmeg towards the end of cooking time.

3 Force vegetables and stock through a fine sieve, or blend until smooth in an electric blender. Chill.

4 Just before serving, stir in cream and taste for seasoning. Serve sprinkled with finely chopped chives.

Lamb Korma

3 lb(1·4kg) boneless leg of lamb
½ pint(3dl) plain yoghourt
½ teaspoon ground cardamom
1 teaspoon ground cumin
1½ teaspoons ground turmeric
¼ lb(100g) dessicated coconut
2 tablespoons butter
½ pint(3dl) milk
4–6 tablespoons olive oil
¾ lb(350g) Spanish onions, chopped
2 cloves garlic, finely chopped
1 teaspoon each ground ginger and
   dry mustard
½ teaspoon each freshly ground black
   pepper, cayenne and cinnamon

Generous pinch of ground cloves
2 medium-sized tomatoes, peeled,
   seeded and diced
Salt
2 teaspoons lemon juice

1 Cut lamb into 1-inch(2·5-cm) cubes, trimming off excess fat.

2 In a bowl, mix yoghourt with cardamom, cumin and turmeric; add lamb and toss until thoroughly coated. Cover bowl and leave to marinate for 1 hour.

3 Place coconut, butter and milk in a heavy pan and bring to the boil over moderate heat, stirring until butter has melted. Simmer for 15 minutes; then strain through a fine sieve. Put coconut and milk aside in separate bowls.

4 In a large pan, heat half the oil; add lamb, together with yoghourt marinade, and cook over high heat, stirring, for 5 minutes. Remove from heat.

5 Heat remaining oil in a frying pan and sauté onions and garlic until soft and golden. Remove pan from heat; add remaining spices and mix well. Cook, stirring, for 2 minutes longer to blend flavours.

6 Add onion mixture to lamb, together with diced tomatoes, coconut milk and a little salt, to taste. Bring to the boil slowly, stirring occasionally, and simmer, covered, for 30 minutes; then uncover pan and simmer for 30 minutes longer, or until lamb is very tender and sauce is rich and thick.

7 Just before serving, stir in lemon juice and season with a little more salt if necessary. If sauce seems too thin, add some of the reserved coconut and simmer for 2 to 3 minutes longer.

8 Serve with **carrot rice** (see next page) and the usual curry accompaniments: chutneys, pappadoms, preserved kumquats, etc.

Carrot Rice

Salt
4 tablespoons lemon juice
1 lb(450g) long-grain rice
¼ lb(100g) coarsely grated raw carrot

1 Bring a large pan of water to the boil with salt and lemon juice. Dribble in rice through your fingers: stir once to dislodge any grains stuck to the bottom of the pan, and simmer for 15 to 18 minutes until the rice is just tender, with each grain separate.

2 Drain rice in a colander, then rinse well with boiling water, shaking out as much moisture as possible.

3 Fold in grated carrot gently with a fork and season to taste with a little more salt if necessary.

Rice with Peas

1 Sauté 1 chopped Spanish onion and 1 lb(450g) rice in 4 level tablespoons butter until rice is translucent. Add water and boil rice as usual (see page 70) with salt and lemon juice, as above. Drain in a colander.

2 Toss a small packet of frozen peas in a small saucepan with 4 level tablespoons butter until tender; add drained rice and heat through. Season with salt and freshly ground black pepper, to taste.

Lamb Korma with Carrot Rice

Petits Pots au Chocolat à l'Orange

½ lb(225g) dark, bitter chocolate
3 oranges (2 large, 1 medium-sized)
2 oz(50g) butter
Grand Marnier or cognac
4 eggs, separated

1 Break chocolate into the top of a double saucepan. Finely grate the rinds of 2 large oranges; squeeze their juice and add both juice and rind to chocolate, together with butter. Heat over simmering water, stirring occasionally, until chocolate has melted. Then remove from heat; add 2 tablespoons Grand Marnier or cognac and beat until smooth.

2 In a bowl, beat egg yolks thoroughly. Strain in chocolate mixture through a fine sieve, beating constantly. Cool.

3 In another bowl, beat egg whites until stiff but not dry. Fold into chocolate mixture gently but thoroughly with a spatula.

4 Pour mixture into 8 individual ¼-pint (1·5-dl) pots or soufflé dishes and chill until set. (Do not use metal pots, as chocolate may discolour.)

5 **Just before serving:** cut 4 thin slices from the centre of remaining orange. Quarter each slice and lay 2 quarters, point to point, on top of each pot. Pour over a teaspoonful of Grand Marnier or cognac; swirl pot around very gently so that entire surface is moistened and serve immediately, accompanied by a dish of **tuiles** (see below).

Tuiles

Makes about 50
5 **tablespoons softened butter**
5 **tablespoons plain flour**
1 **tablespoon cornflour**
2 **egg whites**

3 oz(75g) castor sugar
1 oz(25g) ground almonds
Vanilla and almond essence
2 oz(50g) flaked almonds

1 Put aside 2 tablespoons each butter and flour for baking sheets.

2 Preheat oven to fairly hot (425°F/220°C/Mark 7).

3 Sift remaining flour with cornflour 3 times.

4 Mix egg whites lightly with a fork to break down gelatinous threads.

5 Beat remaining butter with sugar until fluffy. Add egg whites gradually, beating vigorously. Fold in sifted flour, followed by ground almonds. Flavour with a few drops of vanilla and a drop of almond essence.

6 Butter 2 baking sheets and sprinkle generously with flour. Shake off excess.

7 Drop mixture on to them in small globules (about ½ teaspoon each) 2 inches (5cm) apart. With a damp knife blade, spread each globule out into a very thin disc about 1½ inches(4cm) in diameter. Make sure discs are evenly thin throughout: if slightly thicker in the centre, *tuiles* will be spongy instead of crisp. Sprinkle each disc with a few almond flakes.

8 Bake for 5 minutes, or until *tuiles* are golden, with a fine brown fringe.

9 Have ready a rolling pin and/or any other cold metal, glass or wooden object with a similarly curved surface.

10 As soon as *tuiles* come out of the oven, quickly remove each one with palette knife and curve it round prepared shaping tool, nutty side up. Leave for a minute or two to harden; then dislodge and transfer to a cooling rack.

Chilled Pea Soup

¾ lb(350g) shelled fresh or frozen peas
1 medium-sized potato, sliced
1 medium-sized onion, sliced
1 lettuce, quartered
1 pint(6dl) chicken stock
½ pint(3dl) double cream
Juice of ½ lemon
Salt and freshly ground black pepper
Lemon slices and salted whipped
    cream to decorate

1 Place peas, sliced potato, onion and quartered lettuce in a large pan. Add half the chicken stock and bring to the boil. Cover and simmer for 15 minutes.

2 Blend contents of pan to a smooth purée in an electric blender, or press vegetables and stock through a fine sieve.

3 Return purée to pan. Add remaining stock and simmer for 5 minutes.

4 Stir in cream and lemon juice and season to taste with salt and freshly ground black pepper. Cool soup; then correct seasoning and chill until ready to serve.

5 Serve soup in individual bowls, garnished with very thin slices of lemon which you have topped with a swirl of lightly salted whipped cream.

Roast Stuffed Shoulder of Lamb

(illustrated on page 173)

1 boned shoulder of lamb,
    3½–4lb(1·6–1·8kg)
2 tablespoons flour
Salt and freshly ground black pepper
2 tablespoons melted butter
2 tablespoons olive oil

STUFFING:
½ Spanish onion, finely chopped

4 tablespoons butter
Two 6-oz(175-g) packets of frozen
    spinach
½ lb(225g) pork sausage meat
1 egg, beaten
1 tablespoon chopped parsley
Generous pinch each of rosemary and
    thyme
Salt and freshly ground black pepper
Pinch of freshly grated nutmeg

1 Have your butcher bone the shoulder of lamb but leave it unrolled. Lay meat out flat on a board, skin side down. Cut out any excess fat with a sharp knife, taking care not to pierce outer skin.

2 To make stuffing: sauté chopped onion in half the butter until transparent.

3 Heat spinach gently in an uncovered pan until completely defrosted; drain thoroughly in a sieve, pressing firmly with the back of a spoon; then simmer gently in remaining butter until cooked.

4 In a large bowl, combine onion and spinach with sausage meat, beaten egg, chopped parsley, rosemary and thyme. Season with salt, freshly ground black pepper and freshly grated nutmeg. Mix well.

5 Preheat oven to slow (325°F/170°C/ Mark 3).

6 With a needle and thread, 'sew' any holes in outer skin of lamb.

7 Spread stuffing over meat, filling all crevices so that when joint is rolled and sliced stuffing will produce a marbled effect.

8 If there are any loose flaps at the end of meat, bring them up over the stuffing. Then bring sides of meat together and sew securely along every seam, pushing stuffing back into meat if it tends to seep out, and making a neat, smooth roll.

Menu

Chilled Pea Soup

Roast Stuffed
Shoulder of Lamb
with
Avocado Pilaff

Peaches in White
Wine

Serves 4–6

*with this menu I suggest
the following Inexpensive
Red Wines*
**Macon Rouge
Beaujolais
Valpolicella**

9 Dust meat with flour and season with salt and freshly ground black pepper.

10 Place a sheet of foil in a roasting tin and lay meat on top; bring up sides of foil slightly, but do not seal meat. Pour over melted butter and olive oil.

11 Roast for 2 hours, basting occasionally with pan juices. Then raise heat to 400°F/200°C/Mark 6, open foil out and roast lamb for about 30 minutes longer, or until golden brown and cooked to your liking.

12 Serve on a large, heated platter, accompanied by an **avocado pilaff** (see below).

Avocado Pilaff

¼ lb(100g) fresh butter
4 tablespoons finely chopped onion
½ lb(225g) long-grain rice
4 tablespoons dry white wine
1¼ pints(7dl) beef stock
Salt
¼ lb(100g) button mushrooms, sliced
½ teaspoon finely chopped garlic
¼ lb(100g) fresh tomatoes, peeled, seeded and diced
¼ teaspoon dried oregano
Freshly ground black pepper
1 avocado pear
Lemon juice

1 Preheat oven to moderately hot (400°F/200°C/Mark 6).

2 Melt half the butter in a heavy casserole; add onion and sauté for 1 minute. Add rice and cook, stirring over moderate heat for another minute.

3 Pour in wine and stock; season to taste with salt and bring to the boil. Cover tightly and transfer to oven.

4 Bake for 18 minutes, stirring rice once with a fork halfway through cooking time.

5 Sauté mushrooms in 2 tablespoons butter for 3 minutes; add garlic, tomatoes and oregano, and season to taste with salt and freshly ground black pepper. Simmer for 5 minutes.

6 Peel and dice avocado; brush pieces with lemon juice. Add to mushroom mixture, stir once and remove from heat.

7 Toss rice gently with mushrooms and avocado mixture and remaining butter. Serve hot.

Peaches in White Wine

4–6 large peaches or 8–12 small peaches
1 lb(450g) sugar
2 cloves
3 sticks cinnamon
2–3 strips of orange and lemon rind
½ pint(3dl) medium dry white wine

1 In a large, wide saucepan, dissolve sugar in ½ pint(3dl) water over very low heat; add cloves, cinnamon sticks and orange and lemon rind (pared off with an apple peeler). Then carefully drop peaches into syrup and simmer uncovered for 10 minutes.

2 Add wine and continue to simmer for a further 10 minutes, taking care not to let peaches become mushy. Remove from heat.

3 Take peaches, one by one, from syrup with a slotted spoon, and holding gently with a towel so as not to burn your hand, carefully peel off skin with your fingers. Arrange skinned peaches on a serving dish.

4 Simmer cooking juices until reduced to a light syrup. Cool syrup and spoon over peaches. Chill until ready to serve.

Roast Stuffed Shoulder of Lamb with Avocado Pilaff
(pages 171 and 172)

Menu

Caviar
d'Aubergines

Pillows of Chicken
with
Purée Clamart

Souffléed Oranges

Serves 6

*with this menu I suggest
the following Inexpensive
White Wines or Rosés*
**Sancerre
Bourgogne Aligoté
Tavel Rosé**

Caviar d'Aubergines

(illustrated on page 176)

4 large aubergines
2 Spanish onions, finely chopped
2 cloves garlic, crushed
¼ teaspoon oregano
5–6 tablespoons chopped parsley
6 tablespoons olive oil
Two 14-oz(400-g) cans tomatoes,
   drained and chopped
Salt and freshly ground black pepper
Generous pinch of sugar
6 small black olives, pitted and halved

1 Preheat oven to moderate (350°F/180°C/
Mark 4).

2 Bake aubergines for about 20 minutes.

3 In a saucepan, sauté onions, garlic, oregano and 4 tablespoons parsley in olive oil
until onions are soft and golden.

4 Add tomatoes and simmer for about 5
minutes longer until ingredients have amal-
gamated into a sauce.

5 When aubergines are soft, peel off skins;
drain pulp thoroughly and chop finely.

6 Stir aubergine pulp into tomato-onion
mixture; season with salt, freshly ground
black pepper and sugar and simmer for
about 10 minutes longer, stirring until well
blended.

7 Turn mixture into a shallow serving dish
and allow to cool.

8 Serve cold, garnished with remaining
parsley and pitted, halved black olives.

Pillows of Chicken

(illustrated on page 176)

1½ roasting chickens,
   3–3½ lb(1·3–1·5kg) each
Flour
3 tablespoons olive oil
7½ tablespoons butter
Salt and freshly ground black pepper
½ pint(3dl) chicken stock
¾ lb(350g) button mushrooms
9 tablespoons Madeira
4–6 tablespoons cream
¾ lb(350g) puff pastry
Lightly beaten egg yolk, to glaze

1 **Prepare chicken joints:** with a sharp
knife, cut legs off close to body, then
separate drumsticks and thighs.

2 Bone both thighs; roll meat firmly into
sausage shapes.

3 Take drumsticks and cut in down to
bone to loosen flesh. Holding bone firmly
between finger and thumb, pull flesh down
and over the end in one movement, turning
flesh inside out; separate flesh from bone and
turn right side out again.

4 Slice down one side of breast as close to
breastbone as possible; then take knife right
across wing bone and through joint to sever
breast from carcass. Repeat with the other 2
breasts.

5 Remove winglets and the other wing
bone from each breast; cut breasts in half and
roll each piece tightly into a sausage. You
will now have 6 boned leg joints and 6 from
breasts.

6 Make a rich stock with carcass.

7 Dust chicken pieces with flour. In a heavy
casserole, sauté chicken pieces in half the oil
and 3 tablespoons butter until golden
brown, seasoning generously with salt and
freshly ground black pepper.

8 Strain chicken stock over chicken; cover and simmer for 20 minutes, or until tender. Cool.

9 Slice mushrooms thinly. Sauté in remaining oil and 3 tablespoons butter until golden. Season with salt and freshly ground black pepper and moisten with 6 tablespoons Madeira. Cool.

10 Make a sauce: melt $1\frac{1}{2}$ tablespoons butter in a heavy pan; add 3 tablespoons flour and stir over a moderate heat until a deep golden colour. Remove from heat.

11 Beat in remaining Madeira and juices from cooked chicken; return pan to heat and stir in cream. Bring to the boil, stirring constantly to make a smooth sauce.

12 Fold in half the mushrooms and simmer for 20 minutes longer, adding a little more stock if sauce becomes too thick.

13 Preheat oven to fairly hot (425°F/ 220°C/Mark 7).

14 Divide pastry into 6. Roll each piece out and cut into a 6-inch(15-cm) square. Make decorative leaves out of trimmings (2 or 3 per portion).

15 Place 1 piece chicken breast and 1 piece leg on each square of pastry; cover with a sixth of remaining mushrooms. Moisten with some of the mushroom juices; then fold pastry up over filling like an envelope and seal tightly, brushing seams with a little beaten egg yolk.

16 Arrange 'pillows' on a baking sheet, seam side down. Glaze with beaten egg yolk; decorate with pastry leaves and glaze these as well.

17 Bake for 20 to 25 minutes, or until 'pillows' are well risen, crisp and golden.

18 Reheat sauce and serve with chicken.

Purée Clamart

$1\frac{1}{2}$ **lb(675g) frozen peas**
6 tablespoons butter
6 tablespoons strong chicken stock
 (made with a cube if necessary)
$\frac{1}{2}$ **Spanish onion, very finely chopped**
Salt and freshly ground black pepper
About $\frac{1}{2}$ lb(225g) floury potatoes

1 Cover peas with cold water and bring to the boil. Drain.

2 Return peas to pan with butter, chicken stock, very finely chopped onion and a pinch each of salt and freshly ground black pepper; cover and simmer until peas are tender and have absorbed most of liquid.

3 Meanwhile, peel potatoes and boil in salted water. Drain; toss over moderate heat to evaporate remaining moisture; then pass through a sieve. Put about half of purée in a large bowl.

4 Purée cooked peas, together with any remaining liquid, in an electric blender. (Do not use a sieve.)

5 Gradually add blended peas to potato purée in bowl, beating vigorously. If purée does not hold its shape when lifted with a spoon, beat in a little more potato. (Amount of potato depends entirely on moisture of pea purée.)

6 Add more salt or freshly ground black pepper if necessary, and keep hot over a pan of simmering water until ready to serve.

Souffléed Oranges

6 large oranges
6 egg yolks
6 tablespoons castor sugar
6 tablespoons Grand Marnier or
 Marsala
8 fl oz(225ml) double cream, whipped

TO DECORATE:
Whipped cream
Powdered cocoa or grated chocolate
6 lemon, camellia or other glossy leaves

1 Carefully slice off tops of oranges with a sharp knife. Scoop out all the pulp and enough of the pith to leave a firm shell. Reserve pulp and juices for another use.

2 Combine egg yolks, castor sugar and Grand Marnier or Marsala in a bowl. Beat until smooth and creamy.

3 Fold in whipped cream to make a fairly liquid mixture.

4 Fill orange shells with cream mixture and freeze in the top of the refrigerator until firm, preferably overnight.

5 Just before serving, decorate tops with piped whipped cream; dust each orange lightly with cocoa or grated chocolate and spike with a lemon, camellia or other glossy green leaf.

6 Serve with *petits fours* or macaroons.

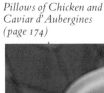

Pillows of Chicken and Caviar d' Aubergines (page 174)

Four Dinners Based on Game

Grouse is the first of our game birds. To make the most of this succulent bird this Autumn, fill it with a 'moistening' mixture of well-seasoned lemon juice and butter, top it with a protective cover of fat bacon and roast it in a fairly hot oven. Grouse should be pink and moist, not dry and overcooked.

The traditional accompaniment to roast game birds – grouse, partridge and pheasant – is a *croûton* of bread, cut in a rectangle or heart shape, fried in clarified butter and a little olive oil. The livers of the birds, drawn from the carcass halfway through its cooking time and allowed to continue to cook in the pan juices, are pounded and spread on the *croûton* with a little *foie gras* and seasoned with a little salt and cayenne pepper.

I like to serve game accompanied by a crisp watercress salad and a choice of bread sauce, browned breadcrumbs and tart rowan or redcurrant jelly; or, for a more substantial meal, with a rich Red Cabbage-in-the-Pot.

Menu

Orange
Vinaigrette

Roast Grouse
with
Red Cabbage-in-
the-Pot

Chocolate Ice
Cream Mexicaine

Serves 4–6

with this menu I suggest the following Medium-priced Red Wines
**Moulin-à-Vent
St Emilion
Pommard**

Orange Vinaigrette

4–6 ripe oranges

OLIVE AND HERB VINAIGRETTE SAUCE:
6 tablespoons olive oil
2 tablespoons wine vinegar
12 black olives, finely chopped
½ Spanish onion, finely chopped
2–3 tablespoons chopped fresh mint
1 tablespoon chopped fresh parsley
Salt and freshly ground black pepper
Cayenne pepper

1 Peel oranges, removing all pith, and slice crosswise.

2 **To make sauce:** combine olive oil, wine vinegar, finely chopped olives, onion and herbs in a mixing bowl. Season to taste with salt, freshly ground black pepper and cayenne. Mix well.

3 Toss orange slices in vinaigrette sauce.

Roast Grouse

4–6 young grouse, ¾–1 lb (350–450g) each
4–6 tablespoons softened butter
Juice of 1 lemon
Salt and freshly ground black pepper
4–6 bacon rashers
4–6 croûtons of bread big enough to serve as base for grouse
Clarified butter
1 tablespoon olive oil
Cayenne pepper
Watercress
Bread sauce or browned breadcrumbs
Tart rowan or redcurrant jelly

1 Combine softened butter and lemon juice in a mixing bowl, seasoning with salt and freshly ground black pepper, to taste.

2 Fill birds with this moistening mixture. Tie a thin rasher of fat bacon over the breast of each bird and roast in a fairly hot oven (425°F/220°C/Mark 7) for 20 to 25 minutes, 25 to 30 minutes if you prefer your birds less rare. When birds are half cooked remove livers; mash them slightly and place in pan to cook with grouse until birds are tender.

3 **Just before serving:** fry *croûtons* in a little clarified butter and olive oil until golden. Spread with mashed livers and crusty bits from pan and season with salt and cayenne.

4 **To serve:** remove bacon and string; place one bird on each *croûton* and arrange on a heated serving dish. Garnish with watercress and serve with bread sauce or browned breadcrumbs and tart rowan or redcurrant jelly.

Red Cabbage-in-the-Pot

1 red cabbage, about 2 lb(900g)
4 tablespoons butter
½ lb(225g) onions, sliced
1 lb(450g) cooking apples, peeled,
    cored and quartered
2 cloves garlic, finely chopped
¼ teaspoon each of powdered nutmeg,
    allspice, cinnamon, thyme and
    caraway seed
Salt
Freshly ground black pepper
1 teaspoon grated orange rind
2 strips orange peel
2 tablespoons brown sugar
½ pint(3dl) red wine
2 tablespoons wine vinegar

1 Wash and shred cabbage, removing central core, ribs and outer leaves. Cook in butter in a covered saucepan for 5 minutes.

2 Place cabbage, onions and apples in a deep ovenproof casserole in layers until casserole is full. Season each layer with finely chopped garlic, spices and salt and freshly ground black pepper, to taste, grated orange rind and orange peel. Sprinkle brown sugar over the top and add wine, wine vinegar and a little hot water.

3 Cover and simmer in a moderate oven (375°F/190°C/Mark 5) until tender, adding a little more wine if necessary.

Chocolate Ice Cream Mexicaine

4–6 scoops chocolate ice cream
12 tablespoons Tia Maria liqueur
Whipped cream, unsweetened
Slivered toasted almonds

1 Place one scoop ice cream in each bowl.

2 Spoon over Tia Maria and garnish with whipped cream and slivered almonds.

Sorrel Soup

1 Spanish onion, finely chopped
3 level tablespoons butter
1 large potato, sliced
3 level tablespoons flour
Salt and white pepper
2 pints(1·2 litres) chicken stock
    (made with a cube)
3–4 packed cups of sorrel leaves,
    washed and stems removed
2 egg yolks
¼ pint(1·5dl) double cream
Lemon juice
Few drops Tabasco

1 Simmer finely chopped onion gently in butter until onion is transparent. Add sliced potato, sprinkle in flour, salt and white pepper to taste and continue cooking over a low heat, stirring constantly, for 3 minutes more.

2 Remove saucepan from the heat and beat in the boiling chicken stock. Add sorrel leaves and allow to simmer for 5 minutes more; then force through a fine sieve.

3 Blend egg yolks and double cream in a small bowl. Pour in a little of the hot soup, beating vigorously. Gradually beat in remainder of soup. Correct seasoning with salt, white pepper, lemon juice and Tabasco to taste. Cool. Chill.

Pheasant with Green Apples

1 pheasant
¼ lb(100g) green bacon, diced
½ Spanish onion, finely chopped
1 clove garlic, finely chopped
2 tablespoons butter
2 tablespoons olive oil
4 small cooking apples, peeled, cored
    and thickly sliced
4 tablespoons Cointreau
½ pint(3dl) cream
Salt and freshly ground black pepper

Menu

Sorrel Soup

Pheasant with Green Apples with Sautéed Mushrooms à la Bordelaise

Fresh Grape Tart

Serves 4

with this menu I suggest the following Medium-priced Red Wines
**Médoc
St Emilion
Pomerol**

1 Sauté diced green bacon and finely chopped onion and garlic in butter and olive oil in a fireproof casserole until golden. Remove and reserve.

2 Brown pheasant on all sides in resulting mixture of fats. Remove and keep warm.

3 Sauté apples in remaining fat until they start to turn golden. Add Cointreau. Remove apples from casserole and skim fat from remaining juices.

4 Return pheasant to casserole; surround with apple slices, bacon, onion and garlic; simmer, covered, for 10 minutes.

5 Stir in cream, add salt and freshly ground

Fresh Grape Tart

black pepper, to taste; cover casserole and cook in a very slow oven (275°F/140°C/Mark 1) until pheasant is tender.

6 When ready to serve, remove pheasant and bacon bits to a clean casserole and keep warm; purée sauce and apples. Correct seasoning; reheat sauce; pour over pheasant and serve immediately.

Sautéed Mushrooms à la Bordelaise

8–12 large flat mushrooms
2 tablespoons olive oil
2 level tablespoons butter
Salt and freshly ground black pepper
2 tablespoons chopped parsley
1–2 cloves garlic, finely chopped

1 Wash mushrooms and trim stalks. Combine oil and butter in a large frying pan; add mushrooms and sauté on both sides until tender, adding a little more oil or butter, if necessary. Season with salt and freshly ground black pepper and keep warm.

2 Just before serving, sprinkle with chopped parsley and garlic and serve immediately.

Fresh Grape Tart

FINGERTIP PASTRY:
$\frac{1}{2}$ lb(225g) plain flour
Pinch of salt
2 tablespoons icing sugar
5 oz(150g) softened butter
1 egg yolk

FILLING:
$\frac{1}{2}$ lb(225g) green grapes
$\frac{1}{2}$ lb(225g) black grapes

APRICOT GLAZE:
$\frac{1}{2}$ pint(3dl) apricot jam
Kirsch

Rabbit with Mustard
(page 182)

DECORATION (optional):
1 egg white
1 small bunch black grapes
Castor sugar

1 To make pastry: sieve flour, salt and sugar into a mixing bowl. Rub in butter with the tips of the fingers until mixture resembles fine breadcrumbs. Do this very gently and lightly, or mixture will become greasy and heavy. Beat egg yolk and add 4 tablespoons cold water; sprinkle over dough and work in lightly with fingers. Shape moist dough lightly into a flattened round; wrap in plastic and leave in refrigerator for at least 1 hour to ripen.

2 If chilled dough is too firm for handling, allow to stand at room temperature until it softens slightly. Then turn it out on to a floured board and roll out as required. Line flan ring and prick with a fork. Bake 'blind'

in a preheated oven 450°F/230°C/Mark 8 for 15 minutes; lower heat to 350°F/180°C/Mark 4 and bake for 30 minutes. If crust becomes too brown at edges, cover with a little crumpled foil.

3 Peel, halve and pip green grapes; halve and pip black grapes. Arrange grapes in colourful segments in baked tart shell, leaving one bunch aside for decoration.

4 To make apricot glaze: add 4 to 6 tablespoons water to apricot jam and heat, stirring constantly, until liquid. Flavour to taste with Kirsch. Spoon over grapes and leave to set.

5 Finally, lightly beat the egg white. Dip the bunch of grapes into the white, holding it by the stalk. Drain slightly and then roll gently in castor sugar. Leave to dry and then place in centre of flan.

Menu

Grilled Pepper Salad

Rabbit with Mustard with Buttered Spinach with Rosemary

Old Fashioned Fruit Pie

Serves 6

with this menu I suggest the following Inexpensive White Wines
Lachryma Christi Chianti Ruffino White
or the following Inexpensive Red Wines
Barolo Valpolicella

Grilled Pepper Salad

6 sweet peppers
12 anchovy fillets
3 cloves garlic, finely chopped
3 level tablespoons finely chopped parsley
4 tablespoons olive oil
2 teaspoons lemon juice
Freshly ground black pepper and salt
Lemon juice, finely chopped parsley and garlic (optional)

1 Place peppers side by side in a grill–pan and grill steadily under moderate heat until their skins blister and blacken all over, and peppers become rather limp. Keep turning them so that every part is exposed to the heat.

2 Plunge grilled peppers into a large bowl of cold water. Leave them for 2 minutes; then drain and peel. Skins will slip off quite easily if peppers have been correctly and evenly grilled. Slice peppers in half; cut out pith and rinse out seeds under cold running water. Pat each piece of pepper dry and cut it in four across the width.

3 Cut anchovy fillets into $\frac{1}{4}$-inch(0·5-cm) lengths and combine them in a deep serving dish with peppers, finely chopped garlic and parsley. Toss lightly until well mixed.

4 Heat olive oil with lemon juice in a small pan. When it is very hot, pour all over the peppers and mix lightly. Leave to become quite cold – the dressing helps to develop and blend flavours together as it cools in a way that a simple cold dressing could never do. Serve chilled.

Note: This dish is so strongly flavoured that you are unlikely to need salt; but taste and judge for yourself before adding freshly ground black pepper, additional lemon juice, if desired, and an additional sprinkling of finely chopped parsley and finely chopped garlic.

Rabbit with Mustard
(illustrated on previous page)

$3-3\frac{1}{2}$ lb(1·3–1·5kg) rabbit, enough to make 12 serving pieces
2 tablespoons flour
Salt and freshly ground black pepper
2 tablespoons olive oil
2 tablespoons butter
$\frac{1}{4}$ lb(100g) fat bacon, diced and blanched
4 shallots, chopped
Bouquet garni
$\frac{1}{4}$ pint(1·5dl) dry white wine
$\frac{1}{4}$ pint(1·5dl) chicken stock
1 teaspoon Dijon mustard
1 teaspoon English mustard
$\frac{1}{2}$ pint(3dl) double cream

1 Cut rabbit into 12 serving pieces; roll pieces in seasoned flour, and sauté until golden in olive oil and butter with bacon.

2 Add chopped shallots and *bouquet garni*; moisten with wine and stock, cover and cook gently until rabbit is tender.

3 Drain rabbit pieces; place them in a heated bowl and keep warm. Skim fat from sauce; whisk Dijon mustard and English mustard thoroughly with fresh cream and add to sauce in pan. Correct seasoning, adding a little more mustard, salt or pepper if desired. Add rabbit pieces; heat through and serve in casserole.

Buttered Spinach with Rosemary

4 level tablespoons butter
$1\frac{1}{2}$ lb(675g) frozen leaf spinach
1–2 level teaspoons crushed dried rosemary
Salt and freshly ground black pepper

1 Melt butter in a heavy pan; add frozen spinach and allow to thaw over very low heat, stirring occasionally.

2 When spinach has thawed completely, sprinkle with crushed dried rosemary and season to taste with salt and freshly ground black pepper. Cover pan and simmer gently, stirring or shaking pan occasionally, for 10–15 minutes longer, or until spinach is tender and fragrant with rosemary.

3 Transfer to a heated serving dish and serve hot.

Note: If using powdered rosemary, cut the amount by about half as it is much more concentrated in flavour.

Old Fashioned Fruit Pie

4 firm pears
4 tart apples
Juice of 1 lemon
Pastry for shell and top
4 tablespoons dark brown sugar
1 tablespoon flour
$\frac{1}{8}$ level teaspoon freshly grated
   nutmeg
$\frac{1}{8}$ level teaspoon powdered cinnamon
Grated peel of $\frac{1}{2}$ orange
2 tablespoons chopped raisins
1–2 tablespoons orange juice
1–2 tablespoons butter
Cream, to serve

1 Peel and core pears and apples; slice thickly. Soak in water with lemon juice added to preserve their colour.

2 Line a deep 9-inch(23-cm) pie dish with pastry, using your own favourite recipe.

3 Combine brown sugar, flour, nutmeg and cinnamon, and rub a little of this mixture into pastry lining. Add grated orange peel to remaining sugar mixture. Cover bottom of the pastry shell with sliced apples and pears and sprinkle with a few chopped raisins and some of the sugar mixture to taste. Repeat layers until pie shell is generously filled.

4 Sprinkle with orange juice; dot with butter and fit top crust over pears, pressing the edges together or fluting them. Cut slits in crust to release steam and bake in a moderately hot oven (400°F/200°C/Mark 6) for 35–40 minutes, or until tender. Serve warm, with cream.

Italian Pumpkin Soup

1 lb(450g) pumpkin
$\frac{1}{2}$ lb(225g) potatoes
1 Spanish onion
2 oz(50g) butter
$\frac{1}{4}$ lb(100g) fresh haricot or
   broad beans
1 pint(6dl) milk
Salt and cayenne pepper
2 oz(50g) leek, cut into fine strips
1 pint(6dl) hot chicken stock
$\frac{1}{4}$ pint(1·5dl) double cream
$\frac{1}{4}$ lb(100g) boiled rice
2 tablespoons chopped parsley

1 Peel and dice pumpkin and potatoes. Chop onion and simmer in half the butter until golden; add diced pumpkin and potatoes, beans and milk. Bring to the boil and simmer for 45 minutes, stirring from time to time to prevent scorching

2 Strain through a fine sieve into a clean saucepan; add salt and cayenne, to taste.

3 'Melt' leeks in the remaining butter; add to soup with stock and bring to the boil.

4 Just before serving, stir in fresh cream, boiled rice and chopped parsley.

**Italian Pumpkin
Soup**

**Partridge with
Lentils**

**Tossed Green
Salad**

**Italian Cheeses
and
Fresh Fruit**

Serves 4–6

*with this menu I suggest
the following Medium-
priced Red Wines*
**Brouilly
Mercurey
Côtes de Bourg**

Poussins with Grapes and Apples (page 191)

Partridge with Lentils

(illustrated on page 177)

2–3 partridges
Salt and freshly ground black pepper
2–3 tablespoons butter
2 tablespoons olive oil
¼ lb(100g) fat salt pork, diced
1 large Spanish onion, sliced
2–3 carrots, sliced
¼ pint(1·5dl) dry white wine
¼ pint(1·5dl) chicken stock

LENTILS:
¾ lb(350g) lentils, pre-soaked
1 onion, stuck with 2 cloves
2 cloves garlic
1 sprig fresh thyme
2 sprigs fresh parsley
Salt and freshly ground black pepper

1 Clean and prepare partridges; sprinkle cavities with a little salt and freshly ground black pepper and sauté birds in a fireproof casserole in butter and olive oil with diced fat salt pork, sliced onion and carrots.

2 When birds are golden, add dry white wine and cook until wine is reduced by half. Add chicken stock and season to taste with salt and freshly ground black pepper; cover casserole and cook over low heat until partridges are tender, about 45 minutes.

3 To prepare lentils: soak overnight; drain and cover with water, adding onion, garlic, thyme, parsley, salt and freshly ground black pepper, to taste. Bring to the boil, reduce heat and simmer until tender but not too soft or mushy. When cooked, drain and remove onion, garlic and herbs.

4 To serve: place partridges on a hot serving dish and surround with cooked lentils. Skim fat from pan juices; strain and pour over birds.

Tossed Green Salad

(for recipe, see **green salad and variations,** page 100)

Italian Cheeses and Fruit

(for **cheese** see page 241)

Right: Vitello Tonnato with Oriental Rice Salad (pages 186 and 187)

Supper Parties

A famous New York hostess once said to me: 'Togetherness is a late-night cheese omelette coupled with the right mood and the right people.'

A wonderfully simple way to entertain, I thought, and late-night suppers immediately became my favourite trouble-free party plan.

What could be easier and more pleasing after an evening at the cinema or the theatre, or, more simply, after an evening spent at home with friends playing cards or watching the late-night thriller? Less important than a formal sit-down dinner, you can centre your late-night supper around a dish as simple as Italian pasta tossed in egg yolks, cream and freshly grated Parmesan (page 117), spaghetti Bolognese (page 159) or a chilled platter of thin slices of rare roast beef and Parma ham served with a delicious potato horseradish salad (pages 189–90).

High on the honours list in today's circles is the informal buffet supper after a cocktail party. Emphasis is on a long table piled with a lavish spread of food. Cold glazed ham or roast turkey, Italian tunnied veal (see below) and a crisp salad are suggestions for the bill of fare

Wine can be served from the cask, or in magnums for festive effect.

Parties-with-a-theme are becoming an intrinsic part of the new supper-party picture.

From France via America comes the French Bistro Party; gay red-checked tablecloths, café-sized tables, guttering candles and hearty French food.

Try a jellied *consommé*, or *filets d'harengs à l'huile*, smoked herrings fillets soaked for 12 hours or more in olive oil with a bay leaf and several slices of onion and carrot. Follow with a French country speciality like *Boeuf en Daube* (page 120) served with plain boiled potatoes, and finish off with individual chocolate puddings (see page 195) or a glazed fruit flan (see pages 108–109).

Serve French bread and red wine throughout the meal.

Or try the following hot weather menu for a supper party with an international flavour: *Vitello Tonnato* from Italy, a fresh-tasting rice salad from Hong Kong, followed by Soused Camembert and a chilled Red Fruit Bowl from France.

A bright new idea for informal entertaining is the Dip-In Supper Party, glamorous, fun and guaranteed to bring out the best and the worst in everyone. Easy-to-produce 'dip-ins' range from Swiss fondue (see page 144) to Italian Bagna Cauda (see page 227), with a fairly recent American invention reminiscent of the Wild West called *fondue bourguignonne* (see page 149).

Vitello Tonnato
(illustrated on previous page)

$2\frac{1}{2}$–3 lb (1·1–1·4kg) boned leg of veal
6 anchovy fillets
Bay leaves
1 Spanish onion, sliced
2 carrots, sliced
2 stalks celery, sliced
2 sprigs parsley
2 cloves

Salt and freshly ground black pepper
$\frac{1}{2}$ pint (3dl) dry white wine (optional)
Lemon slices and capers, to garnish

TUNA FISH SAUCE:
6 oz (175g) canned tuna fish
6 anchovy fillets
1 teaspoon capers
2 tablespoons lemon juice
Freshly ground black pepper

¼ pint(1·5dl) well-flavoured mayonnaise (see page 152)
Olive oil (optional)

1 Start this dish the day before you intend to serve it. Have your butcher bone and tie a piece of leg of veal to make a joint weighing 2½–3 lb(1·1–1·4kg) when boned and trimmed.

2 Cut anchovy fillets into small pieces; push these into holes pierced in surface of meat. Lay several bay leaves along top of joint.

3 Place meat in a heatproof casserole with sliced onion, carrots, celery, parsley sprigs and cloves. Season to taste with salt and freshly ground black pepper. Pour in dry white wine and add just enough water to cover meat (or use water only).

4 Bring to the boil. Skim; lower heat so that liquid barely simmers; cover casserole and simmer gently for 1½–2 hours.

5 When veal is tender, remove cords and skewers and return to stock. Leave to become quite cold.

6 To make tuna fish sauce: pound tuna fish, anchovy fillets and capers to a smooth paste with lemon juice and freshly ground black pepper to taste. Combine with mayonnaise in an electric blender and blend until sauce is smooth. Add a little strained veal stock if sauce seems too thick.

7 Drain cold veal thoroughly and place in a bowl. Cover with prepared sauce and leave to marinate in refrigerator overnight.

8 One hour before serving remove veal from sauce; scrape excess sauce into bowl. Cut veal into thin slices and arrange them in a row, slightly overlapping, on a shallow, oval serving dish. Mask slices with remaining sauce, thinned down with a little more stock or olive oil if necessary, and refrigerate until ready to serve.

9 Serve garnished with lemon slices and capers.

Oriental Rice Salad

(illustrated on page 185)

¾ lb(350g) long-grain rice
Salt
Lemon juice
¼ lb(100g) green peas, cooked
½ green pepper, seeded, cored and finely diced
½ red pepper, seeded, cored and finely diced
6 tablespoons finely chopped parsley
6 tablespoons finely chopped spring onions

DRESSING:
1 tablespoon lemon juice
½ clove garlic, crushed
3 tablespoons olive oil
Salt and freshly ground black pepper

1 Boil rice in plenty of salted water until tender but still very firm. (Add a little lemon juice to keep it white.) Drain thoroughly and allow to cool.

2 In a serving bowl, toss rice with cooked green peas, diced green and red peppers, finely chopped parsley and spring onions.

3 To make dressing: mix lemon juice with crushed garlic. Beat in olive oil with a fork and season generously with salt and freshly ground black pepper.

4 Pour dressing over rice mixture; toss thoroughly and taste for seasoning, adding more salt, freshly ground black pepper, oil or lemon juice if necessary. Chill until ready to serve.

Soused Camembert

(for the recipe see pages 126–127; illustrated overleaf)

Menu

Vitello Tonnato with Oriental Rice Salad

Soused Camembert

Red Fruit Bowl with Raspberry Purée

Serves 6

with this menu I suggest the following Inexpensive White Wines and Rosés
**Lachryma Christi
Soave
Tavel Rosé**

Soused Camembert (pages 127 and 187)

Menu

Sherried
Mushroom
Tartlets

Cold Roast Beef
with Parma Ham

Potato
Horseradish Salad

Walnut Roll

Serves 8

*with this menu I suggest
the following Inexpensive
White Wines and Rosés*
**Soave
Lachryma Christi
Chianti Ruffino
White**

Red Fruit Bowl with Raspberry Purée

$1\frac{1}{2}$ **lb(675g) ripe cherries**
2 punnets ripe strawberries
1 punnet redcurrants
2 punnets ripe raspberries
Cognac
Lemon juice
Icing sugar, sifted

RASPBERRY PURÉE:
2 punnets ripe raspberries
2–3 tablespoons lemon juice
2–3 tablespoons icing sugar

1 Pit cherries; hull strawberries; strip red-currants from their stalks.

2 In a glass bowl, combine prepared fruit with raspberries. Flavour to taste with cognac, lemon juice and sifted icing sugar, tossing fruit gently to avoid crushing them; chill for at least 30 minutes before serving.

3 To make raspberry purée: wash raspberries and rub through a fine sieve (or purée in an electric blender, then rub through a sieve). Flavour to taste with lemon juice and icing sugar. Chill.

4 Serve fruit accompanied by chilled raspberry purée.

Sherried Mushroom Tartlets

16 prebaked small pastry cases

SHERRIED MUSHROOMS:
6 tablespoons butter
2 tablespoons flour
$\frac{1}{2}$ **pint(3dl) chicken stock**
4 tablespoons milk
6 tablespoons double cream
1 lb(450g) button mushrooms, sliced
2 oz(50g) finely chopped shallots
Salt and freshly ground black pepper
4 tablespoons dry sherry

1 Use individual tins with removable bases to shape pastry cases. They should be left in their tins until just before serving.

2 To make sherried mushrooms: in a heavy pan, make a *roux* with 2 tablespoons each butter and flour, stirring over a low heat for 2–3 minutes, taking care *roux* does not burn. Then gradually stir in chicken stock, followed by milk and cream; bring to the boil and simmer for 15 minutes, stirring occasionally.

3 Sauté mushrooms and shallots in remaining butter until soft, 3–5 minutes; season to taste with salt and freshly ground black pepper.

4 Fold into sauce; add sherry to taste and correct seasoning if necessary. Keep hot.

5 Reheat pastry cases in their tins for about 5 minutes in a moderate oven (350°F/180°C/Mark 4). Remove from tins and arrange on a dish. Fill with hot mushrooms and sauce and serve at once.

Cold Roast Beef with Parma Ham

1–2 cloves garlic
**1 joint of roasting beef, at least
    2½ lb(1·1kg)**
**20 thin slices Parma ham, about
    10 oz(275g)**
**1 strip fat salt pork or
    unsmoked bacon**
3–4 tablespoons oil
Salt and freshly ground black pepper
12 gherkins, to decorate

1 Preheat oven to hot (450°F/230°C/Mark 8).

2 Peel and sliver garlic. Make deep slits all over beef with the point of a sharp knife and push in slivers as deeply as possible.

3 Wrap joint in 4 slices Parma ham and then in salt pork or bacon; tie securely with string. Brush with oil; lay in roasting tin and roast until done to your liking, 45–50 minutes for rare beef.

4 Remove meat from oven and allow to cool. When completely cold, remove larding strip and ham and cut beef into 16 slices. Season each slice with a sprinkling of salt and freshly ground black pepper.

5 Arrange beef slices on a long serving platter, alternating them with thin slices of Parma ham.

6 Slice gherkins very thinly lengthwise without cutting right through to the ends, and fan them out attractively. Use them to decorate platter of beef.

189

Potato Horseradish Salad

3 lb(1·4kg) firm salad potatoes
Salt
$\frac{3}{4}$ pint(4dl) thick, home-made
   mayonnaise (see page 152)
3–4 tablespoons horseradish sauce
2–3 tablespoons finely chopped parsley
Freshly ground black pepper

1 Scrub potatoes clean and boil them in their jackets in salted water until cooked but not mushy. Drain; cool slightly and peel off skins. Cool and slice or dice potatoes into a serving bowl.

2 Combine mayonnaise with horseradish, to taste, and finely chopped parsley, and fold into potatoes carefully to avoid breaking slices; season to taste with salt and freshly ground black pepper and chill until ready to serve.

Walnut Roll

(illustrated on page 192)

2 level tablespoons plain flour
Pinch of salt
$\frac{1}{2}$ level teaspoon baking powder
$\frac{1}{4}$ lb(100g) walnuts
6 eggs, separated
Castor sugar
Sifted icing sugar, to decorate

FILLING:
$\frac{3}{4}$ pint(4dl) double cream
3–4 oz(75–100g) castor sugar

1 Select a swiss roll tin 9 × 14 inches(23 × 35 cm) in diameter. Brush tin lightly with oil and line with greaseproof paper; oil paper lightly as well.

2 Preheat oven to moderate (350°F/180°C/Mark 4).

3 Sift flour, salt and baking powder into a bowl.

4 Grind walnuts coarsely in a small *mouli* – they must not be ground too finely, or they will release too much oil and make the cake heavy.

5 Whisk egg yolks with $\frac{1}{4}$lb(100g) castor sugar over hot water until mixture leaves a trail on the surface when beaters are lifted. Remove bowl from heat and continue to whisk mixture until cold.

6 Fold in ground walnuts with a spoon.

7 Whisk egg whites until stiff but not dry. Fold into the walnut mixture gently but thoroughly.

8 Fold in sifted flour mixture.

9 Pour batter into prepared tin and level it out with a spatula. Bake for 20–25 minutes, or until well-risen and springy to the touch.

10 While cake is in the oven, prepare a surface for rolling it: lay a damp cloth on the table, cover with a sheet of greaseproof paper and sprinkle with a teaspoon of castor sugar.

11 Turn cake out on to sugared paper and carefully peel off greaseproof paper.

12 Lay a fresh sheet of greaseproof paper in its place and carefully roll cake up together with papers and cloth, starting at one of the longer sides. Leave to cool.

13 When roll is cool, whip cream until it forms soft peaks and sweeten to taste with castor sugar.

14 Carefully unroll cake and remove top paper. Spread cake evenly with whipped cream and roll it up again, this time without the aid of the cloth and paper underneath.

15 Lay on a long, flat serving dish, seam side down, and dust liberally with sifted icing sugar.

Consommé with Lemon Dumplings

2 long carrots, thinly sliced
2–3 stalks celery, thinly sliced
3–4 leaves of leek, finely diced
2 pints(1·1 litres) clear hot consommé
3–4 tablespoons Madeira
Finely chopped parsley

LEMON DUMPLINGS:
2 oz(50g) coarse stale breadcrumbs
¼ teaspoon grated lemon rind
Generous pinch of thyme
1 teaspoon finely chopped parsley
1 oz(25g) butter, softened
1 egg yolk
Pinch of freshly grated nutmeg
Salt and freshly ground black pepper

1 To make dumplings: knead ingredients to a smooth paste, adding nutmeg, salt and freshly ground black pepper, to taste. Roll into 30 small balls.

2 Poach in lightly salted water for 30–40 minutes; drain well.

3 To finish consommé: simmer vegetables in a little consommé until tender, 8–10 minutes; combine with remaining consommé and flavour to taste with Madeira.

4 Serve hot, garnished with lemon dumplings and sprinkled with parsley.

Consommé Rose
(illustrated overleaf)

1 lb(450g) ripe red tomatoes
2 stalks celery
2 pints(1·1 litres) clear, well-flavoured chicken stock
Salt and freshly ground black pepper

TO GARNISH:
½ lb(225g) firm tomatoes

1 7-oz(198g) can red pimentos
1–2 tablespoons finely chopped parsley or chervil

1 Chop ripe tomatoes and celery roughly. Place them in a large pan with chicken stock; bring to the boil and simmer for 30 minutes.

2 To make garnish: peel and seed tomatoes, and cut them into small dice. Drain pimentos and dice them also.

3 To finish consommé: strain stock through a muslin-lined sieve. Add diced tomato and pimento garnish; season to taste with salt and freshly ground black pepper and bring just to boiling point again.

4 Remove from heat; sprinkle with finely chopped parsley or chervil and serve immediately.

Poussins with Grapes and Apples
(illustrated on page 184)

6 poussins, about 1 lb(450g) each
18–24 oz(500–675g) Philadelphia cream cheese
Salt and freshly ground black pepper
3 tablespoons olive oil
¼ lb(100g) butter
3 lb(1·4kg) cooking apples, peeled, cored and diced
2 lb(900g) black grapes, halved and seeded
6 tablespoons brandy

Menu

Consommé with Lemon Dumplings
or
Consommé Rose

Poussins with Grapes and Apples

Pineapple Bavarian Cream

Serves 6

with this menu I suggest the following Medium-priced White Wines
**Pouilly Blanc Fumé
Chablis
Quincy**

191

Walnut Roll (page 190)

1 Preheat oven to hot (450°F/230°C/Mark 8).

2 Wipe *poussins* clean and dry them thoroughly inside and out.

3 In a large bowl, pound cheese smoothly with a generous seasoning of salt and freshly ground black pepper. Stuff body cavity of each bird with the cheese. Then truss them.

4 Heat oil with half the butter in a large, heavy frying pan. Brown birds one or two at a time over a steady, moderate heat, turning them over so that they colour evenly. Transfer to a large roasting tin which will take them comfortably side by side.

5 When birds are all browned, pour over fat remaining in pan and roast them uncovered for 25 minutes – 10 minutes on each side and a final 5 minutes on their backs – basting

Consommé Rose (page 191)

with pan juices each time you turn them. Check that they are cooked by pushing a skewer through the thickest part of the leg: the juices should run clear. If not, return birds to the oven for a few minutes longer.

6 To make fruit garnish: toss diced apples in remaining butter until golden but not disintegrating. Remove from heat, add grapes and mix carefully.

7 Remove *poussins* from oven. Smother with apples and grapes, and pour a tablespoon of brandy over each bird. Cover the pan securely with a large sheet of foil and return to the oven for a further 10 minutes to develop flavours.

8 To serve: with a large, sharp knife slice each *poussin* in half down the middle. Reform birds and arrange them side by side on a long, heated serving platter. Surround with fruits; pour over cooking juices and serve immediately.

Note: The only accompaniment needed is a large bowl of crisp salad tossed with a light, lemony vinaigrette dressing (see page 100).

Pineapple Bavarian Cream

$\frac{1}{2}$ oz(14g) powdered gelatine
$\frac{1}{4}$ pint(1·5dl) pineapple juice
6 egg yolks
6 oz(175g) granulated sugar
1 level tablespoon cornflour
$\frac{3}{4}$ pint(4dl) milk
5 egg whites
Generous pinch of salt
$\frac{1}{2}$ oz(14g) castor sugar
3 tablespoons lemon juice
$\frac{1}{4}$ pint(1·5dl) double cream, chilled
2–3 slices pineapple, fresh or canned, shredded

TO DECORATE:
Pineapple rings, halved maraschino cherries and angelica

1 Sprinkle gelatine over pineapple juice and leave to soften.

2 In a large bowl, whisk egg yolks with granulated sugar until fluffy and lemon-coloured; add cornflour and continue to whisk until smoothly blended.

3 Scald milk; add to egg yolk mixture in a thin stream, beating vigorously with the whisk. Then pour into the top of a double saucepan and cook over hot water, stirring constantly. As soon as custard coats back of spoon, plunge base of pan into cold water to arrest cooking process.

4 Add gelatine and pineapple juice mixture to hot custard, stirring until completely melted. Pour custard into a large bowl.

5 Beat egg whites with salt until soft peaks form. Add castor sugar and continue to beat to a stiff meringue. Fold gently but thoroughly into warm custard mixture and flavour to taste with lemon juice. Flavour should be rather sharp. Allow mixture to become quite cold, drawing a large metal spoon through it occasionally to prevent it from separating.

6 When custard mixture is on the point of setting, whip chilled cream (by hand for maximum volume) until it almost holds its shape. Fold into custard, together with shredded pineapple.

7 Rinse a 3-pint(1·5-litre) loaf tin (or mould) with cold water, shaking out all excess. Fill to the brim with pineapple cream mixture; cover with greaseproof paper and chill in refrigerator until firmly set, preferably overnight.

8 To serve: plunge mould into very hot water for 1 second only and turn out on to a flat serving dish. Decorate with halved pineapple rings, maraschino cherries and angelica sprigs and return to refrigerator until ready to serve.

with this menu I suggest the following Medium-priced White Wines
**Pouilly Blanc Fumé
Riesling d'Alsace
Pouilly Fuissé**

Oeufs en Cocotte
(and variations)

This dish makes a wonderfully light, elegant appetizer to serve when time is short.

1 Preheat oven to moderate (375°F/190°C/Mark 5).

2 Butter 6 heatproof ramekins (about ¼-pint/1·5-dl capacity) and arrange them side by side in a wide, deep pan.

3 Carefully break 1 or 2 eggs into each ramekin. Season lightly with salt and a turn of the pepper mill, and swirl a little hot cream over the top.

4 Pour hot water into pan to come halfway up sides of ramekins; cover lightly with a sheet of foil and bring back to a simmer. Bake for 12 minutes, or until whites are just beginning to set but yolks are still runny.

5 Serve eggs immediately, as they tend to continue cooking from heat of dishes.

Oeufs en Cocotte with Bacon:
As above, but dust each buttered ramekin with a mixture of 1 tablespoon each crisp-fried crumbled bacon and finely chopped parsley before breaking in eggs. Pour a tablespoon of double cream over each ramekin just before serving.

Oeufs en Cocotte with Ham
Butter 6 ramekins as above.

1 Combine 6 oz(175g) ham, finely chopped, with 6 tablespoons each finely chopped parsley and fresh breadcrumbs.

2 Use three-quarters of the ham-parsley-breadcrumb mixture to coat individual ramekins generously.

3 Break 1 or 2 eggs into each ramekin; cover with remaining ham and breadcrumb mixture and bake as above.

Grilled Salmon Steaks with Snail Butter

**6 salmon steaks, 1 inch(2·5cm) thick
2–3 tablespoons olive oil
Salt and freshly ground black pepper**

SNAIL BUTTER:
**3 oz(75g) butter
1–2 plump cloves garlic, crushed
½ tablespoon very finely chopped shallot
½ tablespoon very finely chopped parsley
Salt and freshly ground black pepper**

1 To make snail butter: work butter with a wooden spoon until slightly softened; add crushed garlic, to taste, and beat until thoroughly blended; then beat in very finely chopped shallot and parsley and season to taste with salt and freshly ground black pepper.

2 Shape butter into six small balls and chill on a dish until firm again. (Cover dish tightly with foil or plastic to avoid strong garlic odour permeating other dishes in refrigerator.)

3 To cook salmon: switch on grill at maximum heat about 20 minutes before cooking salmon.

4 Brush both sides of each steak with olive oil and sprinkle with salt and freshly ground black pepper; arrange steaks side by side on the grid of the grill pan.

5 When ready to cook steaks, turn grill down to moderate and grill steaks for 16–20 minutes, turning them once. Steaks are ready when flesh can be prised away easily from the bone with a fork.

6 Transfer salmon steaks to a heated dish. Top each one with a generous pat of the chilled snail butter and serve immediately.

French Cucumber Salad
(for the recipe, see page 64, illustrated on page 62)

Chocolate Towers

SPONGE:
Butter
3 eggs
3 oz(75g) castor sugar
3 oz(75g) plain flour, sifted

CHOCOLATE FILLING:
3 oz(75g) bitter chocolate, grated
Finely grated rind of 1 orange
¼ pint(1·5dl) milk
1 egg, separated
2 oz(50g) castor sugar
1 teaspoon powdered gelatine
¼ pint(1·5dl) double cream

CRÈME ANGLAISE:
1 pint(6dl) milk
¼ teaspoon vanilla essence
2 level teaspoons cornflour
2 oz(50g) castor sugar
6 egg yolks

1 Grease a swiss roll tin (12 × 8 inches/30 × 20 cm) and line with buttered greaseproof paper. Preheat oven to moderate (350°F/180°C/Mark 4).

2 To make sponge: whisk eggs and sugar over hot water until mixture leaves a trail on the surface. Remove from heat and fold in flour with a metal spoon.

3 Bake for 15–20 minutes, or until sponge is golden and springy.

4 Turn out on to a wire rack; peel off lining paper. Cool.

5 To make chocolate filling: combine grated chocolate with orange rind and milk; bring to the boil, stirring constantly. Remove from heat. Whisk egg yolk with half the castor sugar; then gradually whisk in hot chocolate milk. Sprinkle gelatine over a tablespoon of cold water in a cup and leave for 10 minutes. Place cup in a bowl of hot water and stir until gelatine has completely dissolved. Blend thoroughly with chocolate mixture. Whip cream lightly; fold into chocolate mixture. Whisk egg white until stiff; add remaining castor sugar and continue to whisk until stiff and glossy. Fold into chocolate mixture. Set aside while you prepare moulds.

6 Line 6 ¼-pint(1·5-dl) turret moulds with sponge as follows: cut a circle to fit the bottom of each mould; then cut a strip to fit completely round inside of each mould, trimming ends so that there is no overlap.

7 Fill sponge-lined moulds with chocolate mixture and chill until firmly set.

8 To make crème anglaise: bring milk to the boil with vanilla essence. Mix cornflour with castor sugar; add to egg yolks and beat until smooth. Pour in milk gradually, beating constantly with a whisk; then transfer mixture to the top of a double saucepan and cook over hot water, stirring constantly, until sauce coats back of spoon. Do not let sauce boil, or egg yolks will curdle. Pour into a jug; cool and chill.

9 When ready to serve: turn chocolate towers out on to a wire rack over a flat dish. Mask each tower completely with *crème anglaise* and transfer to individual dishes.

10 Serve with remaining sauce in a separate bowl or jug.

Children's Parties

Think back to the first party you can remember: It was almost certainly a birthday party – your own or one of your best friends'.

I still remember one of my first birthday parties (helped a little over the years by the line-up of ecstatic faces in a faded snapshot in the family album). I was six, and the party – based on a sailor theme, complete with battleships on a blue-sea cake and paper sailor hats – was the highlight of my young life. I boasted about it for years.

Your child's first party will probably be a birthday party, too. So make it as gay and as charming as possible, with lots of brightly coloured balloons and inexpensive paper party favours.

The candle-lit home-made birthday cake will set the theme for the entire party. A gay Carousel Cake supplemented with delicately iced animal biscuits, eggs with rabbit, mice, duck and elephant heads and 'lion' pizzas makes it a Clown and Animal party; for older children – the pre-teens – try a Ranch House 'Western Style' Party complete with Cowboys and Indians and Wild West 'Hero' Sandwiches, or, why not dream up a Space Ship Party for your favourite young astronauts, it could be the launching pad for an afternoon of fun and games they will long remember.

Too many mothers, when faced with the ordeal of a party for young children, get

Hallowe'en Party: Bacon and Apple Skewers, Ranchburgers, and Caramel Apples (pages 204, 205 and 206)

lost in a whirl of indecision: 'Shall I feed them savouries or sweets? Make it plain or fancy?' The answer is really quite easy: keep the party simple. And above all, don't 'cook down' just because the guests are children.

Food for children's parties should look as exciting as it tastes. But bear in mind that the most favourite flavour quickly palls – especially when children are small. So keep each 'course' short: individually prepared portions look less daunting to the average child than large serving dishes piled high with food.

For small children, an overall theme helps you plan both the food and the décor. Keep the latter simple: bright colours, streamers and balloons provide more excitement than some subtly witty arrangement that takes you days to prepare and no one understands anyway. However sophisticated and worldly-wise modern children may seem, in my experience the old favourites – coloured drinking straws and the brightest (paper) tablecloths and napkins you can find – still hold their charm. Use colourful paper plates and cups, too, or at least make sure that the ones you have are not too fragile. Thick enamel or pottery or plastic, but definitely not delicate glass – it is almost impossible to keep all the children sitting at the table all of the time, and a child in motion drinking from a glass is a spine-chilling sight.

Winter Party Western Style: Wild West Hero Sandwiches, Baked Bean and Bacon Hotpot, and Black Bottom Pie (pages 207 and 208)

Some Simple Rules for Children's Parties

1 Use two rooms if possible: one for eating and one for play. Combining the two activities can lead to some sticky results.

2 Remove all breakable ornaments and objects with sharp edges, delicate side tables, etc.
Make a special check for all trailing lamp cords and, especially where really small children are involved, unguarded electric sockets.
All pieces of furniture with keys should be locked and all the keys removed – otherwise it may be years before you find them again, if ever.

3 Nowadays, children are not despatched to parties decked out in satins and lace, but even with sensible, sturdy clothing accidents can happen, so have a spot-remover and a good clothes-brush at hand.

4 A simple first-aid box is essential and it is also a good idea to have a bed clear in a quiet room for any small guest overcome by excitement (or food).

5 As the children arrive, see that each set of coats, gloves, bonnets and overshoes is kept together (tie them up with a ribbon, if necessary) to avoid hunting for missing items when the time comes to put them on again.

6 For small children, a Japanese-style table can be fun – seat them on cushions around a low table made out of the spare leaf of your dining table or a board covered with coloured crêpe paper.
The pre-teens can be served at table but teenagers usually prefer a buffet arrangement.

7 With small and pre-teenage guests an adult should be present all the time to act as master of ceremonies, conciliator, comforter and general all-round encourager.

8 When it comes to entertainment, it is fatal to rely on last-moment inspiration. Work out a programme of activities, alternating quiet games with rowdy ones. Have prizes by all means – but make sure that every child gets one.
If you are having outside entertainment – a film, the neighbourhood magician, Punch and Judy – arrange for the show to come on right after the food. There will be less danger of upset stomachs if the children sit quietly for a bit after eating.

9 Older children can be left to amuse themselves until they drop, but don't make the mistake of taxing the energies of small children beyond their limits, however much they appear to be enjoying themselves. Set a time for the party to end. And stick to it.

10 To counteract the anticlimax which invariably settles on the company when the time comes to leave, send each child on his or her way with a small, gaily wrapped gift, not to be opened until he or she reaches home.

11 For the same reason, mothers collecting tiny offspring should not be pressed with offers of tea or coffee – a happy party can easily turn sour while the adults gossip together in the kitchen. But be prepared in case anyone does hang back for a chat – a drink and unmutilated sandwich, biscuit or cake are quite enough.

The Circus is Coming to Town

Lion Pizzas

PIZZA DOUGH:
1 **level tablespoon dried yeast**
1 **level teaspoon castor sugar**
$\frac{1}{2}$ **lb(225g) plain flour**
Pinch of salt
$\frac{1}{4}$ **pint(1·5dl) lukewarm milk**
  and water
1 **tablespoon olive oil**

TOPPING:
2 **14-oz(400-g) cans peeled tomatoes**
Salt and freshly ground black pepper
$\frac{1}{2}$ **level teaspoon dried oregano**
2 **tablespoons olive oil**
$\frac{1}{4}$ **lb(100g) sliced ham, chopped**
$\frac{3}{4}$ **lb(350g) cheese, grated**
Anchovy fillets, black olives,
  green peppers

1 **To make dough:** dissolve yeast in 3 tablespoons lukewarm water mixed with sugar, following directions on can or packet.

2 Sift flour and salt. Make a well in the centre and pour in frothy yeast mixture. Work into flour with your fingertips, adding enough lukewarm milk and water to make a soft dough; then knead vigorously until dough is springy and leaves bowl and hands clean. Add oil and knead until smooth.

3 Roll dough into a ball. Cover bowl and leave dough to rise in a warm place until doubled in bulk, about 30 minutes.

4 **To make topping:** drain tomatoes, purée through a fine sieve. Season with salt and pepper and add oregano.

5 Make a cardboard stencil of a lion's head 4–4$\frac{1}{2}$ inches(10–11·5cm) deep and wide.

6 Heat oven to hot (450°F/230°C/Mark 8).

7 Divide dough into 8 balls. Roll each ball thinly and, with a sharp knife and the stencil, cut out the shape of a lion's head.

8 Arrange heads on 2 or 3 baking sheets. Brush with a little olive oil and scatter with ham to within $\frac{1}{4}$ inch(0·5cm) of edges. Spread thickly with tomato purée and sprinkle $\frac{1}{2}$lb(225g) grated cheese around heads to resemble 'manes'.

9 Make eyes with rolled anchovy fillets or black olives; noses with pieces of green pepper; and whiskers with slivers of anchovy. Sprinkle with remaining olive oil and bake pizzas for 10–15 minutes.

10 Remove from oven and dust 'manes' with remaining cheese. Serve hot.

Animal Eggs

8 **large eggs, hard-boiled**
2 **tablespoons each finely chopped**
  celery and chives or spring onion
2 **tablespoons softened butter**
1 **tablespoon mayonnaise(see page 152)**
Salt and freshly ground black pepper

1 Shell and halve eggs lengthwise. Scoop out yolks and rub through a fine sieve.

2 Blend yolks thoroughly with remaining ingredients, adding salt and pepper. Chill mixture if it is too soft.

3 Fill egg whites with yolk mixture.

4 Make animal faces as follows, or use your own imagination:
Rabbits: Red pimento for ears and V-shaped noses; strips of cucumber peel for whiskers; small pieces of black olive for eyes. **Mice:** Green pepper ears; black olive eyes; small pimento noses; thin strips of cucumber peel (or chives) for whiskers. **Ducks:** Two wedges of carrot for each beak; capers for eyes; thin fringes of parsley for lashes. **Elephants:** Big green pepper ears; green pepper trunks (use pieces that curve naturally); small black olive eyes; egg-white tusks.

Menu

Lion Pizzas

Animal Eggs

Carousel Cake
and
Animal Biscuits

Serves 8

Carousel Cake and Animal Biscuits

CAKE:
Butter
10 oz(275g) plain flour
6 tablespoons cocoa
1 tablespoon instant coffee
1 tablespoon baking powder
1½ teaspoons baking soda
3–4 teaspoons lemon juice
About ½ pint(3dl) milk
9 oz(250g) castor sugar
3 eggs, well beaten
1 teaspoon vanilla essence

1 Grease 3 8½-inch(21·5-cm) sandwich tins and line bases with buttered paper.

2 Preheat oven to moderate (375°F/190°C/ Mark 5).

3 Sift flour 3 times with cocoa, instant coffee and baking powder.

4 Dissolve baking soda in a tablespoon of warm water.

5 Stir lemon juice into milk until it curdles.

6 Cream 6oz(175g) softened butter with sugar until fluffy; beat in a tablespoon of flour mixture.

7 Add beaten eggs, flour mixture and curdled milk alternately, a little at a time, beating well after each addition. (Stop adding milk if batter becomes too liquid: it should be soft, but hold its shape.)

8 Beat in dissolved soda and vanilla essence.

9 Divide three-quarters of the batter between 2 tins and spread the remainder evenly in third tin.

10 Bake for 20–25 minutes, or until cakes are well risen and have shrunk slightly from sides of tins.

11 Remove from oven and leave for a minute or two before turning out to cool on wire racks.

ANIMAL BISCUITS AND CAROUSEL 'BIG TOP':
¾ lb(350g) plain flour
2 oz(50g) sifted icing sugar
2 oz(50g) castor sugar
½ lb(225g) butter

1 Preheat oven to moderate (375°F/190°C/ Mark 5).

2 Sift flour into a bowl. Stir in icing sugar and castor sugar; rub in butter and knead to a smooth, fairly stiff dough.

3 Cut off 5 oz(150g) dough; roll out $\frac{1}{16}$ inch(0·2cm) thick and cut out a circle 9 inches(23cm) in diameter. Lay on a baking sheet and mark into 8 even triangles.

4 Roll remaining dough about $\frac{1}{8}$ inch (0·3cm) thick. Cut 6 animal shapes for 'carousel' (3 large, 3 small) and 6 clowns' heads with ruffs for sides of cake. Cut remaining dough into as many different animal shapes as possible.

5 Arrange biscuits on baking sheets and bake for 7–10 minutes until crisp and golden.

6 Remove with a spatula and cool on wire racks.

CHOCOLATE FILLING:
2 oz(50g) unsalted butter
¼ lb(100g) icing sugar, sifted
1 egg yolk
¼ lb(100g) bitter chocolate, melted

1 Beat butter until creamy. Add icing sugar gradually, beating vigorously.

2 Beat in egg yolk and when well blended gradually add melted chocolate, beating until smooth.

TO FINISH CAKE:
Sweetened orange juice
2 lb(900g) icing sugar, sifted
Orange, blue, yellow and red food colouring
6 orange-striped or multi-coloured candy sticks about 6 inches(15cm) long
Dolly mixtures, or other small sweets

1 When cakes are cold, place 2 thick layers upside down and prick all over with a fork. Sprinkle generously with sweetened orange juice and sandwich with chocolate filling, reserving a few tablespoons.

2 To make icing: add just enough hot water to 1lb(450g) icing sugar to give a stiff but flowing consistency. Colour it pale orange and beat until smooth. Ice top and sides of sandwiched layers, and leave until set.

3 Make a glacé icing with remaining icing sugar, divide in four and colour pastel blue, yellow, orange and pink.

4 Ice animal and clown biscuits, using different colours.

The Circus is coming to Town: Carousel Cake and Animal Biscuits

5 To assemble cake: push candy sticks firmly into top of cake to resemble poles of carousel.

6 Cut a double thickness of cardboard $8\frac{1}{2}$ inches(21·5cm) in diameter. Lay third layer of cake on it and mask sides with a little of remaining chocolate filling, coming about $\frac{3}{4}$ inch(2cm) over top. Decorate sides with tiny coloured sweets. Place layer on top of candy sticks.

7 Stick a small tube of cardboard about 2 inches(5cm) tall in centre of top layer and arrange iced triangular biscuits around it to make canopy big top.

8 Finally, stick a biscuit animal to each candy pole and the 6 clowns' heads to sides of cake, using dabs of remaining chocolate filling to hold them in place.

9 Serve remaining biscuits separately.

Pre-Teens Tea Party

Stuffed Tomatoes
(illustrated on page 204)

Choose 8 firm, red tomatoes of medium size. Slice off stem end of each tomato and carefully scoop out pulp with a small spoon. Sprinkle each tomato shell with a small pinch of salt and turn upside down on a plate to drain while you prepare one of the following fillings.

SARDINE AND CHEESE FILLING:
Drain a can of sardines (8 large sardines) and mash them with a fork. Blend with 8 tablespoons cream cheese and 1 to 2 teaspoons lemon juice, to taste. Fill tomato shells with this mixture and serve garnished with tiny sprigs of parsley.

CHEESE AND HAM FILLING:
Beat 6 oz(175g) cream cheese until soft and smooth. Add 6 oz(175g) diced cooked ham and 2 tablespoons chopped mustard and cress, and mix well. Season with a little salt and freshly ground black pepper, if necessary, and pile into tomato shells.

RICE AND TUNA FILLING:
Combine 8 tablespoons cooked rice with 2 oz(50g) frozen peas, cooked, 4 tablespoons drained flaked tuna and 4 teaspoons coarsely grated raw carrot. Bind mixture with 2 tablespoons mayonnaise (see page 152) or salad cream and season lightly with salt and freshly ground black pepper, if necessary; pile into prepared tomato shells.

Scotch Eggs

(illustrated overleaf)

1 lb(450g) sausage meat
Flour
8 standard eggs, hard-boiled
3 eggs, well beaten
½ lb(225g) fine white breadcrumbs
Oil, for deep-frying

1 Divide sausage meat into 8 portions of equal size. With lightly floured fingers, flatten each piece into a rectangle 4 × 3 inches(10 × 7·5cm).

2 Put a hard-boiled egg in the centre of each piece of sausage meat and mould meat around it, sealing joins carefully.

3 Roll in beaten egg, allowing excess to drain off, and coat with fresh white breadcrumbs; then repeat egg and breadcrumb coating to prevent sausage meat bursting.

4 Heat a pan of oil for deep-frying to 350°F/180°C.

5 Place eggs in frying basket, a few at a time; lower into hot fat and deep-fry for 5 to 7 minutes, or until eggs are a rich golden colour, making sure temperature of fat stays constant. Drain well on absorbent paper.

6 Serve warm or cold (not chilled), standing on decorated napkin rings or in individual ramekins to hold them steady.

Peanut Loaf Spectacular

1 lb(450g) uncut white sandwich loaf
1 lb(450g) cream cheese
8–10 oz(225–275g) salted peanuts

FILLING 1:
2 oz(50g) softened butter
1 tablespoon mustard and cress
2 oz(50g) cottage cheese
1 tart apple, peeled, cored and diced
2 teaspoons mayonnaise

FILLING 2:
2 oz(50g) cream cheese
2 tablespoons tomato ketchup
1 teaspoon mayonnaise

FILLING 3:
2 oz(50g) softened butter
2 oz(50g) ham, finely chopped
1 tablespoon sweet chutney

1 Cut crusts from loaf, straightening top if it is domed. Cut loaf horizontally lengthwise into 5 slices.

2 Prepare fillings, creaming butter (where used) before adding remaining ingredients. Chill fillings to firm them if necessary.

3 To assemble loaf: spread bottom slice with half the apple filling. Cover with another slice of bread and spread with tomato/cream cheese filling. Place third slice on top and spread with ham filling. Spread fourth slice with remaining apple filling and top with remaining slice of bread.

4 Wrap loaf in foil and chill for 1 hour.

5 Just before serving place loaf on an oblong dish. Spread top and sides evenly with cream cheese and cover with peanuts, pressing them in firmly. Cut in slices as you would an ordinary loaf.

Sundaes

(for recipes – and variations – see page 211)

Hallowe'en Party

Menu

Bacon and Apple Skewers

Bacon and Prune Skewers

Deep-fried Sausages in Batter

Ranchburgers

Cheese-baked Potatoes

Caramel Apples

Brownies

Serves 12

Skewered foods appeal to children of all ages and help to break the ice at the start of a children's party. You can make the skewers very simple – cubes of cheese and pineapple, ham, tiny sausages wrapped in bacon and grilled, olives and grapes – or try the suggestions below.

Always wet wooden skewers to prevent them charring.

Bacon and Apple Skewers

(illustrated on page 196)

4 large cooking apples
¼ lb(100g) Demerara sugar
24 rashers streaky bacon
12 small rounds toasted bread

1 Preheat oven to moderate (350°F/180°C/ Mark 4).

2 Peel, core and cut each apple into 6 segments. Place in an ovenproof dish; sprinkle with sugar and bake for 15 to 20 minutes, or until segments are soft but still hold their shape.

3 Wrap a bacon rasher round each apple segment. Spear 2 at a time on wooden cocktail sticks.

4 Grill until bacon is crisp, turning frequently.

5 Just before serving, spear a round of hot toast on the end of each stick. Moisten with a few drops of pan drippings and serve immediately.

Bacon and Prune Skewers

24 plump prunes, soaked
24 salted almonds
8 long rashers smoked fat bacon
1 tablespoon butter

1 Slit each prune carefully down one side and remove stone. Fill cavity with a salted almond and close up again.

2 Cut each bacon rasher in three crosswise; stretch pieces out thinly with the back of a knife.

3 Wrap each prune in bacon and secure with a wooden cocktail stick.

4 Fry skewers very gently in butter for 6 to 8 minutes, shaking pan to brown them evenly. Serve immediately.

Deep-fried Sausages in Batter

24 frankfurters
Oil, for deep-frying

BATTER:
5 oz(150g) plain flour
Pinch of salt
2 tablespoons olive oil
¼ pint(1·5dl) lager
1 egg white

Pre-Teens Tea Party: Stuffed Tomatoes and Scotch Eggs (pages 202 and 203)

1 To make batter: sift flour and salt into a bowl. Make a well in the centre.

2 Add olive oil; then gradually add lager, stirring lightly to incorporate flour from sides of well. Batter should be smooth and slightly thicker than pancake batter.

3 Leave to rest for 2 hours.

4 When ready to use: beat egg white until stiff but not dry; fold into batter gently but thoroughly.

5 Heat a pan of oil to 375°F/190°C.

6 Coat frankfurters with batter a few at a time and deep-fry for 3 to 5 minutes, until crisp and golden.

7 Drain well and serve immediately, speared on cocktail sticks.

Ranchburgers
(illustrated on page 196)

3 lb(1·4kg) lean beef, coarsely minced
2 Spanish onions, finely chopped
2–3 tablespoons Worcestershire sauce
½ teaspoon each curry powder and paprika
Salt and freshly ground black pepper
Softened butter
Halved toasted baps
Garnishes as below

1 Place minced beef in a bowl with chopped onions, Worcestershire sauce, curry powder, paprika, salt and pepper. Mix well with a fork.

2 Shape into 12 patties.

3 Arrange patties in a grill pan lined with foil. Brush with softened butter and grill until brown and sizzling; then turn and continue to grill until hamburgers are cooked through and a rich brown colour all over, 6 to 8 minutes on each side.

4 Serve burgers on halved toasted baps with some of the following garnishes: sliced tomatoes, sliced cucumbers, deep-fried onion rings, finely chopped spring onions, pickled onions and cucumbers, stuffed olives, slices of cheese (pop burgers back under the grill until cheese melts).

Cheese-baked Potatoes

12 medium-sized baking potatoes
¼ pint (1·5dl) single cream
¼ lb(100g) butter, softened
6 tablespoons finely chopped chives
Salt and freshly ground black pepper
12 slices (about ½ lb[225g]) Gruyère cheese

1 Preheat oven to moderate (375°F/190°C/Mark 5).

2 Scrub potatoes clean; dry them thoroughly and prick all over with a fork. Bake for about 1½ hours, or until soft.

3 When potatoes are cooked, cut a thin slice from the side and with a sharp spoon scoop out pulp into a bowl, leaving a firm shell.

4 Mash potato pulp smoothly with cream and butter. Mix in chopped chives and season to taste with salt and freshly ground black pepper.

5 Pile potato purée back into shells. Cover with a slice of cheese and place under a hot grill for 6 to 8 minutes, or until cheese is golden and bubbling and potatoes are thoroughly hot.

205

Caramel Apples

(illustrated on page 196)

12 small crisp eating apples
$1\frac{1}{4}$ lb(575g) Demerara sugar
5 fl oz(150ml) golden syrup
Butter
$\frac{1}{4}$ lb(100g) walnuts, finely chopped

1 Wash and dry apples thoroughly. Impale them on wooden sticks.

2 To make caramel: combine Demerara sugar with just under $\frac{3}{4}$ pint(4dl) water in a heavy pan, and stir over low heat until dissolved. Have by you a bowl of cold water and a brush to wash down any sugar granules which may stick to sides of pan as you stir.

3 Add golden syrup and 5oz(150g) butter; stir until well blended; then bring to the boil and boil rapidly without stirring until caramel reaches crack stage (310°F/160°C).

4 Butter 2 baking trays (or line a flat surface with buttered greaseproof paper). Spread chopped walnuts out on a flat plate.

5 Remove caramel from heat. Allow bubbles to subside; then dip in apples, one at a time, coating them evenly and twirling them round to remove excess.

6 Dip tops of apples in chopped walnuts. Stand them on a buttered surface and leave until quite cold and set. (If caramel begins to harden before all the apples have been dipped, warm over very low heat until liquid again.)

7 Serve caramel apples on a serving dish, or stuck gaily into a large decorated pumpkin or marrow to make a festive Hallowe'en effect.

Note: If you are preparing apples in advance, store them individually wrapped in greaseproof paper.

Brownies

Makes 16
Butter
2 oz(50g) plain flour
$\frac{1}{2}$ level teaspoon baking powder
$\frac{1}{2}$ level teaspoon salt
2 oz(50g) bitter chocolate
$\frac{1}{2}$ lb(225g) castor sugar
2 eggs
$\frac{1}{2}$ teaspoon vanilla essence
2 oz(50g) walnuts, coarsely chopped

1 Preheat oven to moderate (350°F/180°C/ Mark 4).

2 Butter a swiss roll tin, 12×8 inches (30×20cm).

3 Sift flour with baking powder and salt. Melt bitter chocolate over hot water.

4 Meanwhile, cream $\frac{1}{4}$ lb(100g) softened butter with sugar until fluffy. Beat in eggs, one at a time.

5 Add sifted flour and mix well. Stir in melted chocolate and vanilla essence and beat until smooth. Stir in walnuts.

6 Pour mixture into swiss roll tin and bake for 30 to 40 minutes, or until firm.

7 Remove from oven and cool slightly. (Mixture will settle a little in cooling.) Cut into 2-inch(5-cm) squares with a sharp knife.

8 Allow brownies to cool completely before removing them from baking tin.

Winter Party Western Style

Dried Pea Soup with Cheese Croûtons

2 Spanish onions, chopped
1 clove garlic, crushed (optional)
2 tablespoons bacon fat
1 lb(450g) split peas, soaked overnight and drained
¾–1 lb(350–450g) bacon ends (or smoked ham bones)
4 carrots, roughly chopped
2 tablespoons wine vinegar
2 teaspoons sugar
4 pints(2·3 litres) beef stock (made with a cube)
Bouquet garni
3–4 black peppercorns
Salt
Freshly ground black pepper

CHEESE CROÛTONS:
6 slices of white toast
6 level tablespoons grated Cheddar cheese

1 In a large pan, sauté onions and garlic, if used, in bacon fat until soft and golden.

2 Add remaining ingredients except salt and freshly ground black pepper; top up with 1½ pints(8·5dl) water and bring to the boil. Simmer for 2 hours, or until peas are disintegrating.

3 Remove bacon and *bouquet garni;* rub soup through a fine sieve or purée in an electric blender. Season to taste with salt and freshly ground black pepper.

4 Serve very hot, accompanied by a bowl of cheese *croûtons* to scatter over soup.

To make croûtons: stamp stars or horse-shoes shapes out of toast with a small biscuit cutter. Lay on a baking sheet; sprinkle with grated cheese and slip into a moderate oven (350°F/180°C/Mark 4) for 10 to 15 minutes to dry out *croûtons* and melt cheese.

Wild West Hero Sandwiches

(illustrated on page 197)

Makes 12
3 long French loaves
1 large lettuce
4 large tomatoes, sliced
6 slices processed cheese, halved
6 slices cooked ham, halved
2–3 dill pickles, sliced lengthwise
12 slices salami, halved

HERB BUTTER:
½ lb(225g) butter, softened
1–2 teaspoons oregano (or marjoram)
1–2 teaspoons lemon juice

1 Cut each loaf into 4 chunks; slit through horizontally without separating halves and heat through for 8 to 10 minutes in a very slow oven (300°F/150°C/Mark 2).

2 To make herb butter: beat butter with oregano (or marjoram) and lemon juice.

3 To assemble sandwiches: fill inside of each bread chunk with herb butter and a layer of lettuce, topped with 2 slices tomato, ½ slice cheese, ½ slice ham, a layer of pickle slices and finally 2 pieces of salami.

4 Serve while still hot and crisp.

Baked Bean and Bacon Hotpot

(illustrated on page 197)

4 lb(1·8kg) collar bacon
⅓ pint(2dl) cider
6 oz(175g) dark brown sugar
1 tablespoon dry mustard
3 tablespoons wine vinegar
2 Spanish onions, chopped
3 oz(75g) butter
4 1¼-lb(569-g) cans baked beans
1 teaspoon French mustard
4 tablespoons tomato ketchup
1 teaspoon each ground coriander, cumin and ginger

Menu

Dried Pea Soup with Cheese Croûtons

Wild West Hero Sandwiches

Baked Bean and Bacon Hotpot

Black Bottom Pie

Serves 12

1 Soak bacon in cold water for 24 hours, changing water several times.

2 Next day, cover bacon with fresh water. Bring to the boil slowly and simmer for 45 minutes. Cool under running cold water and strip off skin. Place bacon in a roasting tin, fat side up.

3 Preheat oven to moderate (375°F/190°C/ Mark 5).

4 Combine cider with brown sugar. Blend mustard with wine vinegar and stir into sugar mixture. Pour over bacon.

5 Roast bacon for 45 minutes to 1 hour, or until almost cooked, basting frequently; then increase heat to 450°F/230°C/Mark 8 and continue to roast, basting, for 15 minutes, or until bacon is richly glazed and cooked through.

6 In a large pan, sauté onions in butter until golden. Add beans, French mustard, ketchup and spices, and mix carefully.

7 Cut bacon into bite-sized chunks.

8 Reduce oven temperature to 375°F/ 190°C/Mark 5.

9 Combine some of bean mixture with pan juices in roasting tin, scraping tin thoroughly.

10 Put remaining beans in a large, ovenproof casserole. Add contents of roasting tin and bacon chunks; mix well and return to oven for about 15 minutes. Serve hot.

Black Bottom Pie

(illustrated on page 197)

2 deep 8½-inch(21·5-cm) pastry cases, prebaked
¾ oz(20g) powdered gelatine
½ lb(225g) castor sugar
2 tablespoons cornflour
8 egg yolks, lightly beaten
1½ pints (8·5dl) milk
6 oz(175g) bitter chocolate, melted
2–3 teaspoons vanilla essence
6 egg whites
Generous pinch cream of tartar
4 large bananas
Juice of ½ lemon
Chocolate curls and whipped cream, to decorate

1 Sprinkle gelatine over 3 to 4 tablespoons cold water in a cup and leave to soften.

2 Mix 6 oz(175g) castor sugar with cornflour in the top of a double saucepan. Add lightly beaten egg yolks and mix well.

3 Scald milk and pour over egg yolk mixture, stirring vigorously.

4 Cook over simmering water, stirring, for 15 to 20 minutes, or until custard coats back of spoon.

5 Stand cup with gelatine in a larger container of hot water and stir until completely dissolved. Add to custard and beat well.

6 Pour two-thirds of custard mixture into 1 bowl and rest into another.

7 Beat melted chocolate into larger portion and, when smooth again, flavour to taste with vanilla essence.

8 Divide chocolate custard evenly between prebaked pastry shells; chill until set on top.

9 When remaining custard is on the point of setting, whisk egg whites with cream of tartar until soft peaks begin to form. Add remaining sugar gradually and continue to whisk until stiff and glossy. Fold into plain custard and flavour to taste with vanilla essence.

10 Cut 2 bananas into very thin slices and arrange on top of chocolate custards. Cover pies completely with vanilla fluff, swirling it decoratively. Return to refrigerator until quite set, preferably overnight.

11 Just before serving: cut remaining bananas into thick slices; brush with lemon juice to prevent discolouration and arrange on top of pies. Finish decoration with chocolate curls and piped whipped cream.

Summer Holiday Party

Summer Tomato Soup

Summer Holiday Party: Summer Tomato Soup, Almond Ham Salad and Summer Lemon Cake (pages 209, 210 and 211)

4 14-oz(396–g) cans peeled tomatoes
½ pint(3dl) double cream, chilled
Juice and finely grated rind of
**   1 lemon**
4 teaspoons castor sugar
1–1½ teaspoons onion juice
Salt
½ lb(225g) ham, diced
½ lb(225g) cucumber, diced
Finely chopped parsley

1 Rub canned tomatoes through a fine sieve, together with their juice. Chill purée thoroughly.

2 Just before serving, stir in chilled cream, lemon juice and rind, sugar, onion juice and salt, to taste. Mix well; pour into a bowl and garnish with diced ham, cucumber, and finely chopped parsley.

3 Served chilled with a tray of sandwiches, if desired.

Chicken in a Basket

3 frying chickens, 2½ lb(1kg) each
Salt and freshly ground black pepper
1 level tablespoon dried tarragon
1 level tablespoon dried rosemary
6 level tablespoons finely chopped
    parsley
1½ level teaspoons grated lemon rind
½ lb(225g) plain flour
4 large eggs
6 oz(175g) fine dry breadcrumbs
Oil, for deep frying
Parsley sprigs and lemon wedges, to
    garnish

1 Cut each chicken into 8 pieces: 2 from each leg and 2 from each breast. Season generously with salt and freshly ground black pepper.

2 Combine next 5 ingredients in one bowl and season generously with salt and freshly ground black pepper. In another bowl, beat eggs lightly with 4 to 6 tablespoons cold water. Put breadcrumbs in a shallow dish.

3 Coat each chicken joint with flour mixture and dip in beaten egg, allowing excess to drain off. Repeat this process once more; then coat with breadcrumbs. Chill for about 1 hour to allow coating to set firmly.

4 Heat oil for deep frying to 350°F/180°C (or until a bread cube fries golden brown within 60 seconds). Deep-fry 3 or 4 chicken joints at a time for 20 to 25 minutes, or until juices run clear when chicken is pricked deeply with a skewer and breadcrumb coating is crisp and brown.

5 Drain on absorbent paper. Keep chicken hot and crisp in a moderate oven (350°F/180°C/Mark 4) while chips are fried.

6 Serve 2 pieces of chicken per person in individual baskets lined with paper napkins. Garnish each portion with fried chips, a sprig of parsley and a wedge of lemon.

Potato Chips

1 Peel 4–5 lb(1.8 2.3kg) medium sized potatoes and cut into chips. Rinse off starch with plenty of cold water and dry chips thoroughly on a clean cloth.

2 Heat oil to 350°F/180°C. Deep-fry chips for 5 to 8 minutes until soft but not coloured; drain on paper towels and put aside wrapped in greaseproof paper.

3 Just before serving: reheat oil to 425°F/220°C. Plunge in chips and deep-fry until brown and crisp.

4 Drain thoroughly; sprinkle with salt and serve immediately.

Almond Ham Salad
(illustrated on previous page)

1 lb(450g) cooked ham, in one piece
6 oz(175g) Cheddar cheese
4 small tart apples
½ lb(350g) celery, thinly sliced
4 tablespoons chopped onion
6 oz(175g) flaked almonds, toasted
1 pint(6dl) thick mayonnaise (see
    page 152)
4 tablespoons whipped cream
2–3 tablespoons lemon juice
Tabasco sauce
Salt and cayenne pepper

1 Cut ham, cheese and apples into ¼-inch (0.5-cm) dice.

2 Toss together in a bowl with celery, onion and half the flaked almonds.

3 Fold in mayonnaise and whipped cream; flavour with lemon juice, a few drops of Tabasco, and season to taste with salt and cayenne. Mix well and chill.

4 Serve garnished with remaining toasted almonds.

Summer Lemon Cake

(illustrated on page 209)

Butter
Plain flour
6 eggs, separated
6 oz(175g) castor sugar
Grated rind of 1 lemon
Generous pinch of salt
1 oz(25g) cornflour
Crystallized orange and lemon slices

LEMON TOPPING:
2 eggs
10 oz(275g) castor sugar
Grated rind and juice of 2 lemons
2 oz(50g) plain flour, sifted
1 pint(6dl) double cream, whipped

1 Preheat oven to moderate (350°F/180°C/ Mark 4).

2 Butter 3 8-inch(20-cm) layer cake tins and dust with flour.

3 Beat egg yolks, sugar, lemon rind, salt and 2 tablespoons water until light and fluffy. Sift 3 oz(75g) plain flour with cornflour and gradually blend into mixture.

4 Whisk egg whites until stiff but not dry and fold gently into batter. Divide batter between prepared tins and bake for 45 minutes, until light and golden.

5 Invert layers on wire racks. When cool, loosen edges and remove from tins.

6 **To make lemon topping:** beat eggs, sugar and lemon rind together until foamy; beat in sifted flour, and lemon juice made up to ½ pint(3dl) with water; bring to the boil over low heat, stirring constantly, and cook, stirring, for 5 to 7 minutes, until smooth and thick. Cool. Fold in whipped cream.

7 Sandwich cake layers with some of topping and use rest to decorate top and sides. Finish cake with orange and lemon slices.

Sundaes – with Chocolate and Butterscotch Sauce

You will need: tall glasses and long-handled spoons; a colourful selection of ice creams, say vanilla, chocolate and strawberry; an ice cream scoop; 2 or 3 sweet sauces – chocolate and/or butterscotch, and perhaps a lightly sweetened purée of raspberries for good measure; a piping bag of whipped cream fitted with a rosette nozzle; and a dish of toasted flaked almonds to sprinkle over the top. Demonstrate the first sundae yourself – then stand clear.

CHOCOLATE SAUCE:
Makes about 1 pint(6dl)
9 oz(250g) bitter chocolate
3 oz(75g) butter
6 fl oz(2dl) double cream
6 fl oz(2dl) single cream

1 In a heavy pan, melt chocolate with butter over low heat, stirring. Gradually beat in double and single cream; bring to the boil and simmer for 2 or 3 minutes, stirring.

2 Serve hot or lukewarm.

BUTTERSCOTCH SAUCE:
Makes about 1 pint(6dl)
2 oz(50g) butter
3 oz(75g) granulated sugar
2½ oz(70g) Demerara sugar
6 fl oz(2dl) golden syrup
Pinch of salt
4 fl oz(1·5dl) double cream

1 Combine all ingredients except double cream in a saucepan. Stir over low heat until mixture comes to the boil, then cook very slowly for 20 minutes, stirring occasionally.

2 Remove from heat and allow to cool.

3 Add cream and beat well until smooth.

Note: Sauce keeps well in a screwtop jar in the refrigerator and can also be deep-frozen.

Picnics and Outdoor Meals

A picnic for hot summer days: Roast chicken, a green salad, olives and fresh fruit and cheeses.

A Meal to Serve Out of Doors

The kitchen is a great place to stay out of when the weather is sizzling hot. Cold foods, of course, are appealing in this kind of weather, but every meal – unless it is a picnic or a buffet – should have one hot dish. The rest of the menu can be as simple and as quickly cooked as possible, to avoid spending hours in the kitchen with a hot stove. If you start with a chilled fruit juice or a chilled vegetable soup, have a hot meat or vegetable dish and then cool off again with a fresh fruit dessert.

Watercress and Apple Soup

A chilled, curry-flavoured cream of chicken soup to which puréed watercress and apple add their individual flavours. Dark green watercress leaves and cubes of lemon-flavoured apple add bite and texture to its creamy coldness.

2 tablespoons butter
1 Spanish onion, coarsely chopped
1 bunch watercress
1 pint(6dl) chicken stock
1 level tablespoon curry powder
1 tablespoon cornflour
2 egg yolks
$\frac{1}{4}$–$\frac{1}{2}$ pint(1·5–3dl) hot double cream
2 eating apples
Salt and freshly ground black pepper
Juice of $\frac{1}{2}$ lemon
Extra watercress leaves, for garnish

1 Melt butter; add onion and cook until soft but not brown. Stir in watercress, chicken stock and curry powder; add cornflour mixed with a little water. Bring to the boil, then simmer for 8 minutes.

2 Add egg yolks to hot cream and stir gradually into soup.

213

Menu

**Watercress and
Apple Soup**

**Stuffed Breast of
Veal**

**Cold Lemon
Soufflé**

Serves 4–6

*with this menu I suggest
the following Medium-
priced White Wines*
**Quincy
Sancerre
Chablis**

3 Remove from heat immediately and transfer mixture to electric blender with 1 apple, peeled, cored and sliced. Blend until smooth or pass through a fine sieve. Season to taste with salt and freshly ground black pepper. Chill.

4 Peel, core and dice remaining apple and marinate in lemon juice to prevent discolouration.

5 Just before serving, stir in diced apple and enough watercress leaves to garnish.

Stuffed Breast of Veal

Sausage meat, finely chopped onion, parsley and spinach are combined for the stuffing of this green and pink veal roll. Season it generously with the herbs and spices of your choice. I like fresh tarragon when available, or failing this, a combination of dried thyme, crumbled bay leaf and rosemary. Serve it with tomatoes stuffed with the same mixture (they can be baked at the same time) or with **boiled rice** (see page 70). Any leftovers are excellent cold.

3–4 lb(1·4–1·8kg) breast of veal
Lemon juice
Salt and freshly ground black pepper
Flour
2 tablespoons butter
2 tablespoons olive oil

STUFFING:
½ lb(225g) sausage meat
½ Spanish onion, finely chopped
2 tablespoons butter
1 tablespoon finely chopped parsley
1 beaten egg
**½ lb(225g) spinach, chopped and
    sautéed in butter**
**Salt, freshly ground black pepper,
    herbs or spices**

1 Wipe veal on both sides with a damp cloth; sprinkle with lemon juice and season with salt and freshly ground black pepper.

2 To make stuffing: combine sausage meat, chopped onion sautéed in butter until transparent, finely chopped parsley, beaten egg, sautéed spinach, salt, freshly ground black pepper and herbs or spices, to taste. Mix well.

3 Lay this stuffing in the centre of the veal; make into a neat roll and sew up with fine string. Dust with flour; place it in a roasting pan with 2 tablespoons butter and olive oil and roast in a moderate oven (325°F/170°C/ Mark 4) for about 1½ to 2 hours, basting frequently with fat.

Cold Lemon Soufflé

One of the freshest, tartest sweets imaginable – serve it in a soufflé dish or in individual sorbet glasses.

6 egg yolks
6 oz(175g) castor sugar
Juice of 2 lemons
Grated rind of 1 lemon
6 egg whites, stiffly beaten
½ oz(14g) gelatine
Angelica 'leaves', to decorate
Redcurrant jelly
Kirsch (optional)

1 Beat egg yolks well with sugar, lemon juice and grated lemon rind.

2 Transfer mixture to the top of a double saucepan and cook over hot but not boiling water, stirring constantly with a whisk until mixture thickens.

3 Remove from heat; let it cool slightly and then fold in the stiffly beaten egg whites.

4 Fold in gelatine which you have dissolved in ¼ pint(1·5dl) water. Pour the mixture into a serving bowl and chill. Decorate with angelica 'leaves'.

5 Whisk redcurrant jelly with a little Kirsch to taste, if desired, and serve separately.

Hamper Picnic Makes Portable Feast

There's nothing easier than packing a hamper full of cheeses wrapped in foil, fruits, wines, rolls, a thermos of chilled soup and a cold dish of chicken and setting out in the car for a portable feast.

For events like these, I like to bring the salads washed but not yet prepared, selecting all sorts of greens in season; dark Cos, pale green Salad Bowl lettuce, *mâche*, watercress, tender baby spinach leaves and sprigs of fresh basil and tarragon if available. Always keep salad greens wrapped in foil, of course, complete with bowl, and with a separate cocktail shaker or screwtop jar of dressing. Butter in foil can be kept chilled in a portable ice chest.

My Favourite Gazpacho

(illustrated overleaf)

6 large ripe tomatoes
½ Spanish onion, thinly sliced
1 green pepper, seeded and thinly sliced
½ cucumber, peeled and thinly sliced
1 clove garlic, finely chopped
Salt, Tabasco and freshly ground black pepper
6 tablespoons olive oil
3 tablespoons wine vinegar
¼–½ pint(1·5–3dl) chilled chicken consommé (see page 21)
Finely chopped chives or parsley
Gazpacho accompaniments

1 Seed tomatoes and cut flesh into pieces; combine in a soup or salad bowl with very thinly sliced Spanish onion, green pepper and cucumber. Season to taste with finely chopped garlic, salt, Tabasco and freshly ground black pepper, and marinate in olive oil and wine vinegar in the refrigerator for at least 30 minutes.

2 Just before serving, add chilled chicken consommé and finely chopped chives or parsley. Serve with traditional *gazpacho* accompaniments: diced tomato, green pepper, onion, cucumber and garlic *croûtons*.

Cold Roast Chicken

(for recipe, see **roast chicken with watercress stuffing,** page 32)

Serve with a **green salad** with a **Roquefort dressing** (see **Delmonico salad,** page 138).

Apple Streusel Tart

6 tart eating apples
Juice of 1 lemon
1 unbaked pastry shell
1 oz(25g) sugar
¼ level teaspoon cinnamon
¼ level teaspoon nutmeg or allspice

STREUSEL TOPPING:
3 oz(75g) brown sugar
3 oz(75g) plain flour, sifted
Grated rind of 1 lemon
6 tablespoons softened butter

1 Peel and core apples; cut into eighths and toss in lemon juice. Arrange prepared apples in an unbaked pastry shell. Combine sugar and spices, and sprinkle over apples.

2 **To make Streusel topping:** combine brown sugar, flour and grated lemon rind, and cut softened butter into mixture until crumbly, using a pastry blender or 2 knives. Sprinkle mixture over apples and bake in a hot oven (450°F/230°C/Mark 8) for 15 minutes. Reduce oven temperature to 350°F/180°C/Mark 4 and bake for 30 minutes.

Cheese and Fresh Fruits

(for **cheese,** see pages 240–1)

Menu

My Favourite
Gazpacho

Cold Roast
Chicken

Green Salad with
Roquefort
Dressing

Apple Streusel
Tart

Cheese and Fresh
Fruits

Serves 4–6

with this menu I suggest the following Inexpensive White Wines and Rosés
**Sylvaner d'Alsace
Pouilly Blanc Fumé
Tavel Rosé**

Beach Picnic for the Younger Generation

Red Pepper Salad
with Mustard
Dressing

Hard-boiled Eggs

Club Sandwich
Rolls

Hot Coffee

Fresh Fruit

Gingerbread
Cookies

Serves 4

In America, when I was a boy, we used to like to bring a simple picnic basket to the beach. Easy to carry on a bicycle, or in the car, this light lunch was a winner on many a summer holiday. I've repeated it since with a thermos carrier full of cold bottled beer for more adult tastes. For the weight-conscious, who prefer their portable lunches without bread or rolls, just double the quantities of cooked chicken and bacon, tomatoes and mayonnaise, and serve on individual plates.

The ingredients: red peppers, tomatoes and hard-boiled eggs; 1 screw-top jar of mustard salad dressing; 1 screw-top jar of home-made mayonnaise; 1 large thermos jug of hot coffee (already 'milked and sugared'); rolls or French bread; cooked chicken and bacon; and lettuce leaves, fresh fruit and cookies.

Equipment needed: a sharp knife for vegetables and bread; a bowl for the pepper appetizer; a bread board on which to make the sandwiches; four plates; pepper and salt mills; and paper cups and napkins.

Red Pepper Salad with Mustard Dressing

4 red or yellow peppers

MUSTARD DRESSING:
1–2 teaspoons Dijon mustard
1–2 tablespoons wine vinegar
Salt and freshly ground black pepper
3–6 tablespoons olive oil
**1 tablespoon finely chopped parsley
  and/or chives**

1 Wash the peppers and place them under the grill, as close to the heat as possible. Cook, turning the peppers frequently, until the skin on all sides has charred. Remove charred skin under cold running water.

2 Cut peppers in lengths – 4 to 6 pieces to each pepper – and remove all the seeds and excess fibre. Drain the peppers on absorbent paper.

3 To make mustard dressing: mix the mustard and wine vinegar together. Add salt and freshly ground black pepper to taste; add olive oil and beat with a fork until the mixture emulsifies. Finally, as a garnish, sprinkle over chopped parsley and/or chives.

Hard-boiled Eggs

4–8 eggs
Water

1 Fill a pan with enough water to cover the eggs thoroughly. Bring to the boil and lower eggs into it gently, using a spoon. Lower heat until water is barely bubbling, and cook for about 10 minutes.

2 Remove eggs from water at once and rinse under cold water to stop them from further cooking.

Club Sandwich Rolls

4 **large flat rolls (or 1 loaf French bread cut in quarters)**
¼ **pint(1·5dl) home–made mayonnaise (see page 152)**
1 **lb(450g) sliced cooked chicken**
4 **ripe tomatoes, sliced**
8 **slices cooked bacon**
4 **lettuce leaves**
Salt and freshly ground black pepper

1 Cut each roll, or piece of French bread, in half horizontally. Spread each bottom slice lavishly with mayonnaise. Cover with a layer of sliced chicken; a layer of sliced tomato; top with 2 slices bacon and 1 lettuce leaf. Season with salt and freshly ground black pepper.

2 Spread top half of roll, or French bread, with mayonnaise and assemble sandwich. Wrap a paper napkin around each sandwich.

Fresh Fruit and Hot Coffee

Gingerbread Cookies

Makes about 36 cookies
¾ **lb(350g) sifted plain flour**
1 **teaspoon allspice**
1 **teaspoon ginger**
1 **teaspoon cinnamon**
1 **level teaspoon salt**
½ **level teaspoon soda**
Butter
4 **tablespoons brown sugar**
8 **tablespoons golden syrup**
6 **tablespoons milk**

1 Sift together flour, spices, salt and soda. Blend 6 oz(175g) butter, sugar and golden syrup. Add sifted dry ingredients alternately with milk. Mix well. Chill overnight in the refrigerator.

2 Roll out dough and cut out shapes with cookie cutters. Place cookies on a well-buttered baking sheet, and bake in a moderately hot oven (400°F/200°C/Mark 6) for 10 to 12 minutes.

*with this menu
I suggest the
following Inexpensive
White Wines*
**Soave
Lachryma Christi
Cabernet Blanc
(Yugoslavian)**

*Red Pepper Salad with
Mustard Dressing*

A Fishy Feast for the Garden

There's something festive about eating in the great outdoors, even when your horizons are limited to the confines of your own back garden. Weather permitting, centre your next outdoor meal around a summer spectacular — one of these delicious fish salads from the South of France.

with these recipes I suggest the following Inexpensive White Wines
Pouilly Blanc Fumé
Chevalier d'Alsace
or the following Inexpensive Red Wines
Barolo
Valpolicella

Bouillabaisse Salad

(Serves 6–8)
$\frac{1}{2}$ **lb(225)g frozen prawns**
$\frac{1}{2}$ **lb(225g) cooked lobster meat, diced**
$\frac{1}{2}$ **lb(225g) cooked halibut or sole, diced**
$\frac{1}{2}$ **lb(225g) cooked crabmeat, flaked**
French dressing (see page 100)
1 head lettuce, washed and chilled
1 head Cos lettuce, washed and chilled
4 ripe tomatoes
8 large ripe olives
Finely chopped parsley

1 Defrost prawns and marinate with diced lobster and fish and flaked crab in well-flavoured French dressing in individual bowls.

2 When ready to serve: line salad bowl with lettuce leaves. Arrange prawns, lobster, fish and crabmeat in clusters on a bed of salad greens.

3 Garnish with colourful wedges of tomato, ripe black olives and finely chopped parsley. Serve with additional dressing.

Provençal Fish Salad in Tomato Cases

(Serves 6)
6 large ripe tomatoes
$\frac{1}{2}$ **pint(3dl) well-flavoured mayonnaise (see page 152)**
1 clove garlic, finely chopped
1–2 anchovy fillets, finely chopped
1 tablespoon finely chopped basil or tarragon
2 tablespoons finely chopped parsley
1 tablespoon finely chopped capers

Lemon juice, to taste
$1\frac{1}{2}$ **lb(675g) cold poached fish, diced**
Salt and freshly ground black pepper
Finely chopped parsley

1 **To prepare tomato cases:** plunge tomatoes into boiling water one by one, and remove their skins. Slice cap off each and carefully scoop out all pulp and seeds. Cover loosely with foil and chill in refrigerator until ready to use.

2 Combine mayonnaise, finely chopped garlic, chopped anchovy fillets, chopped herbs and capers, and lemon juice to taste; toss fish lightly in sauce until well coated; season with salt and freshly ground black pepper, to taste, pile mixture into tomato cases and garnish with finely chopped parsley.

Provençal Seafood Salad

(Serves 6)
1 head lettuce
1 head Cos lettuce, washed and chilled
1 lb(450g) cooked white fish, prepared as in recipe above
$\frac{1}{2}$ **lb(225g) cooked prawns**
6 ripe tomatoes
12 black olives
Well-flavoured French dressing (see page 100)

1 Line salad bowl with lettuce leaves and Cos leaves.

2 Combine ingredients for Provençal Fish Salad mixture (see recipe above). Toss well and arrange in centre of bowl with greens.

3 Garnish with cooked prawns and wedges of ripe tomato and black olives. Serve with a well-flavoured French dressing.

Barbecue Parties

Eating outdoors is no longer a choice between uncomfortable picnics by the roadside or rushing plates out into the garden. Thanks to modern electrical equipment that allows us to cook right at the table in our own garden or back yard, and new portable barbecue units that can be carried in the car for grilling chops, steaks and skewers, it can be one of life's finest pleasures. Add to this a selection of specially insulated carriers and thermos jugs to keep food at the right temperature and your outdoor meal can be as informal, or as elaborate, as you choose.

If you embrace the full scope of the barbecue instead of limiting your repertoire to steaks and chops, you will find that you have opened up a whole new range of tastes to your palate, for every dish cooked over charcoal seems to improve in flavour and alter subtly as it cooks to crusty doneness in the wood-scented smoke.

It's not just a trick of the imagination that makes food taste better in the open air. The fire in the grill, the freshness of the air and the beauty of the surroundings add flavour and interest to every dish, whether it is served in a garden, on a terrace, or on a lonely stretch of sandy beach. Skewer cookery can be great fun and delicious, and skewers can be made with practically any food imaginable. Try beef, lamb or pork *kebabs*, cubes of tender meat marinated in olive oil, lemon juice and soy sauce, flavoured with finely chopped shallots, garlic or onions and a bay leaf or two. Let your guests prepare their own *kebabs*, alternating cubes of marinated meat with fresh vegetables, a bay leaf or two, even cubes of bread, brushed with melted butter and finely chopped garlic.

This is a perfectly easy formula for a summer party with a difference. And the choice of combinations is legion: serve bowls of small onions, either raw or poached, strips of green or red pepper, cubes of poached potato, mushroom caps, thin wedges of apple or tomato wrapped in bacon, whole small tomatoes, rum-soaked apricots and port-soaked prunes wrapped in bacon, and cubes of fat salt pork. Guests may then choose their own *kebab* combinations.

Barbecue Cooking Arrangements

Barbecue gear need not be complicated or expensive. You can use a pit, made with a few bricks, some fireproof cement and the grid from an old cooker, or one of the following 'do-it-yourself' suggestions:

A large flower pot covered with a double thickness of chicken wire.

A tin biscuit box: punch holes in the sides for ventilation; use cooker grid for the grill.

A metal wheelbarrow half-filled with stones, with grid from cooker for the grill.

CHARCOAL KNOW-HOW

Charcoal is obtainable from most ironmongers or coal merchants. There are two easy ways to light it: put some in the bottom container of your barbecue and sprinkle with a few drops of lighter fuel, or wrap a few pieces in newspaper, put some more charcoal on top, and set light to the paper.

Don't start cooking too soon. Charcoal should look ash-grey by day and have a red glow after dark. No flames!

CHARCOAL SAVERS

To save charcoal and keep your barbecue new-looking – line the bottom with double-thick aluminium foil. Place gravel or small stones on the foil to insulate it; then put charcoal on top of stones. The foil reflects the heat back on to the food and speeds up cooking time. You'll find it also keeps your equipment cleaner.

When you've finished cooking, don't let charcoal just burn away. If your barbecue has a hood, lower it to snuff out fire. If you have an open grill, use fire tongs to transfer hot coals from barbecue to a fireproof bucket. Then smother fire by covering coals with sand.

MEAT AT ROOM TEMPERATURE

Good barbecue cooks start with their meat at room temperature: 1 to 2 hours out of the refrigerator is a good rule for steaks; big roasts, 2 to 3 hours; chicken, about 30 minutes. Use your own judgment in hot weather.

WARM-UP PERIOD

Always give meats on the spit or grill a chance to warm up over the coals before you start basting. That way you'll find the meat will absorb flavours better.

CHICKEN ON THE GRILL

Place halved young chickens (about 2 lb(900g) each) on charcoal grill, with bony side down. Brush with oil; season well and grill; then turn to finish cooking. The meat will be juicier and better-looking cooked in this way.

FIRE FLAVOURS

Cut a garlic clove in half and toss it on the coals while you're grilling steak or skewered lamb. The flavour is a subtle delight! When roasting pork or ham on the spit, wait until the meat is almost done, then drop a sprig of rosemary or bay leaves on the fire. Wonderful aroma!

COOK IN – COOK OUT

Cooks converted to outdoor grilling can keep at it in winter or in bad weather by getting a grill that goes into the fireplace, or by standing a portable barbecue on the stove under an extractor hood.

Gazpacho Salad
(illustrated on page 232)

2 medium Spanish onions
1 large cucumber
12 large ripe tomatoes
1 large green pepper
8–12 tablespoons dry French bread crumbs

DRESSING:
6 tablespoons olive oil
2–3 tablespoons wine vinegar
1 clove garlic, crushed
Generous pinch of dry mustard
Salt and freshly ground black pepper

1 Slice onions thinly; soak in iced water for 1 hour; drain well.

2 Slice (unpeeled) cucumber thinly. Peel and slice tomatoes. Seed and core pepper, and cut into thin strips.

3 Layer onions, cucumber, tomatoes, green pepper and French bread crumbs alternately in a large glass serving bowl (about 6 pints(3·4 litres) capacity) until all ingredients are used up.

4 Make a well-seasoned dressing with remaining ingredients. Pour over salad and chill until ready to serve.

Barbecued Hamburgers (page 222) and Steak 221

Gazpacho Salad

**Barbecued
Hamburgers
or
Barbecued
Saveloys with
Mustard
with
Barbecued Corn
on the Cob**

**Fruit Brochettes in
Foil**

Serves 12

*with this menu I suggest
the following Inexpensive
Red Wines*
**Rioja Red
Serradayres
Cabernet Red
Gigondas**

Barbecued Hamburgers

(illustrated on page 220)

Try one of the following hamburger combinations, or devise your own. Quantities given are for 1 large hamburger.

1

$\frac{1}{4}$ **lb(100g) steak, coarsely minced**
1 teaspoon chopped parsley
1 teaspoon finely chopped onion
Salt and freshly ground black pepper

2

$\frac{1}{4}$ **lb(100g) steak, coarsely minced**
1 teaspoon tomato ketchup
$\frac{1}{4}$ **teaspoon Worcestershire sauce**
Salt and freshly ground black pepper

3

$\frac{1}{4}$ **lb(100g) steak, coarsely minced**
$\frac{1}{4}$ **teaspoon soy sauce**
2 drops Tabasco
Salt and freshly ground black pepper

1 Combine minced beef with remaining ingredients. Mix well and shape into 1 large hamburger.

2 Spread hamburger with softened butter and grill over very hot coals until underside is brown and crisp; then brush uncooked side with a little more butter, turn over carefully and continue to grill until done to your liking, about 15 minutes in all. (Only hamburgers made with best-quality beef should be served rare.)

3 Serve immediately, accompanied by Dijon mustard and tomato ketchup.

Barbecued Saveloys with Mustard

At their best piping hot, but also good cold.

24 saveloy sausages
Dijon mustard

1 With the point of a sharp knife, make 3 or 4 diagonal slits on both sides of each saveloy. Spread saveloys generously with mustard, pushing it into slits with the side of the knife blade.

2 Arrange saveloys on a grid over hot ashes and grill for 10–15 minutes, or until brown and crisp on the outside and hot through. Turn several times to ensure even cooking.

Barbecued Corn on the Cob

Serve 1 cob per person. When cooking corn, always remember that overcooking will make it tough and hard again.

1 Turn back husks; strip away silk. Brush cobs with softened butter and pull husks back into position. Lay cobs on grid over hot ashes and grill for 15–20 minutes, or until done, turning frequently.

2 Strip off papery brown husks and serve corn with plenty of butter and coarse salt.

To barbecue corn in foil: remove husks; spread each ear with 2 tablespoons butter, sprinkle with salt and freshly ground black pepper and wrap tightly in foil. Grill over hot ashes, turning frequently, for about 20 minutes.

Fruit Brochettes in Foil

3 bananas
Juice of 3 lemons
3 pears
3 oranges
3 peaches
6 plums
4–6 oz(100–175g) granulated sugar
2 teaspoons ground cinnamon
Grand Marnier (optional)

1 Peel and quarter bananas; toss with lemon juice in a large bowl.

2 Peel, quarter and core pears. Add to bananas and toss with lemon juice.

3 Peel oranges, removing every scrap of pith. Cut in four and add to bowl.

4 Pour boiling water over peaches in a sieve one at time and quickly peel off skins. Quarter peaches, discarding stones, and add to the bowl, making sure they are well coated with lemon juice to prevent discolouration.

5 Halve and stone plums and add to the bowl. Sprinkle fruit with sugar and cinnamon; toss lightly. Cover bowl tightly with foil and leave to macerate in the refrigerator for 1 hour.

6 To assemble skewers: drain pieces of fruit thoroughly, reserving juices, and divide evenly between 12 7-or 8-inch (18- or 20-cm) skewers.

7 Wrap each skewer in a rectangle of double-thickness foil, sealing joins carefully. Keep cool until needed.

8 When ready to cook: lay parcels on a grid over hot coals and cook for 10–15 minutes, turning occasionally.

9 Meanwhile, pour reserved juices into a small pan and simmer until reduced by half. Remove from heat and flavour with a little Grand Marnier if liked.

10 Fold back foil wrappings. Spoon a little sauce over fruit and serve immediately.

Orange, Onion and Tomato Salad

1 crisp Cos lettuce
2 large Spanish onions
3 large firm tomatoes
2 large oranges
Pitted black olives, to garnish

DRESSING:
4 tablespoons olive oil
2–3 tablespoons lemon juice
Pinch of sugar
Pinch of dry mustard
Salt and freshly ground black pepper

1 Wash lettuce and pat each leaf dry in a clean towel, wrap in a damp cloth and chill until needed.

2 Peel onions and cut 6 slices from the middle of each one about $\frac{1}{4}$ inch(0·5cm) thick. Soak in iced water for 1 hour.

3 In the same way, cut 4 $\frac{1}{4}$-inch(0·5-cm) slices from the middle of each tomato.

4 Peel oranges and cut 6 $\frac{1}{4}$-inch(0·5-cm) slices from middle of each one.

5 To assemble salad: line a large, flat dish with lettuce leaves. Arrange onion slices in one layer on top; cover each slice with a slice of tomato and top with an orange slice.

6 Make a dressing with olive oil, lemon juice, sugar, mustard, salt and freshly ground black pepper; pour over salad. Garnish with black olives and serve at once.

Chinese Barbecued Spareribs

3 lb(1·4kg) pork spareribs
8 tablespoons soy sauce
3 tablespoons red wine
4 teaspoons castor sugar
1 teaspoon salt
1 clove garlic, crushed

Menu

Orange, Onion and Tomato Salad

Chinese Barbecued Spareribs

Charcoal-baked Cod Steaks with Lemon with Baked Potato Slices in Foil

Bilberry Cheesecake

Serves 6

with this menu I suggest the following Inexpensive White Wines or Rosés
Touraine Sauvignon
Verdicchio
Quincy
Rosé d'Anjou

1 With a sharp knife, score meat between ribs on both sides without separating them completely.

2 Combine remaining ingredients in a flat dish with 4 tablespoons water, stirring until sugar and salt have dissolved. Coat ribs thoroughly and leave to marinate for 1 hour.

3 Drain ribs, reserving marinade; place them on a grid over glowing coals and barbecue for 30 to 40 minutes, turning frequently and brushing with remaining marinade. Pork should be thoroughly cooked, with a rich brown glaze.

4 Separate ribs and serve immediately.

Note: Ribs may also be roasted in a moderate oven (350°F/180°C/Mark 4). Allow 1 to 1½ hours for really well-cooked meat and baste frequently with marinade to glaze and prevent it drying out.

Charcoal-baked Cod Steaks with Lemon

6 cod steaks
Salt and freshly ground black pepper
6 lemons
¼ lb(100g) butter, melted
6 tablespoons dry white wine
2 cloves garlic, crushed
2 tablespoons chopped parsley

1 Season fish generously with salt and freshly ground black pepper.

2 Peel lemons, cutting away all skin and pith as though peeling an apple. Slice lemons thinly.

3 Cut 6 pieces of foil 10 inches(25cm) square. Arrange ½ lemon in slices down centre of each square. Put a cod steak on top and cover with remaining half of lemon in slices.

4 Combine remaining ingredients and spoon over fish.

5 Wrap each cod steak in foil and seal parcel securely.

6 Place parcels on a grid over glowing coals. The fish will be ready in 15 to 20 minutes.

7 Serve immediately, with foil folded back.

Baked Potato Slices in Foil

1 Allow 1 large baking potato per person. Scrub thoroughly; pat dry; cut each unpeeled potato in three vertically.

2 Brush cut surfaces with 2 tablespoons melted butter, a few drops of lemon juice and a generous sprinkling of salt and freshly ground black pepper.

3 Reassemble each potato and wrap securely in foil.

4 Bake over hot coals for 1 hour, or until potatoes feel soft when lightly squeezed.

Bilberry Cheesecake

Fresh bilberries appear all too briefly in English shops in late summer. However, you can also buy excellent bilberries bottled in light syrup, with a full, fresh flavour.

Prepare this cheesecake in your favourite crust – I like a crisp, thin shortcrust shell to act as a foil to the delicate filling, but you may prefer to use a crushed biscuit crust made with 1 lb(450g) crushed digestive biscuits, 6 oz(175g) melted butter, ¼ teaspoon cinnamon and a pinch of salt. Crust should be at least 2 inches(5cm) deep to hold the filling comfortably, and baked in a loose-bottomed tin to facilitate removal.

1 deep 9-inch(23-cm) pastry shell, prebaked

FILLING:

10 oz(275g) cottage cheese, sieved
2 eggs
½ pint(3dl) sour cream
4–6 tablespoons castor sugar
3–4 teaspoons lemon juice
1 teaspoon vanilla essence
3 drops almond essence
Pinch of salt

TOPPING:

1 16-oz(456-g) jar bilberries in light
   syrup
1½ tablespoons cornflour
2 teaspoons lemon juice
Pinch of salt
Pinch of cinnamon

1 Preheat oven to moderate (375°F/190°C/ Mark 5). Leave baked tart shell in tin.

2 To make filling: combine sieved cheese with remaining ingredients and beat vigorously with a wooden spoon until smooth and creamy. (If you have an electric blender, it is not necessary to sieve cheese; simply blend ingredients for 2–3 minutes.)

3 Pour filling into prepared shell and bake for 45 minutes, or until set. Remove from oven and allow to cool completely.

4 To make topping: drain bilberries. Dilute cornflour with a few tablespoons of bilberry syrup and combine with remaining syrup in a small, heavy pan. Stir over moderate heat, stirring until smooth and thick, about 4 minutes from the time mixture comes to the boil. Allow to cool; then stir in bilberries and flavour with lemon juice, salt and cinnamon.

5 Pour bilberry topping over cheesecake and chill until firm.

Note: For a picnic barbecue, leave chilled (or frozen) cheesecake in its tin and wrap in foil or greaseproof paper and several sheets of newspaper to keep it cold.

Salami Appetizer Snack

4 tablespoons each finely diced green
   pepper, cucumber and celery
2 tablespoons diced red pimento
24 large thin slices salami, skinned
Stuffed green olives, to garnish

DRESSING:

½ teaspoon Dijon mustard
Few drops of lemon juice
1 tablespoon olive oil
Salt and freshly ground black pepper

1 Mix diced green pepper, cucumber and celery together.

2 Make a well-seasoned dressing with mustard, lemon juice, olive oil, salt and freshly ground black pepper.

3 Put a little vegetable mixture on each slice of salami and fold in two. Arrange in a tight ring on a round serving dish so that folded slices support each other. (Spear slices with toothpicks if they refuse to stay folded in two.)

4 Fill centre of dish with stuffed olives and serve immediately.

Barbecued Lamb Chops with Herbs
(illustrated on page 230)

8 double loin chops of lamb,
   8–10 oz(225–275g) each
1 teaspoon each dried thyme,
   rosemary and marjoram or
   oregano
3–4 small bay leaves, crushed
Generous pinch of paprika
Finely grated rind and juice of
   1 large lemon
6 tablespoons olive oil
Salt and freshly ground black pepper
Knobs of butter
Finely chopped parsley

Menu

Salami Appetizer
Snack

Barbecued Lamb
Chops with Herbs
with
Vegetables in a
Packet
and
Baked Potatoes
with Blue Cheese
Dressing

Tossed Green
Salad

Fresh Peaches
with Macaroons

Serves 8

*with this menu I suggest
the following Inexpensive
Red Wines*
**Beaujolais
Bourgueil
Côtes-du-Rhône**

1 Combine herbs with crushed bay leaves, paprika and grated lemon rind. Mix well.

2 Rub herb mixture into chops. Lay them side by side in a large, shallow dish. Pour over lemon juice and olive oil; season lightly with salt and generously with freshly ground black pepper, and put chops aside in a cool place to marinate for 3 hours, turning occasionally.

3 When ready to cook chops: drain thoroughly and lay on a grid over hot coals. Grill for 20 to 30 minutes, turning occasionally, until done to your liking.

4 Just before removing chops from grid, throw a good pinch of dried mixed herbs on to the coals, using any or all of the varieties from the marinade. The resulting smoke will impart a delicious flavour to the meat.

5 Serve topped with a knob of butter and sprinkled with finely chopped parsley.

Vegetables in a Packet
(illustrated on page 230)

Makes 1 portion
Salt
2 thick slices aubergine
2 thick slices firm tomato
2 thin slices Spanish onion
2 thick slices courgette
2 small mushrooms, halved
Freshly ground black pepper
Pinch of oregano or marjoram
1 teaspoon olive oil
1 teaspoon butter

1 Rub salt into aubergine slices and leave them to drain in a colander for about 30 minutes. Rinse slices well and squeeze dry between folds of cloth or absorbent paper.

2 Cut a double thickness of foil 10 to 12 inches(25 to 30cm) square. Arrange aubergine slices side by side in the centre; cover each slice with a slice of tomato, followed by a slice of Spanish onion and a slice of courgette. Lay halved mushrooms on top. Sprinkle with salt, freshly ground black pepper and a pinch of oregano or marjoram; moisten with olive oil and top with a nut of butter. Fold over edges of foil and seal packet tightly. All this can be done in advance.

3 When ready to cook: lay packet on a grid over hot coals and cook for 12 to 15 minutes, turning once or twice.

4 Serve packet intact, with foil folded back to act as a plate.

Baked Potatoes with Blue Cheese Dressing

1 Scrub large baking potatoes thoroughly and bake them as usual, either wrapped in foil and arranged on the barbecue grid, or in the ashes of the fire.

2 For each potato blend 1oz(25g) blue cheese with 2 tablespoons sour cream and 1 tablespoon chopped chives or spring onion tops.

3 Just before serving, slash tops of potatoes in criss-cross fashion and squeeze gently to force them open. Fill with cheese mixture and serve immediately.

Tossed Green Salad
(for the recipe see **green salad and variations,** page 100)

Fresh Peaches with Macaroons
Serve fresh ripe peaches accompanied by a dish of these macaroons. They are crisp and hard when first baked – if you prefer them chewy, leave them out overnight.

MACAROONS:
Makes 36
Sheets of rice paper

6 oz(175g) ground almonds
1 oz(25g) icing sugar, sifted
½ lb(225g) castor sugar
3 egg whites (unbeaten)
Few drops of almond essence
36 blanched almonds

1 Preheat oven to very slow (300°F/150°C/ Mark 2).

2 Line 3 baking sheets with rice paper.

3 Mix ground almonds with icing sugar and 2 oz(50g) castor sugar.

4 Make a well in the centre; add 1 egg white and work by hand to a stiff, smooth paste.

5 Gradually work in remaining castor sugar and egg whites until paste is soft and smooth again. Flavour with a few drops of almond essence.

6 Put mixture in a piping bag fitted with a plain ¾-inch(2-cm) nozzle and pipe out 36 rounds on prepared baking sheets. (Or drop on to baking sheets from a teaspoon.)

7 Dust lightly with a little extra castor sugar and decorate top of each macaroon with a blanched almond.

8 Bake macaroons for 25 to 30 minutes until firm and golden.

9 Cool macaroons slightly before removing them from baking sheets and trimming off excess rice paper.

10 Then leave to cool completely on a rack before serving or storing in an airtight container.

Crudités

(illustrated on page 229)

Choose crisp raw vegetables – strips of carrot, celery and Florence fennel, firm tomatoes and sweet peppers cut in wedges, thick slices of cucumber, spring onions, cauliflowerets, tiny white mushrooms, radishes and leaves of chicory – enough to serve 8. Serve with Bagna Cauda and a Herbed Cheese Dip.

Bagna Cauda

½ lb(225g) butter
3–4 tablespoons olive oil
3–4 cloves garlic, finely chopped
6–8 anchovy fillets, crushed
1 small white truffle, thinly sliced (optional)

1 This sauce is traditionally prepared in a flameproof earthenware dish with a short handle. Melt butter in it with olive oil and sauté finely chopped garlic until golden.

2 Remove dish from heat; add anchovies and mix thoroughly. Return to low heat and simmer, stirring constantly, until anchovies have dissolved into a paste. Stir in sliced truffle, if used.

3 Serve in the pan, keeping it hot over a small burner.

Herbed Cheese Dip

3 small packets Philadelphia cream cheese
2 teaspoons lemon juice
4 tablespoons double cream
1–2 tablespoons milk
½ clove garlic, crushed
Freshly ground black pepper
1–2 tablespoons each finely chopped parsley, basil and chives
Dried thyme

Menu

Crudités
with Bagna Cauda
and
Herbed Cheese
Dip

Corn-husk
Barbecued Trout
with
Grilled Aubergines

Chocolate Beer
Cake

Serves 8

with this menu I suggest the following Inexpensive White Wines or Rosés
**Chianti Ruffino
White
Riesling
Tavel Rosé**

1 Beat cream cheese with a wooden spoon until smooth.

2 Stir lemon juice into double cream; beat into softened cheese, together with milk.

3 Season to taste with about $\frac{1}{2}$ clove crushed garlic and a little freshly ground black pepper.

4 Finally, beat in finely chopped parsley, basil and chives, and a generous pinch of dried thyme.

Corn-husk Barbecued Trout

A way to make use of the husks from fresh boiled corn. If corn husks are not available, wrap fish in lightly oiled foil instead.

$\frac{1}{4}$ lb(100g) softened butter
8 bay leaves, crushed
2 teaspoons lemon juice
Salt and freshly ground black pepper
8 fresh trout, about $\frac{1}{2}$ lb(225g) each, gutted
2 tablespoons finely chopped parsley
1 teaspoon dried marjoram
16 rashers unsmoked fat bacon
8 corn husks
Lemon wedges, to garnish

1 Combine butter with crushed bay leaves, lemon juice, salt and freshly ground black pepper, to taste. Divide into 8 even-sized portions.

2 Stuff a piece of butter into each trout. Season fish and sprinkle with finely chopped parsley and dried marjoram.

3 Wrap 2 rashers bacon round each trout. Put each fish inside a corn husk (in place of the ear of corn) and tie at the silk end.

4 Set husks in glowing embers and surround with live coals. Cook for 7–8 minutes on each side, or until fish flakes easily with a fork.

5 Serve immediately, accompanied by a dish of lemon wedges.

Grilled Aubergines

4 large long aubergines
Salt and freshly ground black pepper
2–3 teaspoons oregano
Olive oil

1 Cut aubergines across width into $\frac{1}{2}$-inch (1·5-cm) slices. Sprinkle salt on both sides; place in a colander and leave for 1 hour to allow salt to draw out bitter juices.

2 Rinse slices thoroughly and press dry between folds of cloth or sheets of absorbent paper.

3 Sprinkle slices with freshly ground black pepper and oregano; brush all over with olive oil.

4 Grill over hot ashes for 5 to 7 minutes, or until slices are soft and lightly browned, turning once.

Chocolate Beer Cake

Butter
Plain flour
2 oz(50g) bitter dessert chocolate
$\frac{1}{4}$ level teaspoon salt
1 level teaspoon baking powder
$\frac{1}{4}$ level teaspoon bicarbonate of soda
6 oz(175g) castor sugar
2 eggs
8 fl oz(3dl) lager
3 oz(75g) walnuts, coarsely chopped (optional)

FILLING:
2 oz(50g) softened butter
$\frac{1}{4}$ lb(100g) icing sugar, sifted
1–2 tablespoons lager
2 oz(50g) bitter dessert chocolate, melted and cooled

Crudités with Herbed Cheese Dip and Bagna Cauda (page 227)

1 Butter 2 8-inch (20-cm) sandwich tins and dust lightly with flour. Preheat oven to moderate (350°F/180°C/Mark 4).

2 Melt dessert chocolate in the top of a double saucepan and allow to cool to lukewarm.

3 Sift $\frac{1}{2}$ lb(225g) flour, salt, baking powder and bicarbonate of soda into a bowl.

4 In another bowl, cream $\frac{1}{4}$ lb(100g) butter; add sugar gradually and beat until light and fluffy. Beat in eggs, one at a time, followed by melted chocolate. Then add flour mixture gradually, alternating it with lager (save 1 or 2 tablespoons for the filling) and beating vigorously until batter is well blended. Fold in walnuts, if used.

5 Pour batter into prepared tins and bake for 25 to 30 minutes, or until layers spring back when pressed lightly with the finger.

6 Remove tins from oven; allow to cool for 5 minutes, then turn layers out on wire racks and leave to become quite cold.

7 To make filling: cream softened butter with icing sugar until very light. Add lager and lukewarm melted chocolate and beat vigorously until well blended. Chill until firm before using.

8 Sandwich cake layers with chocolate filling and spread remainder smoothly over top and sides. (If you have not included nuts in the batter, you can decorate top of cake with walnut halves.)

229

Left, above: Vegetables in a Packet (page 226)
Left, below: Skillet Salad and Barbecued Lamb
Chops with Herbs (pages 225 and 233)

Barbecue Parties

French Garlic Bread in Foil (page 234)

Skillet Salad

(illustrated on page 230)

4 lb(1·8kg) green peppers
10 Spanish onions
6–8 tablespoons olive oil
12 ripe tomatoes
2 7-oz(198-g) cans red pimentos
Salt and freshly ground black pepper

1 Cut peppers in half lengthwise and remove pith and seeds. Slice lengthwise into strips ½ inch(1·5cm) wide.

2 Peel Spanish onions and cut into slices ¼ inch (0·5cm) thick.

3 Sauté green peppers and onions in olive oil over moderate heat, stirring frequently, for about 8 minutes, until vegetables have lost some of their crispness and are slightly coloured.

4 Cut tomatoes into slices ¼ inch(0·5cm) thick. Drain pimentos and cut into ½-inch(1·5-cm) strips.

5 Add to peppers and onions, together with salt and freshly ground black pepper, to taste, and continue to cook for 4 or 5 minutes longer, until tomatoes are soft and coloured but not mushy. Serve hot.

Note: For a picnic barbecue, finish cooking the salad with tomatoes and pimentos in a large pan or skillet over the barbecue fire. Alternatively, cook salad completely at home and serve cold.

Spatch-cocked Chicken

Nothing could be simpler or more delicious than a tender young chicken grilled over charcoal. Serve half a chicken per person, garnished with a generous knob of butter and a squeeze of lemon.

6 grilling chickens, about 2½ lb (1·1kg) each

Olive oil
Salt and freshly ground black pepper
Paprika

1 Wipe chickens and split in half lengthwise. Break drumstick, hip and wing joints so that chickens will lie flat on the grid.

2 Brush each chicken generously with olive oil and season to taste with salt, freshly ground black pepper and a generous pinch of paprika per side.

3 Place on grid, cut side down, and grill for 10 to 15 minutes; then turn over, brush with more oil and continue to cook for a further 15 minutes, or until the juices run quite clear when chicken is pierced with a skewer through the thickest part of the leg.

For a more adventurous version, try the following:

Spatch-cocked Chicken with Honey Fruit Marinade

6 grilling chickens (about 2½ lb[1kg] each)

MARINADE:
6 tablespoons clear honey
2 tablespoons Dijon mustard
2 tablespoons oil
¾ pint(4dl) pineapple juice
¾ pint(4dl) orange juice
6 fl oz(175ml) tomato ketchup
Salt and freshly ground black pepper
Cayenne pepper
Ground ginger

1 To make marinade: bring the first six ingredients to the boil in a pan and simmer gently for about 40 minutes until slightly thickened. Season generously with salt, freshly ground black pepper and a generous pinch or two of cayenne pepper and ground ginger.

Menu

Skillet Salad

Spatch-cocked
Chicken
or
Spatch-cocked
Chicken with
Honey Fruit
Marinade

French Garlic
Bread in Foil

Apple Turnovers

Serves 12

*with this menu I suggest
the following Inexpensive
White Wines or Rosés*
**Touraine Sauvignon
Verdicchio
Quincy
Rosé d'Anjou**

233

2 Split chickens in half down the breast; break drumstick, hip and wing joints as above. Brush generously with marinade and leave for at least 1 hour to absorb flavours.

3 Drain chicken halves thoroughly and thread on spits (or place flat on a grid) over hot coals. Barbecue slowly, brushing occasionally with remaining marinade, for 15 to 20 minutes on each side, or until chickens are crisply browned on the outside, and juices run clear when a skewer is pushed into the thickest part of the leg.

French Garlic Bread in Foil
(illustrated on page 231)

1 One long French loaf will serve 3, possibly 4. Cut each loaf on the slant into slices about 1½ inches(4cm) thick, taking care not to cut through base at any point.

2 Spread each slice with garlic butter (see below).

3 Wrap loaf tightly in foil and grill over hot ashes, turning frequently, for about 20 minutes, or until butter has melted and bread is crisp and hot.

GARLIC BUTTER:
(Enough for 1 French loaf about 16 inches (40cm) long)
¼ lb(100g) softened butter
1–2 cloves garlic, crushed
1 tablespoon finely chopped parsley
Salt and freshly ground black pepper

To make garlic butter: pound softened butter smoothly with crushed garlic, finely chopped parsley, salt and freshly ground black pepper, to taste.

Apple Turnovers

Makes 12
1 lb(450g) puff pastry
Butter for baking sheets
Beaten egg, to glaze

FILLING:
1½ lb(675g) cooking apples, peeled, cored and thinly sliced
2 tablespoons granulated sugar
2 tablespoons dark brown sugar
2 oz(50g) mixed raisins and sultanas, chopped
1 tablespoon flour
½ teaspoon freshly grated nutmeg
½ teaspoon ground cinnamon
Grated rinds of ½ orange and ½ lemon
Juice of 1 lemon
2 tablespoons orange juice

1 Preheat oven to moderately hot (400°F/200°C/Mark 6). Butter 2 large baking sheets.

2 Combine filling ingredients in a bowl and toss until well mixed.

3 Roll out pastry very thinly and cut into 12 circles 6 inches(15cm) in diameter.

4 Heap filling on one half of each pastry circle, leaving a ¼-inch(0·5-cm) rim clear. Brush edges lightly with water; fold each circle in half and seal tightly, turning edges over on themselves attractively.

5 Arrange turnovers on prepared baking sheets. Cut 2 or 3 small slits on top with a sharp-pointed knife, and glaze with beaten egg.

6 Bake for 15 to 20 minutes, or until pastry is puffed and golden, and apples feel soft when pierced (through one of the slits) with a toothpick.

7 Serve hot, or reheated on a barbecue grid lined with foil.

Christmas Entertaining

Informality is creeping more and more into the daily ritual of our meals. This very informality is a boon at Christmas, when entertaining is such an important part of our activities. From the traditional family Christmas dinner (roast turkey, game or goose with all the trimmings) to the more sophisticated approach of a midnight supper for lovers and friends (Avocado and Orange Salad, *Timbale* of Duck and *Tulipes Glacées à l'Ananas*), Christmas entertaining becomes a positive joy instead of a problem when close ones are carried gaily – drink in hand – into the preparations for the party. It's a great deal more fun to be brought right into the picture, to help serve the drinks, carve the bird or make the salad dressing.

That preparing the Christmas feast was already a family affair in Victorian England we know from the mouth-watering descriptions of the Cratchits' Christmas dinner as described by Charles Dickens. Mrs Cratchit made the gravy 'hissing hot'; Master Peter mashed the potatoes with all his force; Miss Belinda sweetened the apple sauce, and the young Cratchits, 'mounting guard, crammed spoons into their mouths lest they should shriek for goose before their turn came to be helped'.

After the whole family had been 'steeped in sage and onion to their eyebrows' came the Christmas pudding. 'Hallo! A great deal of steam! The pudding was out of the copper.' And then Mrs Cratchit entered, proudly bearing the great round pudding 'like a speckled cannon ball blazing in a half a quartern of ignited brandy and bedight with Christmas holly stuck in the top'.

Centre your Christmas dinner around a golden turkey in the traditional manner; surround it with cranberry baked apples. Accompany it with mashed potatoes, green beans and a delicious winter salad of curly endive dressed with a mustard-flavoured vinaigrette. The apples are placed in the roasting pan with the bird 45 minutes before serving.

Precede the great golden bird with a chilled turbot salad with green olives, and end the meal with a traditional yule log cake, or, more simply, cheese and fresh fruits.

Christmas Turbot Salad with Green Olives

2 lb(900g) turbot
Salt
1 quart(1 litre) water
¼ pint(1·5dl) milk
5 tablespoons olive oil
Juice of 1 lemon
Freshly ground black pepper
2–4 tablespoons chopped parsley
2–4 level tablespoons chopped onion
¼ pint(1·5dl) home-made mayonnaise (see page 152)
12–18 green olives

1 Cut turbot into slices about ¾ inch(1·5cm) thick and place in boiling salted water to which you have added milk to make fish white. Reduce heat so that water barely bubbles. It is important that the turbot cooks very slowly so that it does not lose its juices in the stock. When fish can be flaked with a fork, remove from heat and drain.

2 Remove skin and bones while fish is still warm. Dress immediately with olive oil, lemon juice and salt and freshly ground black pepper to taste. Add chopped parsley and onion; toss once and allow to cool.

3 Just before serving, correct seasoning, adding more olive oil and lemon juice if necessary. Spoon over mayonnaise and toss gently. Garnish with green olives.

235

Roast Turkey with Sausage and Chestnut Stuffing

1 medium-sized turkey, about
  10 lb(4·5kg) dressed weight
Salt and freshly ground black pepper

SAUSAGE MEAT STUFFING:
3 oz(75g) fat bacon slices
2 level tablespoons butter
4 oz(100g) stale trimmed white bread,
  cut into $\frac{1}{3}$-inch(0·5-cm) cubes
1 lb(450g) pork sausage meat
$\frac{1}{2}$ lb(225g) boned pork sparerib,
  minced
1 small onion, finely chopped
2 level tablespoons finely chopped
  parsley
$\frac{1}{4}$ level teaspoon dried thyme
$\frac{1}{4}$ level teaspoon dried marjoram
Pinch of dried sage
4 tablespoons turkey giblet or
  chicken stock
1 egg, beaten
Salt and freshly ground black pepper

CHESTNUT STUFFING:
2 lb(900g) chestnuts, peeled and
  skinned
Turkey giblet or chicken stock
  (optional)
1–2 tablespoons butter
Salt and freshly ground black pepper

BASTING SAUCE:
8 oz(225g) butter
$\frac{1}{2}$ pint(1·5dl) turkey giblet or
  chicken stock

1 **To make sausage meat stuffing:** in a large frying pan, cook bacon slices until fat runs and bacon turns crisp. Remove from pan with a slotted spoon and crumble into a large bowl.

2 Add butter to fat remaining in pan. Heat until frothy. Then add bread cubes and toss over a moderate heat until they are crisp on the outside but still feel soft and spongy inside when pressed. Add sautéed bread cubes to the crumbled bacon.

3 Add remaining ingredients. Mix by hand until thoroughly blended.

4 Having peeled and skinned chestnuts (see opposite★), cook them in boiling stock, or simply in salted water, until they are quite tender, about 20 minutes.

5 Drain chestnuts thoroughly, reserving stock; return them to the hot, dry pan. Add butter; moisten with 1 or 2 tablespoons of the stock, and swirl around until chestnuts are coated with buttery liquid. Season with salt and freshly ground black pepper.

6 Preheat oven to fairly hot (425°F/220°C/ Mark 7).

7 Wipe turkey both inside and out with a damp cloth or absorbent paper.

8 Free the skin from the breast by working your hand down under the skin from the neck end. If skin refuses to come away at any point, do not force it or you may cause it to tear. Instead, separate the meat from the underside of skin with the tip of a small knife, or snip it free with a pair of scissors. Proceed carefully until you have loosened skin almost to the end of the breast and down each side to the legs.

9 Stuff breast with sausage meat mixture, pushing it right down and over sides of breast to keep the meat moist. Try not to pack it too tightly, however, as it does tend to swell. Draw the neck skin over the back, not too tightly, and either sew or fasten it in position with metal skewers or toothpicks.

10 Chestnuts should be stuffed loosely into the body cavity. (Any left over can be added to the pan juices to reheat about half an hour before bird is ready to come out of the oven; then strained out of the sauce with a slotted spoon just before serving.)

11 To truss bird: sew or skewer vent tightly to prevent juices escaping. Cut off ends of wings to use for the giblet stock. Tie legs together with string and fasten string around tail.

12 Lay bird, breast side up, in a roomy roasting tin. Season generously with salt and freshly ground black pepper, and with a sharp toothpick or skewer, prick the breast skin all over – this, too, helps to prevent it bursting should the stuffing swell.

13 Cover bird with butter-soaked muslin and roast turkey on lowest shelf of oven for 15 minutes. Then reduce temperature to moderate (350°F/180°C/Mark 4) for the rest of the cooking time.

14 Using remainder of butter mixed with stock as your basting sauce, baste turkey with some of this buttery liquid at the end of the first 15 minutes, and every 15 minutes thereafter, making sure that the muslin is completely remoistened with this liquid.

15 The total roasting time, including the first 15 minutes at the higher temperature, is calculated at between 12 and 15 minutes per lb/450g, but this can only be a guide. The important thing to remember is that with a turkey you are dealing with two different kinds of meat, the delicate white meat of the breast, and the dark leg meat, which needs longer cooking. A balance must therefore be struck by roasting the bird just long enough to cook the legs through without drying out the breast. Test the leg by pushing a skewer into the thickest part close to the body – the juices should just run clear. If you then cut the string, the leg joint should wiggle loosely in its socket.

16 When turkey is cooked, discard muslin, trussing threads and skewers, and transfer to a hot serving dish. Keep hot in the turned-off oven while you finish gravy.

17 Skim pan juices. You may find this easier to do if you pour them off into a bowl first. Leave gravy for a couple of minutes to allow all the fat to come to the surface so that you can skim it off.

18 Correct seasoning if necessary. Gravy may also be thickened with a teaspoon of cornflour, worked to a smooth paste with cold water before it is stirred in and brought to the boil. Pour gravy into a hot sauce boat and serve.

19 Serve the turkey and trimmings surrounded by cranberry baked apples, and accompany it with **mashed potatoes** (see page 42), **haricots verts** (see page 126) and a **curly endive salad** dressed with **mustard-flavoured vinaigrette** (see page 238).

★To Peel Chestnuts

1 With the tip of a small knife, cut a slit in the shell on the rounded side of each chestnut.

2 Heat 3 tablespoons cooking oil in a wide, heavy saucepan.

3 Add enough chestnuts to make more or less a single layer, and sauté over a high heat for about 5 minutes, shaking pan to keep chestnuts on the move and prevent them charring.

4 Transfer chestnuts to a colander with a slotted spoon. Rinse briefly so that they are cool enough to handle.

5 Shell chestnuts and peel away thin inner skins. They are now ready for cooking.

If you are preparing anything over 1 lb(450g) of chestnuts, you will probably have to fry them off in batches. The oil in the pan will do for several batches.

Allowing for shells, skins and the odd bad or wormy nut, you can, on average, count on getting $\frac{1}{2}$ lb(225g) from 1 lb(450g) chestnuts.

Cranberry Baked Apples

6 large baking apples
1 can whole-berry cranberry sauce
2 oz(50g) sugar
8 marshmallows, cut in eighths
2 oz(50g) finely chopped walnuts

1 Spread half the cranberry sauce in shallow baking pan. Add sugar and enough water to fill pan to a depth of about $\frac{1}{2}$ inch(1·5cm).

2 Core apples, peel about $\frac{1}{4}$ inch(0·5cm) down from stem end; place peeled side down on cranberry sauce in pan. Bake at 350°F/180°C/Mark 4, for 30 minutes. Turn apples peeled side up.

3 Combine remaining cranberry sauce, marshmallows and chopped walnuts. Fill apples heaping full. Return to oven; bake 15 minutes longer or until apples are tender.

Curly Endive Salad with Mustard Dressing

1 head curly endive (frisé)
6 button mushrooms
Lemon juice
6 walnut halves
2 level tablespoons chopped parsley

MUSTARD VINAIGRETTE:
1 tablespoon lemon juice
1–2 tablespoons wine vinegar
$\frac{1}{2}$ level teaspoon dry mustard
$\frac{1}{2}$ clove garlic, finely chopped
6–8 tablespoons olive oil
Salt and freshly ground black pepper

1 Separate curly endive leaves from base of head. Wash well and discard any tough or damaged leaves. Shake dry and chill.

2 Wash mushrooms and trim stems; slice thinly and toss in lemon juice to preserve colour.

3 **To make the dressing:** mix together lemon juice, wine vinegar, and dry mustard. Add finely chopped garlic, olive oil and salt and freshly ground black pepper, to taste.

4 **To serve:** pour mustard vinaigrette into salad bowl, arrange prepared curly endive leaves on top. Sprinkle with sliced mushrooms, walnut halves and finely chopped parsley. Toss well to ensure that every leaf is glistening with dressing. Check seasoning and serve.

Christmas Yule Log Cake

Elegant, exciting, and as festive as the season: Christmas Yule Log Cake from France. The cake itself is a delicate sponge roll filled with Vanilla Butter Icing; the chocolate-flavoured covering is shaped and surfaced like natural bark; and bright red glacé cherries and 'leaves' of green angelica complete the traditional yule log look.

Serve this rich, delectable cake to aunts and uncles for tea; or let it make your Christmas dinner the most important family gathering of the year.

6 eggs, separated
$\frac{1}{2}$ lb(225g) sugar
2 tablespoons lemon juice
Grated rind of $\frac{1}{2}$ lemon
Salt
3 oz(75g) flour
1 oz(25g) cornflour
Butter

VANILLA BUTTER ICING:
6 oz(175g) softened butter, diced
$\frac{3}{4}$ teaspoon vanilla essence
$1\frac{1}{2}$ tablespoons Grand Marnier
$\frac{3}{4}$ lb(350g) icing sugar

CHOCOLATE BUTTER ICING:
4–5 squares unsweetened chocolate
$\frac{3}{4}$ lb(350g) icing sugar
1 egg
1 egg yolk
6 oz(175g) softened butter, diced

GARNISH:
Apricot jam
Powdered coffee or chocolate
Angelica
Glacé cherries

1 Preheat oven to 350°F/180°C/Mark 4.

2 Beat together egg yolks, sugar, lemon juice, 1 tablespoon water, lemon rind and a generous pinch of salt until light and fluffy (5 minutes at high mixer speed).

3 Sift 3 oz(75g) flour and cornflour and mix into egg yolk mixture a little at a time.

4 Whisk egg whites until soft peaks form and fold gently into yolk mixture.

5 Butter and lightly flour a $9\frac{1}{2} \times 13\frac{1}{2}$-inch (24.5 × 34.5-cm) baking tin. Pour in cake mixture. Cut through mixture gently several times to break up any large air bubbles.

6 Bake cake for about 25 minutes, or until surface springs back when gently pressed with fingertip. Invert tin on a cake rack and allow to cool for 10 minutes. Remove cake from tin on to a sheet of waxed paper and cut off all the edges of the cake. Roll cake as for a jelly roll, without removing the paper. Cool and chill.

7 **To make vanilla butter icing:** cream diced, softened butter with vanilla essence and Grand Marnier in an electric mixer (medium speed). Gradually beat in icing sugar alternately with 3 tablespoons hot water until smooth.

8 **To make chocolate butter icing:** melt unsweetened chocolate in the top of a double saucepan; combine chocolate, icing sugar and 6 tablespoons hot water in bowl of electric mixer. At high speed beat in egg and additional egg yolk. Add diced, softened butter a little at a time, beating until smooth. Continue to beat until thick enough to spread.

9 Unroll cake, remove waxed paper, brush with apricot jam and spread with vanilla butter icing. Roll as jelly roll, wrap in waxed paper and chill until icing becomes firm.

10 **To decorate cake:** when ready to decorate, remove waxed paper from cake; cut off a thin slice at one end diagonally; trim this slice to an approximate circle and place on top of cake to represent a sawn-off branch when iced. Ice cake generously with chocolate butter icing, using a pastry bag with a flattened, notched tube, running strips of icing along cake to look like bark. Ice two ends of cake with vanilla butter icing, then top of sawn-off branch; smooth these with a spatula dipped in hot water and then decorate with thinly piped rings of chocolate. Dust bark with a little powdered coffee or chocolate and decorate with angelica leaves and glacé cherries. Store cake in a cool place until ready to serve.

CHEESE

A Guide to Serving Cheeses

Cheese, like its natural partners, bread and wine, is made by a process of fermentation which can turn one substance, just as it is about to spoil, into something better than it was in the first place.

Cheese is one of the most versatile foods known to man. It can be soft and creamy, firm, or tangy and blue-veined; and it can be served at every course throughout the meal, from appetizer to dessert.

Bring out a cheese tray of three or four different kinds of cheese with biscuits at cocktail time; serve it at the end of the meal with crusty French bread, fruit, nuts and wine; try a snack of cheese with pumpernickel, dark rye bread, crusty French loaf or stone-ground wholemeal.

To bring out its full flavour, well-ripened cheese should be removed from the refrigerator at least two hours before serving.

Cheddar (English) Most popular English cheese, close and buttery in texture, with a full, clean, slightly nutty flavour. Crumbles when aged. Cooks well, if a trifle too greasily, when fresh for soufflés and fine sauces. Good with beer and red wine.

Stilton (English) Perhaps the world's most regal blue cheese. Its blue mould should be evenly distributed in wide-branching veins, the cheese itself being a rich cream, not anaemic white. Best season is between November and April. Serve with port, nuts and raisins.

Cheshire (English) Oldest of our cheeses, probably dating from pre-Roman Britain. Crumbly in texture, slightly salty in flavour and excellent with apple pie.

Blue Cheshire (English) A much rarer cheese, and a great favourite with epicures. It has a rich flavour.

Leicester (English) Crumbly and flaky, very like Cheshire in texture but a deep orange-red in colour. A good keeper, but best when young and mild. Good with salads and watercress; excellent as one of the components of Welsh rarebit. Goes well with beer.

Sage Derby (English) Made from bruised sage and parsley steeped in milk. The sage imparts a distinctive 'herby' flavour. Try this country cheese with pale ale or beer, a crusty cottage loaf and fresh butter. A most attractive cheese for the cheese board.

Maribo (Danish) Mild, creamy, whipped milk cheese. Good with grapes or for sandwiches.

Danish Blue (Danish) Blue-veined, white, creamy, sharp-flavoured. Use it, creamed with butter and brandy, as a spread or to fill celery stalks; crumble a little into French dressing for salads.

Emmenthal (Swiss) Comes in large wheels, aged to achieve a faintly waxy texture and huge 'eyes'. A perfect table cheese, and one of the great cooking cheeses. (Not to be confused with Gruyère, which has no eyes, and from which Swiss fondue is made.)

Edam (Dutch) A red cannonball, mild or sharp according to age. Ideally, cut a 'lid' from top and spoon out cheese, replacing 'lid' to keep soft.

Gouda (Dutch) A junior version of Edam. Sometimes rubbery when bought; let it age. Melts well; use for toasted cheese sandwiches.

Camembert (French) One of the world's favourite cheeses, 'invented' by a farmer's wife in 1790. Best when pale yellow, rather runny and soft. Eat it with crusty French bread, claret or burgundy, and a slice of ripe pear; try it soused in dry white wine.

Chèvre (French) A variety of cheeses made of goat's milk, creamy and chalky in texture; they come in various shapes. Most types are eaten fresh, but are at their best when skin has a little green mould. Serve with French bread and butter and a robust red wine or dry rosé.

Pont L'Evèque (French) One of the noblest French cheeses, ripe and strong in flavour. Made in square moulds and cured for four months to develop heavy crust and typical odour. Best avoided in its early stages and when past its prime. Goes with all red wines.

Brie (French) Talleyrand called this soft, creamy cheese 'the king of cheeses'. Comes in thin, yellow-crusted wheels dusted with powdery white mould. Apt to be chalky when under-ripe; smells of ammonia when past its prime. Good with red Burgundy or Beaujolais.

Tomme (French) Mild-flavoured cheese from Savoy. There are several varieties: for example, Tomme with fennel – very popular in Britain – and Tomme with a protective and flavour-giving cover of dry grape stalks, pips and skins (not to be eaten).

Bel Paese (Italian) Soft but firm, rich yet delicately flavoured; delicious with fruit. Served almost entirely as a dessert cheese, it can be used instead of Mozzarella in cooked dishes. Keeps well, sharpening with age. Serve it at room temperature.

Gorgonzola (Italian) Originated in Gorgonzola, near Milan, more than 1,000 years ago. Riper in flavour than other blue cheeses, but softer and creamier in texture. Very good with fruit, and combines well with butter and oil for dips, spreads and sauces.

Burrini (Italian) Small, pear-sized cheese of a soft but firm texture, with an earthy tang. Encloses a small 'egg' of butter in its outer layer; cut it in slices across so butter and cheese are combined in each. Cheeses are strung together with raffia.

Christmas Eve Menu

In France it is customary to celebrate Christmas Eve with a late-night supper. Menus range from oysters in the half shell and *pâté de foie gras* to superb casseroles or galantines of chicken and duck.

Our menu for Christmas Eve–or for any other festive evening during the holidays–is based on a spectacular *Timbale* of Duck, tender fillets of duckling encased in a highly flavoured forcemeat stuffing. This hot duck loaf, with its gay Christmas dressing of rounds of stuffed green olives is turned out on a platter just before serving and garnished with diced duck, stuffed green olives and a delicately flavoured Madeira sauce.

Menu

Avocado and
Orange Salad

Timbale of Duck

Tulipes Glacées à
l'Ananas

Serves 4

*with this menu I suggest
the following Medium-
priced Red Wines*
**Moulin-à-Vent
St Emilion
Pommard**
or Champagne

Avocado and Orange Salad

2 ripe avocado pears
Lemon juice
2–3 oranges
Lettuce
Vinaigrette sauce (see page 100)
Finely chopped garlic
Dry mustard

1 Cut avocado pears in half lengthwise. Remove stones, and peel carefully with a knife. Cut avocados into $\frac{1}{4}$-inch(0·5-cm) slices crosswise and soak in lemon juice to keep colour. Peel and segment oranges.

2 Arrange avocado slices and orange segments in nests of crisp lettuce. Serve with vinaigrette sauce highly flavoured with garlic and dry mustard.

Timbale of Duck

1 tender duckling, about 5lb (2·25kg)
Softened butter
Salt and freshly ground black pepper
Rubbed thyme
4 carrots, sliced
2 Spanish onions, sliced
2 stalks celery with tops, sliced
1 clove garlic
1 bay leaf
8 peppercorns
1 lb(450g) stuffed olives, sliced

MARINADE:
2–4 tablespoons Madeira

2 tablespoons cognac
1 clove garlic, finely chopped
2 tablespoons finely chopped parsley
Salt and freshly ground black pepper

FORCEMEAT:
5 slices white bread
Chicken stock, to moisten
1 lb(450g) minced veal
2 eggs
2 tablespoons finely chopped onion
2 tablespoons finely chopped parsley
4 tablespoons melted butter
4 tablespoons double cream
Salt and freshly ground black pepper
Nutmeg and cayenne pepper

SAUCE:
2 tablespoons butter
2 tablespoons flour
Pan juices from duckling (strained)
4 tablespoons Madeira
$\frac{1}{2}$ pint(3dl) chicken stock
Salt and freshly ground black pepper

1 **On the day before the party:** clean and singe duckling and rub inside and out with softened butter combined with salt, freshly ground black pepper and thyme.

2 Cover the bottom of an oval casserole with sliced carrots, onions and celery. Add garlic, bay leaf, peppercorns and salt, to taste. Place duckling on this bed of aromatics; cover casserole tightly and simmer duck and vegetables gently for 1 to $1\frac{1}{4}$ hours, or until tender. Remove duck and strain sauce into a bowl. Cool.

3 On the day of the party: skim fat from surface of stock. Discard skin of duck and cut meat from bones in long thin strips. Marinate strips for at least 2 hours in a little Madeira and brandy combined with finely chopped garlic, parsley, salt and freshly ground black pepper, turning once or twice during this time to allow flavour to impregnate meat thoroughly.

4 To make forcemeat: trim crusts from bread and soak slices in a little chicken stock until well moistened. Place minced veal in a large mixing bowl; add eggs, chopped onion, parsley, melted butter, double cream and moist bread, which you have shredded. Mix well; add salt, freshly ground black pepper, nutmeg and cayenne, to taste, and work mixture into a smooth paste.

5 To make sauce: melt butter in the top of a double saucepan; stir in flour and cook over water, stirring constantly, until *roux* is smooth. Add strained pan juices from duck, Madeira and chicken stock and stir until smooth. Season to taste with salt and freshly ground black pepper and a little more Madeira if desired. Allow sauce to simmer over hot water, stirring from time to time, until sauce is thick and smooth.

6 To assemble timbale: butter a loaf tin or oval *terrine* generously. Cut stuffed olives into thin slices. Line bottom inside walls of loaf tin or *terrine* with olive slices so that bottom and sides are completely covered with olive rings. Carefully press a little of the forcemeat stuffing against olives, keeping your fingers wet so that stuffing does not adhere to them, continuing until mould is entirely lined with a layer of forcemeat. Then place a layer of duck strips in the *terrine;* cover with a layer of sliced olives; pour in 2 tablespoons of the sauce and top with remaining duck, finishing with 2 tablespoons of sauce. Close the mould with a layer of forcemeat; top with a piece of buttered aluminium foil and place the *timbale* in a large pan containing enough hot water to come halfway up the sides of the *terrine*. Bring the water to the boil; cook *terrine* in a preheated moderate oven (350°F/180°C/Mark 4) for 1 to 1¼ hours.

7 Unmould the *timbale* carefully on a large heated serving dish. Garnish with remaining duck strips, diced, remaining olives, and sauce. Serve remaining sauce separately. This dish is equally good served cold.

Tulipes Glacées à l'Ananas

5 oz(150g) flour
5 oz(150g) icing sugar
2 egg yolks
3 egg whites
1 large orange, greased, to form pastry shapes
1 fresh pineapple, peeled and diced
Kirsch
Vanilla ice cream
Double cream, whipped

1 Sift flour and icing sugar into a bowl; add egg yolks and whites, and mix well.

2 Grease a cold baking sheet and mark 4 circles on it with a saucer. Spread 1 dessertspoon of mixture over each circle, using the back of a teaspoon. Bake in a moderate oven (350°F/180°C/Mark 4) for 5 to 6 minutes, or until edges just turn brown.

3 Remove each round from baking sheet; turn over and, working quickly, place each circle over top of a greased orange. Place tea towel over pastry to prevent burning hands, and mould pastry to fit orange. Remove and continue as above, baking 2 to 4 circles each time, and shaping them over oranges as you go. Cases will keep for days in a biscuit tin. This recipe makes 12 to 16 *tulipes*.

4 To serve: fill 8 cases with diced fresh pineapple which you have marinated in Kirsch; add a scoop of vanilla ice cream and decorate with whipped cream.

243

A Gala Christmas Breakfast

To begin Christmas Day with an elaborate meal may seem a lot of trouble. It is. But the British are famous for their breakfasts, so here is my menu for a memorable morning party. The Cold Gammon will give plenty of meat for the rest of the day.

Menu

Fresh Fruit Compote
or
Orange and Grapefruit Segments in Lemon Juice

Creamed Finnan Haddie

Cold Gammon of Bacon with Cumberland Jelly

Hot Popovers

Serves 6

with this menu I suggest Champagne Cup, Tea, Chocolate or Coffee

Fresh Fruit Compote

2 oranges
2 pears
2–3 Cox's orange pippins
2–3 plums
1 bunch grapes
Icing sugar, to taste
2 tablespoons brandy
2 tablespoons lemon juice
$\frac{1}{4}$ bottle champagne

1 Peel oranges and slice. Peel, core and slice pears and apples. Slice and pit plums, and halve and seed grapes. Combine fruits in a bowl and dust with icing sugar to taste; moisten with brandy and lemon juice; toss well and chill.

2 Just before serving, transfer to a serving bowl; pour over chilled champagne and serve immediately.

Orange and Grapefruit Segments in Lemon Juice

3–4 large juicy oranges
2 large grapefruit
Lemon juice
Sifted icing sugar
6 leaves fresh mint

1 Prepare oranges and grapefruit as follows, working over a shallow dish so that no juice is lost: using a sharp knife, slice off top and bottom of each fruit, taking all the pith and outer membrane away with the peel.

2 Stand fruit on one cut end and, with sharp, straight, downward strokes, whittle off peel and membrane all around sides.

3 Turn fruit on its other end and again

whittle off peel and membrane all around sides.

4 Finally, slice off ring of peel left around centre. You should be left with a slightly angular-shaped fruit, completely free of pith as well as peel. With a little practice, and providing your cutting tool is really sharp, this method takes far less time than the more conventional one.

5 Now take fruit in one hand and slip your knife between each segment and the membrane holding it on either side. Cut segment out, keeping it whole if possible; remove any pips and drop segment into the juice below. Proceed in this manner until all you have left is the central core and empty membranes, fanned out like the leaves of a book.

6 Squeeze out any remaining juice into the dish.

7 Toss orange and grapefruit segments with lemon juice and sweeten to taste with icing sugar. Chill.

8 Serve in individual glass dishes, decorated with a fresh mint leaf.

Creamed Finnan Haddie

2 lb(900g) smoked haddock
Water and milk, to cover
3 tablespoons butter
3 tablespoons flour
$\frac{3}{4}$ pint(4dl) cream
Freshly ground black pepper and nutmeg
Triangles of bread
Butter

1 Soak haddock in water for 2 hours.

Drain; place in a saucepan and cover with equal amounts of water and milk and bring to a fast boil. Remove from heat and allow to stand for 15 minutes, then drain, reserving stock for use in step 2.

2 Melt butter in the top of a double saucepan; stir in flour and cook over direct heat for 3 minutes, stirring continuously until smooth. Place top of double saucepan over hot water, add cream and ½ pint(3dl) haddock stock and continue to cook, stirring from time to time. Season to taste with freshly ground black pepper and a little grated nutmeg.

3 Remove skin and bones from haddock and break into pieces. Fold pieces into sauce and simmer gently until ready to serve. Serve in a shallow casserole with triangles of bread which you have sautéed in butter.

Cold Gammon of Bacon

1 gammon of bacon
  10–12 lb(4·6–5·3kg)
2 Spanish onions, peeled
6 large carrots, scraped
2 stalks celery
2 cloves
2 bay leaves
6 peppercorns
Toasted breadcrumbs (or cloves,
  brown sugar, dry mustard and cider
  or fruit juice)

1 Wash gammon well; do not take off rind; soak for 24 to 48 hours to remove salt, changing water several times.

2 Cover gammon completely with cold water and bring very slowly to boiling point to open pores gradually, extract salt and at the same time help increase the temperature of any cold core in the joint.

3 Change water; add peeled onions, scraped carrots and celery, cloves, bay leaves and peppercorns, and bring slowly to boiling point again; reduce heat immediately boiling point is reached and allow temperature to drop to simmering point. Cover and simmer until cooking is complete – about 20 minutes per lb/450g for an average-sized gammon.

4 Allow gammon to cool in water in which it was cooked. Do not remove rind until well set if you are going to serve it cold. (I leave mine overnight.) Then remove skin and sprinkle fat with toasted breadcrumbs; or, if you prefer, score fat criss-cross, stud with cloves, sprinkle with brown sugar and a little dry mustard and brown in the oven for 20 to 30 minutes, basting from time to time with cider or fruit juice.

Cumberland Jelly

½ jar redcurrant jelly
Rinds of 1 orange and 1 lemon
Juice of 2 oranges and 1 lemon
1 level tablespoon dry mustard
½ oz(14g) gelatine
¼ pint(1·5dl) port wine
2 tablespoons Cointreau

1 Pare rinds of orange and lemon as thinly as possible; cut into fine short strips and blanch for 5 minutes in boiling water.

2 Combine redcurrant jelly and strained orange and lemon juice in a saucepan and simmer until jelly is melted. Add a small quantity of this to the mustard, mix well and return to pan.

3 Soak gelatine in port wine and Cointreau for 5 minutes; then dissolve gently over heat and add to redcurrant mixture. Allow to cool a little before spooning into glass serving dish or crock. Just before setting, stir in blanched rind.

Hot Popovers

(for recipe, see Breakfast Bakery, page 88)

Making the Most of Christmas Leftovers

If for Christmas this year you had a turkey – a fine, fat bird often seems the answer to a cook's holiday prayer – cheer up. There is no need to restrict your post-Christmas meals to cold sliced turkey and stuffing, or to turkey warmed up in gravy. Far better to whet family appetites this week with chilled turkey salad garnished with orange segments, black olives, almonds and seeded grapes; curried turkey and rice; American turkey pie with a golden pastry crust; and last – but certainly not least – a delicious turkey soup.

Turkey Soup

Makes about 2¼ pints(1·3 litres)
Carcass and bones (drumsticks, wing tips, etc.) of 1 roast turkey
3 pints(1·7 litres) chicken stock
4 celery stalks with leaves, sliced
2 Spanish onions, sliced
2 bay leaves
Salt and freshly ground black pepper
Sprigs of parsley
4–6 level tablespoons rice

1 Scrape stuffing from interior of turkey and discard.

2 Put carcass and bones in a large saucepan or casserole. Add chicken stock, sliced celery, onions, bay leaves, salt, freshly ground black pepper and a few sprigs of parsley. Bring to the boil; skim froth from soup; lower heat and simmer gently for 2 hours. Strain. Remove any meat from bones and add to soup.

3 Fifteen minutes before serving, add rice; return to heat and cook until rice is tender. Correct seasoning and serve.

American Turkey Pie

1 lb(450g) cooked turkey, cut into cubes
4 level tablespoons butter
4 level tablespoons flour
1 pint(6dl) chicken stock
¼ pint(1·5dl) milk
1 packet frozen peas
1 lb(450g) cooked carrots, sliced
1 lb(450g) button onions, cooked and drained
Salt and freshly ground black pepper
½ lb(225g) flaky pastry
1 egg yolk, for glazing

1 Melt butter in the top of a double saucepan; add flour and stir until well blended. Add well-flavoured chicken stock and milk and stir until sauce is smooth.

2 Put carcass and bones in a large saucepan or casserole. Add chicken stock, sliced button onions and turkey meat. Season with salt and freshly ground black pepper and pour into a large pie dish.

3 Top with flaky pastry; brush with egg yolk mixed with 1 tablespoon water and bake in a preheated hot oven (450°F/230°C/Mark 8) for about 15 to 20 minutes, or until pastry is cooked and golden.

Curried Turkey

1½ lb(675g) cooked turkey, diced
4 tablespoons butter
1 Spanish onion, finely chopped
2 stalks celery, thinly sliced
1 apple, peeled, cored and diced
1 garlic clove, finely chopped
1 tablespoon curry powder
1 tablespoon flour

$\frac{3}{4}$ **pint(4dl) chicken stock**
2 tablespoons finely chopped parsley

1 Melt butter and sauté finely chopped onion and thinly sliced celery until onion is transparent; add peeled, cored and diced apple, finely chopped garlic and curry powder mixed with flour; continue to cook, stirring constantly, until mixture begins to turn golden.

2 Add chicken stock and cook sauce, stirring, until it is smooth and thick.

3 Add turkey and finely chopped parsley and simmer until heated through. Serve curried turkey in a ring of cooked rice.

Turkey and Orange Salad

1$\frac{1}{2}$ lb(675g) cooked turkey, diced
4 shallots, finely chopped
2 stalks celery, sliced
4 small oranges, peeled and divided into sections
Lettuce leaves

DRESSING:
Olive oil
Wine vinegar
Salt and freshly ground black pepper
Rosemary

GARNISH:
8–10 black olives
Grapes, halved and seeded
Slivered toasted almonds

1 Combine diced turkey, finely chopped shallots and sliced celery with a dressing made with 3 parts olive oil to 1 part wine vinegar. Season with salt, freshly ground black pepper and rosemary. Toss well and leave to marinate for at least 2 hours.

2 Just before serving, add orange sections; toss again, adding more dressing if required.

3 Line a glass salad bowl with lettuce leaves;

fill with salad and garnish with black olives, grapes and toasted almonds.

Super Turkey Hash

1$\frac{1}{2}$ lb(675g) cooked turkey, diced
$\frac{1}{2}$ **Spanish onion, finely chopped**
$\frac{1}{2}$ **green pepper, finely chopped**
1 clove garlic, finely chopped
Butter
Salt and freshly ground black pepper
1 egg yolk, beaten
2–4 tablespoons whipped cream
Fresh breadcrumbs

SAUCE:
2 level tablespoons butter
2 level tablespoons flour
$\frac{1}{2}$ **pint(3dl) milk**
$\frac{1}{4}$ **pint(1.5dl) double cream**
Salt and freshly ground black pepper

1 Sauté finely chopped onion, green pepper and garlic in 2 level tablespoons butter until vegetables are soft. Add diced turkey meat and continue to cook, stirring constantly, until meat is heated through. Season with salt and freshly ground black pepper, to taste. Keep warm.

2 To make sauce: melt butter in a saucepan; add flour and cook until *roux* just starts to turn golden. Add milk and cook, stirring constantly, until sauce is reduced to about two-thirds the original quantity. Stir in double cream. Season with salt and freshly ground black pepper, to taste.

3 To assemble dish: add $\frac{1}{2}$ pint(3dl) sauce (see above) to the turkey mixture; season to taste with salt and freshly ground black pepper, and pour into a heatproof *gratin* dish. Combine remaining sauce with beaten egg yolk and fold in whipped cream. Spread over creamed turkey mixture. Sprinkle with fresh breadcrumbs; dot with a little butter, and brown in a hot oven (450°F/230°C/Mark 8) or under the grill.

Your Emergency Shelf

Every cook should have a selection of canned, packaged and dried foods in the larder ready for unexpected guests or an impromptu meal.

When shopping for emergency shelf items, remember that most can be kept for an almost unlimited time. So buy in quantity when they are on sale; you'll save both time and money.

I always have eggs, butter, milk, cream, Parmesan cheese and a small supply of sliced bacon, Spanish onions, carrots, garlic, tomatoes, lemons and lettuce on hand. In addition to these perishables I like to keep the following staples for emergency entertaining:

Canned Fruits

Pears
Pineapple
Peaches
Apricots
Cherries

Canned Vegetables

Mushrooms
Small White Onions
Italian Peeled Tomatoes
Tomato Concentrate
Tomato Juice
Artichoke Hearts
Peas

Canned or Bottled Meats

Ham
Chicken
Liver Pâté
Luncheon Meat

Canned Fish

Lobster
Salmon
Tuna
Crabmeat
Sardines
Anchovies
Minced Clams
Cod's Roe

Canned Soups and Stock Cubes

Cream of Mushroom
Tomato
Turtle
Green Pea
Clam Broth
Chicken Stock Cubes
Beef Stock Cubes

Dried Vegetables

Lentils
Haricots Blancs
Kidney Beans
Peas
Chick Peas

Dried Fruits

Apricots
Prunes
Raisins
Sultanas
Currants

Miscellaneous

Olive Oil
Wine Vinegar
Canned Milk
Mayonnaise
Olives
Pickles
Relishes
Truffles
Pine Nuts
Pistachio Nuts
Almonds

Pasta and Rice

Spaghetti
Noodles
Green Noodles
Long-grain Rice
Risotto Rice

INDEXES
PART 1 – GENERAL

PART II – INDEX OF COURSES